Communications in Computer and Information Science 441

Editorial Board

T0236190

More information about this series at http://www.springer.com/series/7899

Alexander B. Sideridis · Zoe Kardasiadou
Constantine P. Yialouris · Vasilios Zorkadis (Eds.)

E-Democracy, Security, Privacy and Trust in a Digital World

5th International Conference, E-Democracy 2013
Athens, Greece, December 5–6, 2013
Revised Selected Papers

 Springer

Editors
Alexander B. Sideridis
Constantine P. Yialouris
Agricultural University of Athens
Athens
Greece

Zoe Kardasiadou
Vasilios Zorkadis
Hellenic Data Protection Authority
Athens
Greece

ISSN 1865-0929   ISSN 1865-0937   (electronic)
ISBN 978-3-319-11709-6   ISBN 978-3-319-11710-2   (eBook)
DOI 10.1007/978-3-319-11710-2

Library of Congress Control Number: 2014950836

Springer Cham Heidelberg New York Dordrecht London

Printed on acid-free paper

Springer is part of Springer Science+Business Media (www.springer.com)

5th INTERNATIONAL CONFERENCE

e-Democracy 2013:
Security, Privacy, and Trust in Digital World

Preface

The 5th International Conference on e-Democracy held in Athens, Greece, during December 5–6, 2013, focused on the following topics: security, privacy, e-Government and e-Governance applications, politics, legislation and relative European initiatives. Research and technological innovations in information and communication sciences, as well as advances in law that aim at improving the performance of e-Government systems and, at the same time, protecting and guaranteeing the citizen's rights were also presented in a full two-day program. A number of workshops, namely on the latest cybersecurity threats and best practices in protecting e-Gov infrastructures, on crypt-analytic attacks and how to design secure cryptosystems and on new encryption concepts, enriched the knowledge of young researchers attending the conference with the latest efficient tools in further shielding vulnerable systems.

The 5th e-Democracy 2013 International Conference was organized by the Scientific Council for Information Society of Greece and supported by a large number of academic organizations. Greek Universities and Technological Institutes joined forces with the University of East London and the Greek Lawyers' Association "e-Themis", to bring together their experiences in this biannual scientific event. The conference also included three keynote addresses, which brought to the audience's attention issues varying from day-to-day European Union trans-boarder e-Government implementation and privacy and trust problems in the digital world that we live in, to philosophical ideas in relation to human integrity and civil rights protection.

All papers presented in the conference were blind peer reviewed at least by two internationally recognised specialists in relevant scientific fields. Furthermore, papers included in this volume are a subset of the above papers, selected for post-conference proceedings, on an additional blind review round, performed under the guidance of a publication advisory group, especially established for this purpose.

The 5th e-Democracy 2013 International Conference took place in Athens, Greece, the centre of the deepest economic crisis among the southern countries of the European Union since the great depression. Taking this into account, the Organizing Committee decided to offer free registration to the conference to all postgraduate students. This explains the large number of young researchers and PhD students, among the audience.

Dear colleagues,

Holding this research book in your hands and keeping in mind that it represents an important part of the essence in e-Government science and technology, don't forget to join us for the next e-Democracy 2015 International Conference.

August 2014   Alexander B. Sideridis

Organization

Organizing Committee

Conference Chair

Alexander B. Sideridis   President of the Scientific Council for the
Information Society, Greece

General Co-chair

Zorkadis Vasilios   Hellenic Data Protection Authority, Greece

Co-chairs

Anastassopoulos D.	Greek Lawyers' Association "e-Themis", Greece
Iliadis L.	Democritus University of Thrace, Greece
Karyda M.	University of the Aegean, Greece
Patrikakis Ch.	Technological Educational Institute of Piraeus, Greece

Finance and Patronage Chair

Middleton F.   Scientific Council for the Information Society,
Greece

Organizing Committee Members

Anagnostou M.	National Technical University of Athens, Greece
Catsikas S.	Piraeus University, Greece
Chrissikopoulos V.	Ionian University, Greece
Costopoulou C.	Agricultural University of Athens, Greece
Gritzalis S.	Aegean University, Greece
Iliadis L.	Democritus University of Thrace, Greece
Manthou V.	University of Macedonia, Greece
Ntaliani M.	Agricultural University of Athens, Greece
Pagonas J.	Greek Lawyers' Association "e-Themis", Greece
Pimenidis E.	University of East London, UK
Vassilaki E.	Hellenic Scientific Council for Information Society, Greece

Technical Program Committee Chair

Pimenidis E.   University of East London, UK

Tutorials Chair

Anastassopoulos D.   Greek Lawyers' Association "e-Themis", Greece

Workshops Chair

Costopoulou C.   Agricultural University of Athens, Greece

Publications Co-chairs

Zorkadis Vasilios   Hellenic Data Protection Authority, Greece
Kardasiadou Zoe   Hellenic Data Protection Authority, Greece
Makedon F.   University of Texas at Arlington, USA
Patrikakis Ch.   Technological Educational Institute of Piraeus,
                                     Greece

Program Coordinator

M. Ntaliani   Agricultural University of Athens, Greece

Scientific Committee

Alexandris N.   University of Piraeus, Greece
Alexandropoulou E.   University of Macedonia, Greece
Alikakou M.   Hellenic Data Protection Authority, Greece
Anastasopoulos D.   Democritus University of Thrace, Greece
Andreopoulou Z.   Aristotle University of Thessaliniki, Greece
Assimakopoulos N.   University of Pireaus, Greece
Athanasiadis E.   National & Kapodistrian University of Athens,
                                     Greece
Atil H.   Ege University, Turkey
Bouras C.   University of Patras, Greece
Bourka A.   Hellenic Data Protection Authority, Greece
Chao H.C.   National Ilan University, Taiwan
Chatziliassi E.   Hellenic Data Protection Authority, Greece
Chrissikopoulos V.   Ionian University, Greece
Crearie L.   University of West Scotland, UK
Costopoulou C.   Agricultural University of Athens, Greece
Doulamis A.   Technical University of Crete, Greece

Douligeris Ch.	University of Piraeus, Greece
Edelmann N.	Department for Governance and Public Administration, Greece
Georgiadis Ch.	University of Macedonia, Greece
Gupta M.P.	Indian Institute of Technology, India
Herdon M.	University of Debrecen, Hungary
Iliadis L.	Democritus University of Thrace, Greece
Jahankhani H.	Williams College, UK
Kaklamani D.	National Technical University of Athens, Greece
Kanellopoulou - Boti M.M.	Ionian University, Greece
Kantzavelou I.	Technological Educational Institute of Athens, Greece
Kardasiadou Zoe	Hellenic Data Protection Authority, Greece
Karetsos S.	Technological Educational Institute of Larissa, Greece
Katos V.	Democritus University of Thrace, Greece
Katsikas S.	University of Piraeus, Greece
Kokolakis S.	University of the Aegean, Greece
Kolokotronis N.	University of Peloponeese, Greece
Lambrinoudakis C.	University of Piraeus, Greece
Lambrou M.	University of the Aegean, Greece
Limniotis K.	National & Kapodistrian University of Athens, Greece
Lorentzos N.	Agricultural University of Athens, Greece
Loukis E.	University of Aegean, Greece
Magkos E.	Ionian University, Greece
Makedon F.	University of Texas at Arlington, USA
Manthou V.	University of Macedonia, Greece
Margaronis P.	University of Aegean, Greece
Marianos N.	University of the Aegean, Greece
Marias I.	Athens University of Economics and Business, Greece
Merunka V.	Czech Technical University, Czech Republic
Molhanec M.	Czech Technical University, Czech Republic
Najjar J.	Synergetics NV, Belgium
Nouskalis G.	Aristotelean University of Thessaloniki, Greece
Ntaliani M.	Agricultural University of Athens, Greece
Ntalianis F.	University of Piraeus, Greece
Ntalianis K.	Technological Educational Institute of Athens, Greece
Ochos X.	Esquela Superior Polytéchnica del Litoral, Equador
Patrikakis Ch.	Technological Educational Institute of Piraeus, Greece
Paulsson F.	Umeli University, Sweden
Pawlowski J.	University of Jyväskylä, Finland
Polemi N.	University of Piraeus, Greece

Publications Advisory Board

Prasad N.   Aalborg University, Denmark
Pucihar A.   University of Maribor, Slovenia
Voulgaris S.   University of Amsterdam, Holland

Web and Technical Support

Gazis F.   Technological Educational Institute of Piraeus,
                              Greece
Mouhtaropoulos A.   University of Warwick, UK
Protopappas L.   Agricultural University of Athens, Greece

Contents

Politics - Legislation - European Initiatives

e-Governance II

Security, Privacy

Ensuring Cloud Security: Current Concerns and Research Challenges

Nikos Vesyropoulos[1], Christos K. Georgiadis[1],
and Elias Pimenidis[2(✉)]

[1] University of Macedonia, 156 Egnatia Str., 540 06 Thessaloniki, Greece
{Nvesyrop,geor}@uom.edu.gr
[2] University of the West of England, Frenchay, Bristol BS16 1QY, UK
Elias.Pimenidis@uwe.ac.uk

Abstract. Over the past few years Cloud computing has been widely accepted and adopted as an alternative way for businesses to store data, communicate and operate. Consumers and enterprises regard this as a compelling opportunity to reduce or even in some cases completely eliminate costs, since Software as a Service (SaaS) offers a software delivery model in which software and the corresponding user data are being hosted on Cloud computing data centers. This shifts the costs of acquiring hardware and software and the additional costs for maintenance and personnel expenses from the enterprises to the Cloud providers, thus enabling business to reallocate IT operations costs. Alongside the emerging opportunities provided by the Cloud, security threads and concerns are also being raised. Providers and consumers must be aware and cautious of risks of data loss due to breaches. Security issues and current research challenges in securing cloud computing systems are reviewed here.

Keywords: Cloud computing · Cloud security · Cloud services

1 Introduction

With the term Cloud computing we refer to an alternative use of computing resources. Computers loosely connected in a global scale, provide data, storage and software in a new paradigm, which is providing them as services. Gartner in its revision defines cloud computing as "a style of computing in which scalable and elastic IT-enabled capabilities are delivered as a service to external customers using Internet technologies" [11]. While enterprises can have access to newly released applications and acquire vast storage solutions with minimal cost, and reap benefits such as flexibility, scalability, universal access to data from any terminal and low-cost backup solutions, awareness should be raised regarding security issues [2].

The cloud provider may also be the publisher of certain services, or could act solely as an intermediate. In both ways service providers can reap benefits from the cloud modeling approach as they can enable their works (e.g. software) to be easier reachable to clients as services. Additionally they offer the opportunity to end users, to use the latest and most updated versions of their software, usually regardless of the platform that the end user works on. As a result clients can have access to up to date software

A.B. Sideridis et al. (Eds.): E-Democracy 2013, CCIS 441, pp. 3–10, 2014.
DOI: 10.1007/978-3-319-11710-2_1

and developers can focus more on functionality and security issues instead of compatibility issues during each update.

2 Deployment Models

In Cloud computing, there are four known deployment models. These models can be classified as private, public, community, and hybrid. As mentioned below, a number of security concerns depend heavily on the delivery model [14].

   (i)   Private: With the term Private Cloud we refer to an infrastructure that belongs to an organization and is used to fulfill its own private needs. Private Clouds are often used for data sharing and management of internal applications.

  (ii) Public: A Public cloud is an infrastructure provided by a specific service provider (for example Google, Microsoft and Amazon) to the public. The End-users are charged according to the usage of the provided services and resources.

 (iii) Community: In Community cloud models, resources and applications are used and can be shared, by a community of people with similar interests. Usually there is an administrator outside the scope of the community that operates the Cloud, but in some cases it can also be operated in conjunction by a number of the community members.

 (iv) Hybrid: A Hybrid cloud is the combination of two or more cloud infrastructures, which enables a flexible transition between the aforementioned infrastructures, in order to comply with the End-users needs.

3 Security Concerns

The introduction of the Cloud computing paradigm has created the need for additional security measures, as new challenges rise. While issues such as authorization, authentication and availability of services, are dominant concerns even in locally stored systems, these issues are gravely exacerbated in Cloud computing systems [5]. Regarding authentication and authorization concerns include the policies and protocols used by the cloud provider and the storage of sensitive enterprise data externally. In regard to the subject of availability, as all physical hardware is being managed externally, and a provider handles requests from a plethora of enterprises, any hardware failure can impact more end-users [3, 10].

Software as a Service (SaaS) is an emerging software delivery paradigm, where users instead of buying applications and installing them on their terminals, can have on-demand access to them, thus consuming them as services. Those applications are being remotely hosted on a service provider and provide unparalleled benefits such as increased efficiency at a significantly lower cost. Nevertheless, enterprises show resilience in adopting this delivery model [6]. Security concerns may include breach of data both from the Cloud provider, and from external threats. Major enterprises are reliant as to how safe are their sensitive data, when their storage is outsourced. In addition, system and software availability of the Cloud provider is also extremely important, as inconsistencies could lead to the unavailability of requested data or even worse in corruption of sensitive information resulting to financial losses. As a result enterprises often avoid adopting SaaS applications.

Security measures are almost entirely the provider's responsibility. As a result the end user usually has limited knowledge as to how his data is being protected.

The sensitive enterprise data is stored in one or more Cloud computing data centers, with common practice within cloud providers being creating multiple synchronized copies of the data and storing them in a number of data centers globally. This ensures that data will be reachable to the users in high speeds regardless of his location and in case of system failure in a data center the data will still be available. Since the enterprise data are not stored within the enterprise the provider has to block other users of the service as well as external malicious threats from having access to the data.

External malicious users can utilize one of many known techniques, such as cross-site scripting, SQL database injection flaws, manipulation of cookies and manipulation of Hidden fields to identify and exploit weaknesses in the data center.

4 Classification of Security Concerns

4.1 Data Confidentiality and Privacy

As end-users utilize the cloud services and store their data in the provider's infrastructure, the most critical security concern is about privacy and user data confidentiality. When we refer to confidentiality we refer to issues regarding the authorization of the end-user prior to providing access to sensitive data [7]. If a malicious user gains authentication privileges, there can be a breach of sensitive data or an alteration to them which can in time harm the owner of the data. Nevertheless confidentiality is not limited solely on data as it also regards the access to specific provider applications. Software confidentiality refers to the confidentiality of applications that handle sensitive personal or enterprise data. In more detail, the handling of data is undertaken by applications that are owned by the service provider, and usually the end-user cannot choose which applications we approve. As a result these applications must provide insurances regarding their maintenance, keep a log file regarding changes between versions, provide assurances regarding the lack of known vulnerabilities and in general provide assurances that are not a source of a potential threat. As a large scale distributed model, cloud computing includes more hardware, software and protocols as well as an overwhelming number of end-users and third parties, in relation to traditional platforms. As a result there are more security threats that need to be addressed. While the data center provider should ensure that their own administrators and other employees will not be able to view sensitive enterprise information, it is also very important that authorization rules, which the enterprise casts on its own employees, are maintained when the enterprise shifts to the cloud. These authorizations must remain unchanged to avoid intrusion of data by unauthorized users [9]. The service provider must enforce security measures against application vulnerabilities and provide assurances that employees will not be able to access the data, or the physical storage drives that contain those data without authorization. The problem is two-fold: first of all, all data must be properly encrypted [8]. Firstly, all sensitive data should be properly encrypted when stored in data center. Many encryption algorithms have been proposed, though analysis is outside the scope of this research. Secondly access to the physical drives should be monitored and employees must have proper authorization, when they do routine checks on the hardware. Administrators of the cloud provider should only be able to log in using unique access keys (such as Secure Shell (SSH) keys) and have their activities monitored and logged when performing routine software maintenance. As a precaution, and to avoid data loss due to above two reasons, enterprises should also perform their own encryption, before storing data to a data center.

Regarding the data confidentiality issue, current research concerns include addressing the multitenancy and data remanence issues.

(i)   Multitenancy refers to the sharing of resources by a plethora of users. Resources include applications, sensitive data, bandwidth, storage or memory. While users operate on different instances of the same resources, it is inevitable that they use the same hardware. This sharing of resources creates the threat of unauthorized access from other users when executing the same applications. And while the reusability of resources is a profound advantage of the cloud computing paradigm, it is also a possible vulnerability threat. As users nowadays tend to store their sensitive data to the cloud with less resilience, and as more and more cloud providers are available this is building up to be an important issue.

(ii) As Data remanence we refer to traces of data representations that remain on a physical drive even through the data has been erased. When a new user is given access to a segment of a hard disk drive, data remanence may lead to unauthorized access to sensitive data of previous users. This security threat is often exploited in cloud scenarios, as malicious users try to gain access to large segments of disk space and then apply data remanence identification algorithms.

4.2   Trust

Trust is a concept directly related to the terms credibility and reliability. In cloud computing environments, trust refers to the assumption by each involved party, that other party members that are involved in a transaction will behave as expected [15]. In addition from the scope of an end-user trust refers to the assumption that the enterprise is capable of delivering the services and/or products that are expected. In addition the end user trusts that the enterprise will use all necessary precautions and perceptional measures to ensure that no data leakage will occur. Trust between parties should result in a mutual feeling of reduced risks and high levels of safety [7].

But in cloud scenarios, most of the safety mechanisms and responsibility for them, shifts from the enterprise to the cloud provider. The end-user has limited information regarding the security standards that are applied and enforced by the cloud provider which can be very different from his conceived level of security when he opted to select a specific enterprise to fulfill his needs. This is usually the case in public or hybrid cloud delivery models.

4.3 Integrity

With the term integrity we refer both to the inability of unauthorized users, or personnel, to access, modify or permanently delete data and to their inability to access or perform any changes to hardware, such as hard disk drives. One of the greatest risks in these scenarios is the intended alteration of data, which may result in wrong decisions later from the side of the enterprise [12, 18].

Usually enterprises keep a log of personnel that access data and hardware, and can prevent unauthorized interventions. But in cloud environments access to data can be achieved from many endpoints and with the existence of intermediaries, there is an increased risk for sensitive data or hardware.

Breach of data can be both internal and external. Internal breaches are the result of malevolent behavior for the cloud provider's employees, while external breaches can be the result of malicious software or users, that try to exploit weaknesses in the provider's software (software integrity), or in the interfaces that enable access to the legal end users [13].

4.4 Availability

With the term availability we refer to the on-demand ability to access a specific resource (software, data or hardware) [18]. A high level of availability means that a provider ensures that critical operations can be achieved even when hardware failure occurs, or external attacks are happening [4]. In traditional local environments availability is mainly a concern regarding the frequency of hardware-based system failures, and their recovery mechanisms. In cloud environments this risks shift towards the network infrastructure, the protocols applied and the bandwidth provided [12]. A vast amount of data is being exchanged daily, by a plethora of users, from many endpoints. As a result the provider must take the necessary measures, in order to be able to comply with such network load. As a result, the term availability in cloud computing refers mainly to the ability to continue operations even when malicious users try to gain unauthorized access to the system, or when they try to bring the system down by DDOS attacks.

4.5 Authorization

Authorization in cloud environments is a vital issue. Clients (enterprises), end-users and employees of the provider, may have access to the externally stored resources (data, software or hardware), but should each have differentiated privileges [17]. As a result identification of user's based simply on credentials (username and password) is not a sufficient measure [18]. The end user should be provided with assurances that data stored externally (not locally but on the cloud) will not be modified without with approval. By altering a user's sensitive data, severe damage can be caused. For example if a file regarding an early stage of an application model is altered, this alteration may be identified at a later stage of development leading to severe financial and scheduling issues [18].

Access policies should be enforced, providing access to specific resources with differentiated level of restrictions. Users should have roles assigned to them, based on specific attributes, which determine the level of the restrictions enforced. Authorization should be accomplished through the transfer of security certificates, issued by a trusted party.

5 Additional Research Challenges

Resource location: In the cloud computing model, providers must handle enormous amounts of data. Thus they often opt to store data in many data centers around the globe in order to lower data circulation in each data center and achieve higher availability. The end users are not aware of the location of the physical drives that store the data [16]. That can occasionally lead to legal issues as privacy laws differ in many countries and thus by storing data in various locations can raise questions over the jurisdiction that applies to that data.

Application vulnerabilities: Cloud applications are mostly managed over a web browser [1]. Thus vulnerabilities that originate in the web application can have consequences to the end users. These vulnerabilities do not apply solely to the network layer, and as an effect security issues rise in both the network and application layer. As a result firewalls and secure network protocols are necessary but not sufficient for the protection of the end users.

Monitoring: Cloud providers rarely provide monitoring logs to their clients as these logs could contain clues regarding the operational functions of the provider. For example information regarding the platforms used, or the maintenance schedules could be derived from these logs. Nevertheless monitoring can under conditions prove useful to both the clients and providers.

Encryption: Since the data is not being stored within the enterprise, the service provider must enforce security measures against application vulnerabilities and provide assurances that employees will not be able to access the data, or the physical storage drives that contain those data without authorization. The problem is two-fold: first of all, all data must be properly encrypted. Firstly, all sensitive data should be properly encrypted when stored in data center. Many encryption algorithms have been proposed, though analysis is outside the scope of this research. Secondly access to the physical drives should be monitored and employees must have proper authorization, when they do routine checks on the hardware [18].

Administrators of the cloud provider should only be able to log in using unique access keys (such as Secure Shell (SSH) keys) and have their activities monitored and logged when performing routine software maintenance. As a precaution, and to avoid data loss due to above two reasons, enterprises should also perform their own encryption, before storing data to a data center.

In order to ensure that data exchanges between the enterprises and the Cloud provider are secure, messages and data packages should be properly encrypted. The use of traffic encryption techniques are considered mandatory. The most common protocols used are the Secure Socket Layer (SSL) and the Transport Layer Security (TLS). Apart from the transfer protocol Cloud providers should also implement well known service protocols. In a cloud environment where data from various enterprises are being stored together in a central data center and applications are presented, invoked and consumed as services, web service security protocols such as the WS-Security, WS-Transaction and WS-Reliability should be taken into account when performing transactions. Although it is of fundamental importance to include such protocols, not many Cloud providers have implemented them. In addition, in order for the data to remain intact transactions should follow the atomic ACID properties. Failure to do so, may lead to corrupted data, due to the existence of multiple databases for multiple services within an enterprise and the vast number of enterprises shifting towards the Cloud computing model.

6 Conclusion

As Cloud has gained an increased popularity during the past few years, the need to ensure security in such computing environments, is higher than ever. A vast number of security concerns are documented in modern literature, which can be classified in a number of categories. The main differences that originate from this distributed computing paradigm, related to traditional computing systems originate from the fact that in Cloud computing, data centers can store data from a plethora of users and enterprises. As a result providers must ensure that data can only be accessed by their respective owners and cannot be accessed by other Cloud service users. Malicious users could exploit platform weaknesses and attempt to insert malware into the system, in an attempt to have that code executed, giving them access to other users data. Additional security risks have been documented and categorized in this work, in an attempt to shed light into the most recent developments in this area.

References

1. Aguiar, E., Zhang, Y., Blanton, M.: An overview of issues and recent developments in cloud computing and storage security. In: High Performance Cloud Auditing and Applications, pp. 1–31. Springer, New York (2013)
2. Ahuja, S.P., Komathukattil, D.: A survey of the state of cloud security. Netw. Commun. Technol. 1(2), 66–75 (2012)
3. Behl, A.: Emerging security challenges in cloud computing: an insight to cloud security challenges and their mitigation. In: World Congr. on Information and Communication Technologies, pp. 217–222. IEEE (2011)
4. Behl, A., Behl, K.: Security paradigms for cloud computing. In: 4th International Conference on Computational Intelligence, Communication Systems and Networks, pp. 200–205. IEEE (2012)
5. Carlin, S., Curran, K.: Cloud computing security. Int. J. Ambient Comput. Intell. 3(1), 38–46 (2011)

6. Chen, D., Zhao, H.: Data security and privacy protection issues in cloud computing. In: International Conference on Computer Science and Electronics Engineering, vol. 1, pp. 647–651. IEEE (2012)

7. Fugini, M.: Security and trust in Cloud scenarios. In: 1st International Workshop on Securing Services on the Cloud (IWSSC), pp. 22–29, September 2011

8. Gul, I., Rehman, A., Islam, M.: Cloud computing security auditing. In: The 2nd International Conference on Next Generation Information Technology, pp. 143–148. IEEE (2011)

9. Meetei, Z.M., Goel, A.: Security issues in cloud computing. In: 2012 5th International Conference on Biomedical Engineering and Informatics (BMEI), pp. 1321–1325 (2012)

10. Paquette, S., Jaeger, T.P., Wilson, C.S.: Identifying the security risks associated with governmental use of cloud computing. Gov. Inf. Quart. 27(3), 245–253 (2010)

11. Plummer, C.D., Smith, M.D., Bittman, J.T., Cearley, W.D., Cappuccio, J.D., Scott, D., Kumar, R., Robertson, B.: Five refining attributes of public and private cloud computing, May 2009

12. Popovic, K., Hocenski, Z.: Cloud computing security issues and challenges. In: 2010 Proceedings of the 33rd International Convention, MIPRO, pp. 344–349 (2010)

13. Rong, C., Nguyen, S.T., Jaatun, M.G.: Beyond lightning: a survey on security challenges in cloud computing. Comput. Electr. Eng. 39, 47–54 (2012)

14. Subashini, S., Kavitha, V.: A survey on security issues in service delivery models of cloud computing. J. Netw. Comput. Appl. 34(1), 1–11 (2011)

15. Sun, D., Chang, G., Sun, L., Wang, X.: Surveying and analyzing security, privacy and trust issues in cloud computing environments. Science Direct, 2852–2856 (2011). Published by Elsevier Ltd

16. Tianfield, H.: Security issues in cloud computing. In: 2012 IEEE International Conference on Systems, Man, and Cybernetics (SMC) (2012)

17. Tsai, H., Siebenhaar, M., Miede, A., Huang, Y., Steinmetz, R.: Threat as a service? virtualization's impact on cloud security. IT Prof. 14(1), 32–37 (2012)

18. Zissis, D., Lekkas, D.: Addressing cloud computing security issues. Future Gener. Comput. Syst. 28, 583–592 (2012). Science Direct 2012

A Hybrid Network Anomaly and Intrusion Detection Approach Based on Evolving Spiking Neural Network Classification

Konstantinos Demertzis[(⊠)] and Lazaros Iliadis

Department of Forestry and Management of the Environment
and Natural Resources, Democritus University of Thrace, 193 Pandazidou st.,
68200 N. Orestiada, Greece
{kdemertz,liliadis}@fmenr.duth.gr

Abstract. The evolution of network services is closely connected to the understanding and modeling of their corresponding traffic. The obtained conclusions are related to a wide range of applications, like the design of the transfer lines' capacity, the scalar taxing of customers, the security violations and the spotting of errors and anomalies. Intrusion Detection Systems (IDS) monitor and analyze the events in traffic, to locate indications for potential intrusion and integrity violation attacks, resulting in the violation of trust and availability of information resources. They act in a complimentary mode with the existing security infrastructure, aiming in the early warning of the administrator, offering him details that will let him reach proper decisions and correction actions. This paper proposes a network-based online system, which uses minimum computational power to analyze only the basic characteristics of network flow, so as to spot the existence and the type of a potential network anomaly. It is a Hybrid Machine Learning Anomaly Detection System (HMLADS), which employs classification performed by Evolving Spiking Neural Networks (eSNN), in order to properly label a Potential Anomaly (PAN) in the net. On the other hand it uses a Multi-Layer Feed Forward (MLFF) ANN to classify the exact type of the intrusion.

Keywords: Security · Network intrusion and anomalies · Machine learning · Evolving spiking neural networks · Multi-layer neural network

1 Introduction

An IDS [4] monitors network traffic for suspicious activity or anomalous behavior and alerts the system or network administrator accordingly. There are network based (NIDS) and host based (HIDS) intrusion detection systems. Some of them are looking for specific signatures of known threats, whereas others are spotting anomalies by comparing traffic patterns against a baseline. There are three basic approaches for designing and building IDS, namely: the Statistical, the Knowledge based and the Machine Learning one which has been employed in this research effort.

The concept of the Statistical-based systems (SBID) is simple: it determines "normal" network activity and then all traffic that falls outside the scope of normal is

© Springer International Publishing Switzerland 2014
A.B. Sideridis et al. (Eds.): E-Democracy 2013, CCIS 441, pp. 11–23, 2014.
DOI: 10.1007/978-3-319-11710-2_2

flagged as anomalous (abnormal). These systems attempt to learn network traffic patterns on a particular network. This process of traffic analysis continues as long as the system is active, so, assuming network traffic patterns remain constant, the longer the system is on the network, the more accurate it becomes. The Knowledge Based Intrusion Detection systems (KBIDES) classify the data vectors based on a carefully designed Rule Set or they use models obtained from past experience in a heuristic mode. The Machine Learning Anomaly Detection (MLAD) approach automates the analysis of the data vectors, and they result in the implementation of systems that have the capacity to improve their performance as time passes.

Artificial Intelligence and data mining algorithms have been applied as intrusion detection methods in finding new intrusion patterns [3, 11, 12, 17], such as clustering (unsupervised learning) [7, 13, 21] or classification (supervised learning) [5, 14, 18, 26]. Also, a few hybrid techniques were proposed like Neural Networks with Genetic Algorithms [23] or Radial Based Function Neural Networks with Multilayer Perceptron [1, 16]. Besides, other very effective methods exist such as Sequential Detection [22], State Space [15], Spectral Methods [27] and combinations of those.

This research effort aims in the development and application of an innovative MLAD approach towards the trace of anomalies in the network. The methodology will be using spiking (biologically inspired) Artificial Neural Networks (SANN). SANN are modular connectionist-based systems that evolve their structure and functionality in a continuous, self-organized, on-line, adaptive, interactive way from incoming information. Also, it can learn both data and knowledge in a supervised and/or unsupervised way. For the aforementioned reasons, many studies attempt to use SANN for practical applications, some of them demonstrating very promising results in solving complex real world problems [8, 19, 28].

The Hybrid Evolving Spiking Anomaly Detection Model (HESADM) that has been developed and discussed herein is based in the "*Thorpe*" neural model [24] which intensifies the importance of the spikes taking place in an earlier moment, whereas the neural plasticity is used to monitor the learning algorithm by using one-pass learning. In order to classify real-valued data sets, each data sample, is mapped into a sequence of *spikes* using the Rank Order Population Encoding (ROPE) technique [2, 25]. The topology of the developed eSNN is strictly feed-forward, organized in several layers and weight modification occurs on the connections between the neurons of the existing layers.

2 Rank Order Population Encoding

The ROPE method [2, 25] is an alternative to conventional rate coding scheme that uses the order of firing neuron's inputs to encode information which allows the mapping of vectors of real-valued elements into a sequence of spikes. Neurons organized into neuronal maps which share the same synaptic weights. Whenever the synaptic weight of a neuron is modified, the same modification is applied to the entire population of neurons within the map. Inhibition is also present between each neuronal map. If a neuron spikes, it inhibits all the neurons in the other maps with neighboring positions. This prevents all the neurons from learning the same pattern. When propagating new information, neuronal activity is initially reset to zero. Then, as the propagation goes on, neurons are progressively desensitize each time one of their inputs fire, thus making neuronal responses dependent upon the relative order of firing of the neuron's afferents. More precisely, let $A = \{a_1, a_2, a_3 \ldots a_{m-1}, a_m\}$ be the ensemble of afferent neurons of neuron i and $W = \{w_{1,i}, w_{2,i}, w_{3,i} \ldots w_{m-1,i}, w_{m,i}\}$ the weights of the m corresponding connections; let mod $\in [0,1]$ be an arbitrary modulation factor. The activation level of neuron i at time t is given by Eq. (1):

$$\text{Activation}(i,t) = \sum_{j \in [1,m]} \text{mod}^{\text{order}(a_j)} w_{j,i} \tag{1}$$

where order(a_j) is the firing rank of neuron a_j in the ensemble A. By convention, order (a_j) = +8 if a neuron a_j is not fired at time t, sets the corresponding term in the above sum to zero. This kind of desensitization function could correspond to a fast shunting inhibition mechanism. Whenever a neuron reaches its threshold, it spikes and inhibits neurons at equivalent positions in the other maps so that only one neuron will respond at any particular location. Every spike also triggers a time based Hebbian-like learning rule that adjusts the synaptic weights. Let t_e be the date of arrival of the Excitatory PostSynaptic Potential (EPSP) at synapse of weight W and t_a the date of discharge of the postsynaptic neuron.

$$\begin{aligned} \text{if } t_e < t_a \text{ then} \quad & dW = a(1 - W)e^{-|\Delta o|\tau} \\ \text{else} \quad & dW = -aWe^{-|\Delta o|\tau} \end{aligned} \tag{2}$$

Where Δo is the difference between the date of the EPSP and the date of the neuronal discharge (expressed in term of order of arrival instead of time), a is a constant that controls the amount of synaptic potentiation and depression [2].

ROPE technique with receptive fields allows the encoding of continuous values by using a collection of neurons with overlapping sensitivity profiles [8, 28]. Each input variable is encoded independently by a group of one-dimensional receptive fields (Fig. 2). For a variable n, an interval $\left[I_{min}^n, I_{max}^n\right]$ is defined. The Gaussian receptive field of neuron i is given by its center μi:

$$\mu i = I_{min}^n + \frac{2i - 3}{2} \frac{I_{max}^n - I_{min}^n}{M - 2} \tag{3}$$

The width σ is given by Eq. (4):

$$\sigma = \frac{1}{\beta} \frac{I_{max}^n - I_{min}^n}{M - 2} \tag{4}$$

where $1 \leq \beta \leq 2$ and the parameter β directly controls the width of each Gaussian receptive field.

Figure 1 depicts an example encoding of a single variable. For the diagram ($\beta = 2$) the input interval $\left[I_{min}^n, I_{max}^n\right]$ was set to $[-1.5, 1.5]$ and M = 5 receptive fields were used. For an input value v = 0.75 (thick straight line in left figure) the intersection points with each Gaussian is computed (triangles), which are in turn translated into spike time delays (right figure).

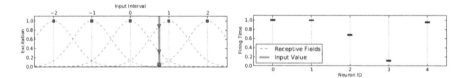

Fig. 1. Population encoding based on Gaussian receptive fields. Left Figure: Input Interval – Right Figure: Neuron ID [28]

3   One-Pass Learning

The aim of the one-pass learning method is to create a repository of trained output neurons during the presentation of training samples. After presenting a certain input sample to the network, the corresponding spike train is propagated through the SANN which may result in the firing of certain output neurons. It is also possible that no output neuron is activated and in this case the network remains silent and the classification result is undetermined. If one or more output neurons have emitted a spike, the neuron with the shortest response time among all activated output neurons is determined. The label of this neuron represents the classification result for the presented input sample. The procedure is described in detail in the following Algorithm 1 [8, 28].

Algorithm 1. Training an evolving Spiking Neural Network (eSNN) [28]

Require: m_l, s_l, c_l **for a class label** $l \in L$

1:   initialize neuron repository $R_l = \{\}$
2:   **for all** samples $X^{(i)}$ belonging to class l **do**
3:      $w_j^{(i)} \leftarrow (m_l)^{\text{order}(j)}, \forall j \mid j$ pre-synaptic neuron of i
4:      $u_{\max}^{(i)} \leftarrow \sum_j w_j^{(i)} (m_l)^{\text{order}(j)}$
5:      $\theta^{(i)} \leftarrow c_l u_{\max}^{(i)}$
6:   **if** $\min(d(w^{(i)}, w^{(k)})) < s_l, w^{(k)} \in R_l$ **then**
7:      $w^{(k)} \leftarrow$ merge $w^{(i)}$ and $w^{(k)}$ according to Equation 6
8:      $\theta^{(k)} \leftarrow$ merge $\theta^{(i)}$ and $\theta^{(k)}$ according to Equation 7
9:   **else**
10:     $R_l \leftarrow R_l \cup \{w^{(i)}\}$
11: **end if**
12: **end for**

For each training sample i with class label $l \in L$ a new output neuron is created and fully connected to the previous layer of neurons resulting in a real-valued weight vector $w^{(i)}$ with $w_j^{(i)} \in R$ denoting the connection between the pre-synaptic neuron j and the created neuron i. In the next step, the input spikes are propagated through the network and the value of weight $w_j^{(i)}$ is computed according to the order of spike transmission through a synapse j: $w_j^{(i)} = (m_l)^{\text{order}(j)}$, $\forall j | j$ pre-synaptic neuron of i.

Parameter m_l is the modulation factor of the Thorpe neural model. Differently labeled output neurons may have different modulation factors m_l. Function order(j) represents the rank of the spike emitted by neuron j. The firing threshold $\theta^{(i)}$ of the created neuron I is defined as the fraction $c_l \in R, 0 < c_l < 1$, of the maximal possible potential $u_{max}^{(i)}$:

$$\theta^{(i)} \leftarrow c_l u_{max}^{(i)} \tag{5}$$

$$u_{max}^{(i)} \leftarrow \sum_j w_j^{(i)} (m_l)^{\text{order}(j)} \tag{6}$$

The fraction c_l is a parameter of the model and for each class label $1 \in L$ a different fraction can be specified. The weight vector of the trained neuron is then compared to the weights corresponding to neurons already stored in the repository. Two neurons are considered too "similar" If the minimal *Euclidean* distance between their weight vectors is smaller than a specified similarity threshold s_l (the eSNN object uses optimal similarity threshold s = 0.6). All parameters modulation factor m_l, similarity threshold s_l, PSP fraction c_l, $1 \in L$ of ESNN which were included in this search space, are optimized according to the Versatile Quantum-inspired Evolutionary Algorithm (vQEA) [19]. In this case, both the firing thresholds and the weight vectors are merged according to Eqs. 7 and 8:

$$w_j^{(k)} \leftarrow \frac{w_j^{(i)} + N w_j^{(k)}}{1 + N}, \forall j \mid j \text{ pre-synaptic neuron of i} \tag{7}$$

$$\theta^{(k)} \leftarrow \frac{\theta^{(i)} + N \theta^{(k)}}{1 + N} \tag{8}$$

It must be clarified that integer N denotes the number of samples previously used to update neuron k. The merging is implemented as the (running) average of the

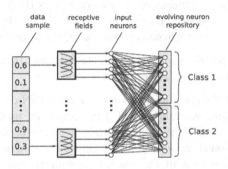

Fig. 2. The Evolving Spiking Neural Network (eSNN) architecture [28]

connection weights, and the (running) average of the two firing thresholds. After the merging, the trained neuron i is discarded and the next sample processed. If no other neuron in the repository is similar to the trained neuron i, the neuron i is added to the repository as a new output neuron.

Pattern recognition aims to classify data (patterns) based on either a priori knowledge or on statistical information extracted from the patterns. The patterns to be classified are usually groups of measurements or observations, defining points in an appropriate multidimensional space. Methods like classification, regression and clustering according to the type of learning procedure are used to generate the output value based on template matching, statistical classification, syntactic or structural matching and neural networks. The HESADM uses a two-layer feedforward neural network with sigmoid function both in hidden and output layer, scaled conjugate gradient backpropagation as the learning algorithm. The performance metric used is the Mean Squared Error (MSE).

4   Description of the HESADM Methodology

The HESADM methodology uses eSNN classification approach and Multi-Layer Feed Forward ANN in order to classify the exact type of the intrusion or anomaly in the network with minimum computational power.

The general methodology is described in detail below:

Step 1: We choose to use the traffic oriented data, which is related to only 9 features. We import the required classes that use the variable ***Population Encoding***. This variable controls the conversion of real-valued data samples into the corresponding time spikes. The encoding is performed with 20 Gaussian receptive fields per variable (Gaussian width parameter beta = 1.5). We also normalize the data to the interval [−1, 1] and so we indicate the coverage of the Gaussians using i_min and i_max. For the normalization processing the following function 9 was used:

$$x_{1_{norm}} = 2 * \left(\frac{x_1 - x_{min}}{x_{max} - x_{min}} \right) - 1, \quad x \in R \tag{9}$$

The data is classified in two classes namely: class 0 which contains the normal results and class 1 which comprises of the abnormal ones (DoS, r2l, u2r and probe). The eSNN object using modulation factor m = 0.9, firing threshold ratio c = 0.7 and similarity threshold s = 0.6 in agreement with the vQEA algorithm [19, 28].

Step 2: We train the eSNN with 70 % of the dataset vectors (*train_data) a*nd we test the eSNN with 30 % of the dataset vectors *(test_data).*

Step 3: If the result of the classification is normal, the eSNN classification process is repeated but this time the relevant normal data vectors are used. These vectors are comprised of 11 features [9]. If the result is normal then the process is terminated. If the result of the classification is abnormal, a two-layer feedforward neural network is used to perform pattern recognition of the attack type with all features of KDD dataset

(41 inputs and 5 outputs). In the hidden layer 33 neurons are used, based on the following empirical function 10 [6]:

$$\left(\frac{2}{3} * \text{Inputs}\right) + \text{Outputs} = \left(\frac{2}{3} * 41\right) + 5 = 33 \qquad (10)$$

The outcome of the pattern recognition process is submitted in the form of an *Alert* signal to the network administrator. A Graphical display of the complete HESADM methodology can be seen in Fig. 3.

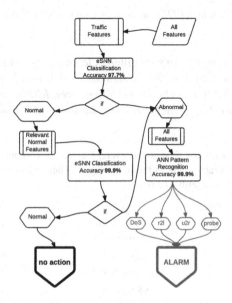

Fig. 3. The Hybrid Evolving Spiking Anomaly Detection Model (HESADM) methodology

5   Data

The *KDD Cup* 1999 data set [20] was used to test the herein proposed approach. This data set was created in the LincolnLab of MIT [20] and it is the most popular free data set used in evaluation of IDS. It contains recordings of the total network flow of a local network which was installed in the Lincoln Labs and it simulates the military network of the USA air force. The method of events' analysis includes a connection between a source IP address and a destination IP, during which a sequence of TCP packages is exchanged, by using a specific protocol and a strictly defined operation time. The KDD Cup 1999 data includes 41 characteristics which are organized in the following 4 basic categories: *Content Features, Traffic Features, Time-based Traffic Features, Host-based Traffic Features.* Also the attacks are divided in four categories, namely: DoS, r2l, u2r and probe.

6 Results

The analysis of the data set, the eSNN classifications and the pattern recognition was performed on a dual boot laptop machine with an AMD Phenom X3 N830 at 2.1 GHz CPU and 4 GB RAM.

In the first classification the data classified as normal or abnormal. The dataset Traf_Red_Full.data has 145,738 records and the 70 % (102,016 rec.) used as train_data and the 30 % (43,722 rec.) used as test_data. The results are shown below:

Classification Accuracy: 97.7 %.
No. of evolved neurons: Class 0/794 neurons - Class 1/809 neurons.
Elapsed time: 2068.23 s.

In order to perform comparison with different learning algorithms the Weka version 3.7 software was used (http://www.cs.waikato.ac.nz/ml/weka). Table 1 reports the results obtained with 10 different classifiers (*NaiveBayes, RBFNetwork, MLP, LibSVM, k-NN, J48, RandomForest, LogisticRegression, BayesNet, AdaBoost*) (Table 2).

Table 1. The Training Accuracy reports the average accuracy computed over 10-fold cross-validation. The testing accuracy refers to the percentage of data that were correctly detected by each classifier in the Traf_Red_Full_Dataset.

Traf_Red_Full Dataset		
Classifier	Train Accuracy	Test Accuracy
NaiveBayes	96.387 %	95.3981 %
RBFNetwork	94.9734 %	93.3281 %
MLP	97.9475 %	97.3743 %
LibSVM	98.9691 %	97.0335 %
k-NN	97.5435 %	97.4452 %
J48	97.619 %	97.4909 %
RandomForest	97.57 %	97.5046 %
LogisticRegression	97.8937 %	96.9008 %
BayesNet	97.9025 %	96.9237 %
AdaBoost	96.0311 %	95.947 %
eSNN	98.9 %	97.7 %

In the second classification case, the relevant normal features comprising of 11 features were used. The data were classified as normal or abnormal. The dataset normalFull.data has 145,738 records and the 70 % (102,016 rec.) used as train_data and the 30 % (43,722 rec.) used as test_data. The results are shown below:

Classification Accuracy: 99.9 %.
No. of evolved neurons: Class 0/646 neurons - Class 1/136 neurons.
Elapsed time: 1345.25 s.

Table 2. The Training Accuracy reports the average accuracy computed over 10-fold cross-validation. The testing accuracy refers to the percentage of data that were correctly detected by each classifier in the normalFull_Dataset.

normalFull Dataset		
Classifier	Train Accuracy	Test Accuracy
NaiveBayes	99.5112 %	98.895 %
RBFNetwork	99.9351 %	99.4412 %
MLP	99.9818 %	99.8992 %
LibSVM	99.673 %	99.1088 %
k-NN	99.2554 %	98.9278 %
J48	99.7751 %	99.719 %
RandomForest	99.8463 %	98.9561 %
LogisticRegression	98.998 %	98.9855 %
BayesNet	98.9933 %	98.9718 %
AdaBoost	99.2784 %	98.9357 %
eSNN	99.999 %	99.9 %

We can consider the Testing Accuracy as an estimate of the generalization ability of our classifiers. The best results on the testing dataset were obtained by using the eSNN classifier.

A MLFF ANN was developed with 41 input neurons, corresponding to the 41 input parameters of the KDD cup 1999 dataset, 33 neurons in the Hidden Layer and 5 in the output one corresponding to the following output parameters: DoS, r2l, u2r, Probe, normal. The KDD cup 1999 dataset was divided randomly in 70 % (102,016 rec.) the train_data, 15 % (21,861 rec.) as test_data and the rest 15 % (21,861 records) as validation_data. The training process finished in 11 min 54 s and 178 iterations were performed. The performance of the classification is shown in the following matrices and it supports the validity of the model:

ROC analysis: The ROC curve is a plot of the true positive rate (sensitivity) versus the false positive rate (1 - specificity) as the threshold is varied. A perfect test would show points in the upper-left corner, with 100 % sensitivity and 100 % specificity. For this problem, the network performs very well (Fig. 4).

Performance analysis: Mean Squared Error gives the difference between observation and simulation. The lower the better. In this case all curves converging to the same point mean that network performs perfect (Fig. 5).

Training State: The Figure shows variation in gradient coefficient with respect to number of epochs. Minimum the value is better will be training and testing of networks. From figure it can be seen that gradient value goes on decreasing with increase in number of epochs (Fig. 6).

Error histogram: this shows how the error sizes are distributed. Typically most errors are near zero, with very few errors far from that (Fig. 7).

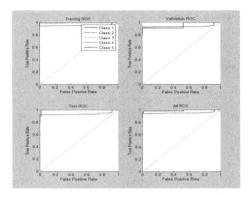

Fig. 4. ROC analysis

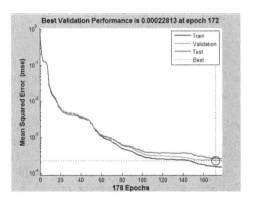

Fig. 5. Performance analysis

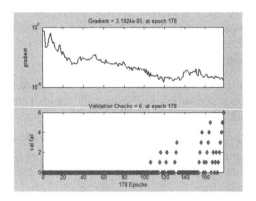

Fig. 6. Training State

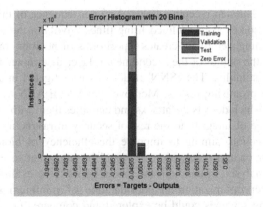

Fig. 7. Error histogram

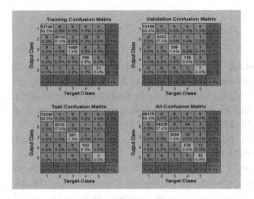

Fig. 8. Confusion Matrix

Confusion Matrix: The network outputs are very accurate, by the high numbers of correct responses in the green squares and the low numbers of incorrect responses in the red squares. The lower right blue squares illustrate the overall accuracies (Fig. 8).

7 Conclusion

In this paper we have proposed a Hybrid Evolving Spiking Anomaly Detection Model which intended to classify the normal and attack patterns in a computer network. This was based on an evolving Spiking Neural Network model and on MLFF ANN techniques. An effort was done to use minimum computational power and resources. The classification performance of eSNN and the accuracy of MLFF ANN were experimentally explored based on KDD cup 1999 dataset. The topology of the eSNN model consists of two layers. The first layer receives an input stimulus obtained from the mapping of a real-valued data sample into spike trains using a rank order population encoding based on Gaussian receptive fields. As a consequence of this transformation input neurons emit spikes at pre-defined firing times, invoking the one pass learning algorithm. The learning iteratively creates repositories of neurons, one repository for each class. Finally, the output of the second neural layer determines the class label of the presented input stimulus. The eSNN model was investigated in a number of scenarios and reported promising results. Moreover the MLFF ANN system is a pattern recognition system which detects the attacks and classifies them with high accuracy and adds a greater degree of integrity to the rest of security infrastructure of HESADM.

As a future direction, aiming to improve the efficiency of biologically realistic neural networks for pattern recognition, it would be important to extend the eSNN model with ROC analysis. In addition, the model needs to be evaluated further, with respect to parameter optimization in consideration of minimum processing time. Finally, other coding schemes could be explored and compared on the same security task.

References

1. Dahlia, A., Zainaddin, A., Hanapi, Z.M.: Hybrid of fuzzy clustering neural network over NSL dataset for intrusion detection system. J. Comput. Sci. **9**(3), 391–403 (2013)
2. Delorme, A., Perrinet, L., Thorpe, S.J.: Networks of integrate-and-fire neurons using rank order coding B: spike timing dependant plasticity and emergence of orientation selectivity. Neurocomputing **38–40**(1–4), 539–545 (2000)
3. Denning, E.D.: An Intrusion-Detection model. IEEE Trans. Softw. Eng. **13**, 222–232 (1987). doi:10.1109/TSE.1987.232894
4. Garcia, P., Verdejo, J., Fernandez, G., Vazquez, E.: Anomaly-based network intrusion detection: techniques, systems & challenges. Comput. Secur. **28**, 18–28 (2009). Elsevier
5. George, H.J.: Estimating continuous distributions in Bayesian classifiers. In: Proceedings of the UAI' 95, pp. 338–345. Morgan Kaufmann Publishers Inc., San Francisco (1995)
6. Heaton, J.: Introduction to Neural Networks with Java (2008). ISBN 097732060X
7. Jakir, H., Rahman, A., Sayeed, S., Samsuddin, K., Rokhani, F.: A modified hybrid fuzzy clustering algorithm for data partitions. Aust. J. Basic Appl. Sci. **5**, 674–681 (2011)
8. Kasabov, N.: Evolving Connectionist Systems: The Knowledge Engineering Approach. Springer, New York (2006)
9. Günes, K.H., Heywood, A.N.Z., Heywood, M.I.: Selecting Features for Intrusion Detection: A Feature Relevance Analysis on KDD 99 Intrusion Detection Datasets, Natural Sciences and Engineering Research Council of Canada (1999)
10. Kohavi, R.: A study of cross-validation and bootstrap for accuracy estimation and model selection. In: 14th International Joint Conference on Artificial Intelligence, vol. 2, no. 12, pp. 1137–1143 (1995)
11. Bharti, K., Shweta, J., Sanyam, S.: Fuzzy K-mean clustering via random forest for intrusion detection system. Int. J. Comput. Sci. Eng. **02**(06), 2197–2200 (2010)
12. Mehdi, B., Mohammad, B.: An overview to software architecture in intrusion detection system. Int. J. Soft Comput. Softw. Eng. (2012). doi:10.7321/jscse.v1.n1.1
13. Muna, M., Jawhar, T., Mehrotra, M.: Design network intrusion system using hybrid fuzzy neural network. Int. J. Comput. Sci. Secur. **4**(3), 285–294 (2009)

14. Mehdi, M., Zulkernine, M.: A neural network based system for intrusion detection and classification of attacks. In: IEEE International Conference on Advances in Intelligent Systems - Theory and Applications (2004)
15. Mukhopadhyay, I.: Implementation of Kalman filter in intrusion detection system. In: Proceeding of International Symposium on Communications and IT, Vientiane (2008)
16. Novikov, D., Yampolskiy, R.V., Reznik, L.: Anomaly detection based intrusion detection. In: Proceedings of the Third International Conference on IT: New Generations, 10–12 April. IEEE (2006)
17. Puketza, N., Zhang, K., Chung, M., Mukherjee, B., Olsson, R.A.: A methodology for testing intrusion detection system. IEEE Trans. Softw. Eng. **22**, 719–729 (1996)
18. Han, S.-J., Cho, S.-B.: Evolutionary neural networks for anomaly detection based on the behavior of a program. IEEE Trans. Syst. Man Cybern. **36**, 559–570 (2005)
19. Schliebs, S., Defoin-Platel, M., Kasabov, N.: Integrated feature and parameter optimization for an evolving spiking neural network. In: 15th International Conference, ICONIP 2008 (2009)
20. Stolfo, S.J., Wei, F., Wenke, L., Prodromidis, A., Chan, P.K.: Cost-based modeling and evaluation for data mining with application to fraud and intrusion detection: results from the JAM project. In: DISCEX '00 (2000)
21. Suguna, J., Selvi, A.M.: Ensemble fuzzy clustering for mixed numeric and categorical data. Int. J. Comput. Appli. **2012**(42), 19–23 (2012). doi:10.5120/5673-7705
22. Tartakovskya, A.G., Rozovskii, B.L., Blazek, R.B., Hongjoong, K.: A novel approach to detection of intrusions in computer networks via adaptive sequential and batch-sequential change-point detection methods. IEEE **54**(9), 3372–3382 (2006)
23. Zhou, T.-J.: The research of intrusion detection based on genetic neural network. IEEE Xplore Press, Hong Kong, pp. 276–281 (2008). doi:10.1109/ICWAPR.2008.4635789
24. Thorpe, S.J., Delorme, A., van Rullen, R.: Spike-based strategies for rapid processing. Neural Networks **14**(6–7), 715–725 (2001)
25. Thorpe, S.J., Gautrais, J.: Rank order coding. In: CNS '97, pp. 113–118 (1998)
26. Vapnik, V.: The Nature of Statistical Learning Theory, 2nd edn, p. 188. Springer, New York (1995). ISBN 10:0387945598
27. Wei, L., Ghorbani, A.A.: Network anomaly detection based on wavelet analysis. EURASIP **2009**, 1–16 (2009). (Article No. 4, Hindawi Publishing Corp., New York)
28. Wysoski, S.G., Benuskova, L., Kasabov, N.: Adaptive learning procedure for a network of spiking neurons and visual pattern recognition. In: Blanc-Talon, J., Philips, W., Popescu, D., Scheunders, P. (eds.) ACIVS 2006. LNCS, vol. 4179, pp. 1133–1142. Springer, Heidelberg (2006)

Security Risk Assessment Challenges in Port Information Technology Systems

Georgios Makrodimitris[(⊠)], Nineta Polemi, and Christos Douligeris

Department of Informatics, University of Piraeus, 80, Karaoli & Dimitriou St.,
185 34 Piraeus, Greece
{geomakro,dpolemi,cdoulig}@unipi.gr

Abstract. Port Information Technology Systems are of critical importance for the uninterrupted and effective operation of commercial ports. However, as shown in this paper the current safety and security approaches have several weaknesses and they are not thoroughly harmonized with the current demanding global collaborative environment. An analysis of the major current risk assessment methodologies shows that they aim to identify risks through resources (time, manpower, cost), which are time and resource consuming procedures and their results depend not only on the specific characteristics of the entity analyzed but also on the quantitative or the qualitative approach of the methodology. This paper concludes that current risk assessment methodologies demand significant parameterization and suggest the development of a new approach with less complexity that will sufficiently cover the identified weaknesses.

Keywords: Critical infrastructures · Collaborativeness · Information and communication technologies · Port information systems · Risk assessment · Safety · Security

1 Introduction

As information and communication technology (ICT) systems become an integral part of the everyday operations of entities and organizations, the associated potential internal and external risks increase at a fast pace. The absence of sectorial, targeted, security risk assessment methodologies is becoming a major requirement for the successful adaptation of the applicable security policies.

Moreover, current methodologies address either safety or security concerns but, in most cases, they do not view them simultaneously. The term "security" is associated with the assets' protection regarding the four dimensions of confidentiality, integrity, authenticity/access control and availability. "Safety" deals with the access control and the availability of physical assets. It is understandable that safety is a subset of security.

The scope of this paper is to identify and assess several well-known risk assessment methodologies proposed for risk assessment in critical information infrastructures (CIIs), with a focus in ports. This paper reveals the weaknesses of the existing methodologies and proposes criteria and requirements that need to be fulfilled by a

© Springer International Publishing Switzerland 2014
A.B. Sideridis et al. (Eds.): E-Democracy 2013, CCIS 441, pp. 24–35, 2014.
DOI: 10.1007/978-3-319-11710-2_3

holistic (cyber and physical) risk assessment methodology applicable to CIIs, and in particular to ports which constitute very demanding and dynamically changing infrastructures.

2 Existing Methodologies and Open Issues

Most CIIs include complex ICT systems with dynamic interactions with several other entities. This complex interaction of a critical infrastructure is illustrated in Fig. 1. For example, ports interact with other ports, ships (with their passengers, crew and/or cargo), port authorities, maritime and insurance companies, customs, ship-industry administrators, banks, government ministries, other commercial providers and other critical infrastructures (e.g. railroads, airports).

Fig. 1. Interconnections of the ICT environment in a critical infrastructure

Regarding the protection of this complex ICT infrastructure, the existing related standards, methodologies and tools focus either on safety (physical security) or on IT security. Moreover, one finds a common misunderstanding between the methodologies used and the tools available for the methodologies' implementation. A methodology describes the sequence of the generic steps needed to implement a risk assessment analysis. These steps are the processes of identifying, quantifying and associating risk to assets. On the other hand, a risk assessment tool is oriented towards the measurement of the potential for losses that a threat could have on an organization. Tools are based on methodologies and most often a specific tool is developed for a specific methodology [1, 26].

These methodologies must be compliant to standards that deal with critical infrastructures' safety and security. Table 1 provides a list of standards as well as of some best practices that address security and safety issues in ports.

Table 1. Safety and Security Standards relative to Ports [18–21].

| Standards | |
Safety	Security
International Labour Organization (ILO) Code of Practice for Safety and Health in Ports (2005)	ISO/IEC 27005:2008 - Information technology - Security techniques - Information Security Risk Management
General Conference of the International ILO Convention concerning Occupational Safety and Health in Dock Work, C-152 (1979)	ISO/IEC 27001 - Information technology - Security techniques - Specification for an Information Security Management System
General Conference of the ILO Recommendation concerning Occupational Safety and Health in Dock Work, R-160	ISO/IEC 27002:2005 - Information technology - Security techniques - Code of practice for information security management
IMO Code of Practice for Solid Bulk Cargo (BC Code)	
International Code for the Construction and Equipment of Ships carrying Dangerous Chemicals in Bulk (IBC Code)	
International Code for the Safe Carriage of Grain in Bulk (International Grain Code)	
Code of Practice for the Safe Loading and Unloading of Bulk Carriers (BLU Code)	
International Maritime Dangerous Goods Code (IMDG Code)	

2.1 Cyber Risk Assessment Methodologies

According to El Fray I. [13], there exist more than 200 risk assessment methodologies. The most known and market-accepted methodologies are CRAMM, OCTAVE, EBios, MAGERIT, MEHARI, STORM, IT - Grundschutz and ISAMM. A common characteristic of these methodologies is that they deal only with IT security risk assessment and do not deal with safety. Table 2 presents the basic characteristics of each methodology and shows some of each methodology's unique characteristics.

Table 2. Characteristics of current risk assessment methodologies.

		Characteristics			
		Evaluation scale	**Impact evaluation**	**Collaboration capabilities**	**Required skills**
Methods	**OCTAVE**	Qualitative	Based on critical assets	Medium	Standard
	CRAMM	Qualitative	Based on open damage scenarios	Low	ICT Experts
	Ebios	Qualitative	Based on security needs	Medium	Standard
	MAGERIT	Quantitative / Qualitative	Based on open damage scenarios	Low	ICT Experts
	MEHARI	Qualitative	Based on fixed damage scenarios	Low	ICT Experts
	STORM	Qualitative	Based on open damage scenarios	High	Low
	IT-Grundschutz	Qualitative	Based on open damage scenarios	Low	Standard
	ISAMM	Qualitative	Based on monetary loss	Low	Standard

2.1.1 OCTAVE

OCTAVE is a suite of tools, techniques and methods for risk-based information security strategic assessment and planning. OCTAVE consists of three methods: the original OCTAVE method forms the basis for the OCTAVE body of knowledge, OCTAVE-S, is proposed to be used for smaller organizations while OCTAVE-Allegro is a streamlined approach for information security assessment and assurance. All of them are based on specific criteria for risk evaluation, which form the basis of the principles and attributes of the risk analysis and management [29].

The common feature of this family of methods is that they are based on the same criteria. Moreover, they use the same technique in order to examine the organizational and technology issues. These methods are implemented by three to five persons from the organization's own personnel, who work on the same forms of the tool they use. This personnel needs to have a thorough knowledge and understanding of the operations of the organization. They are responsible for the implementation of the methodology in order to identify the critical assets and their threats, as well as the vulnerabilities of the organization and to protect the organization from all potential risks [2].

Since OCTAVE is implemented in an organization by a specific team, the required skills of the participants are very high and the collaborativeness of the methodology is low.

2.1.2 CRAMM

CRAMM can be used to undertake a risk analysis of information systems and networks, to identify security requirements and possible solutions, and to detect contingency requirements and possible solutions. CRAMM materializes the asset identification and valuation, the threat and vulnerability assessment, and the counter-measures recommendations [16].

CRAMM is implemented by an analyst or by a group of analysts, who are responsible for evaluating the security and risk level of the organization analyzing and combining the diverse knowledge located distributed in the corporate environment [13]. As it is understood, the required skills of the participants are very high and the collaborativeness of this methodology is also low.

2.1.3   Ebios

Ebios is a methodology for assessing and treating risks in the field of information systems security (ISS) which can be implemented in various organizations and businesses, from small to large ones. Ebios is quite collaborative, since it gathers and combines the corporate knowledge through a qualitative approach. Ebios builds its ISS repository and integrates ISS into existing projects or systems regardless of their level of advancement [12].

Although the methodology is collaborative, there does not exist an advanced computational schema for the correlation and determination of the results. This characteristic is a significant disadvantage of the methodology.

2.1.4   Magerit

Magerit is a methodology to identify and mitigate security risks in an organization, either no matter whether it is a complex or a basic one. Magerit can be used in several parts of IT systems, such as in communications, and electronic media, which brings evident benefits for the users [8–10].

Magerit can be used and maintained only by expert IT users. These users are responsible to implement the risk analysis process using workshops and interviews with specific representatives of the organization. They participate only in specific phases of the assessment process. Therefore, the required skills of the participants are very high and the collaborativeness of the methodology is low, even though there exist interactions between the experts and some of the organization's personnel.

2.1.5   MEHARI

MEHARI is a methodology most appropriate for medium to large scale organizations, such as governmental agencies and medium and large size companies. Its features are the risk model, the consideration of the efficiency of the security measures in place or planned and the capability to evaluate and simulate the residual risk level resulting from additional measures [7].

In this methodology, there exists considerable participation of some users in specific phases, especially in the identification of assets and vulnerabilities [13], resulting in a low collaborativeness. Moreover, the participants need to know have a thorough understanding of the breadth and depth of the organization, thus their required skills are very high.

2.1.6   STORM-RM

STORM-RM is a collaborative, multi-criteria risk management methodology. It allows all organization users to participate in the various risk assessment and treatment phases. Different users are involved in its implementation in order to calculate the risk, provide input for the impact assessment, identify threat/vulnerability and risk, and evaluate and select the appropriate countermeasures [25, 27, 28, 31]. Based on the above, it seems that STORM-RM is the appropriate methodology in a demanding and dynamically changing system, such as ports.

The problem in the use of STORM is the computational schema of the total risk. In order to compute the risk, it takes into account the maximum value of each answer. This means that if the users give extreme values in their responses, the resulting outcome will not correspond to the organization's expected risk and the selection of countermeasures will be erroneous and non-efficient.

2.1.7   IT-Grundschutz

IT-Grundschutz (IT-G) is a methodology which has been designed for organizations with complex infrastructures, such as governmental agencies and large companies. IT-G uses simple modules and, thus, can also be implemented in smaller businesses, as well.

IT-G needs first to be configured for the establishment of an integrated and effective IT security management. The proposed IT security process consists of two steps:

- Initialization of the process, where the IT security goals and business environment is defined, and an organizational structure for IT security is established
- Creation of the IT Security Concept, where the IT structure analysis it is defined, the protection requirements are assessed,
- IT-G first checks the security by addressing the verification of current counter-measures in the organization. The risk assessment identifies threats, which can be eliminated by additional security measures. IT-G is a qualitative risk analysis approach, where the analysis and the correlation are made with a unique primitive computational technique.

IT-G can be implemented by users who know the IT standards very well and undertake the responsibility to implement the entire process. The collaborative abilities of IT-G can be considered low, because the users participate only in some specific steps of the risk assessment [4–6].

2.1.8   Information Security Assessment and Monitoring Method (ISAMM)

ISAMM can be implemented either by governmental agencies or by various size companies. ISAMM is a quantitative methodology consisting of three parts, namely the scoping, the assessment, and the analysis of the compliance and threats, and results in the necessary calculations and reporting.

In this methodology, the differentiation from the others is that the risks are expressed in monetary units. Having implemented ISAMM, the assessed risks are expressed via the Annual Loss Expectancy (ALE). ALE is a threat or a group of threats being implemented. Also, ALE expresses the annual expected loss or cost in the organization [17].

2.1.9   Comparison and Evaluation

From the above, it is clear that the presented methodologies cannot capture the complexity of infrastructure interconnections, cross-sector impacts, dependencies on other systems or infrastructures and the cascading effects within a sector or across sectors. They consider risk so as a combination of the likelihood and the impact of a threat to hit a group of assets, and as the vulnerability level of this group of assets [24].

Regarding compliance to international standards, only Ebios and MAGERIT are fully compliant with the rules and procedures of ISO [32]. The other methodologies cover only partially the obligations imposed by the ISO family of standards. Moreover, only STORM achieves a high degree of collaborativeness while the other methodologies are either not collaborative at all or they are at a remarkably low level.

2.2   Physical Risk Assessment Methodologies/Tools

The most well-known methodologies are implemented in ports and, generally, in maritime environments in order to be compliant with the ISPS Code, are the following: Port Security Risk Assessment Tool, Maritime Security Risk Analysis Model, Maritime Security Risk Analysis Model-PLUS/FORETELL, MAritime RISk Assessment and Comprehensive Maritime Awareness System. These methodologies are used to analyze and manage the risks in these infrastructures but they study only the safety in maritime environment.

2.2.1   Port Security Risk Assessment Tool (PSRAT)

The U.S. Coast Guard has developed PSRAT. PSRAT is a tool for security assessment. This tool examines if a port's infrastructure is compliant with the security requirements specified by the ISPS Code. It also assesses terrorism risks and helps to and protect the physical assets, services and people (personnel, travelers, etc.) leading in a sager maritime environment [15].

2.2.2   Maritime Security Risk Analysis Model (MSRAM)

The U.S. Coast Guard has also developed the Maritime Security Risk Analysis Model (MSRAM), a specialized tool assessing terrorism risk. This tool is used to evaluate the terrorist risks and to protect the port infrastructure and vessels with specific security plans. This methodology estimates and rolls up risk through different types, modes and levels. The consequences of a successful attack are divided into five levels: death and injury; primary and secondary economic impact; symbolic effect; national security; and environmental impact [11].

2.2.3   Maritime Security Risk Analysis Model-PLUS/FORETELL (MSRAM-PLUS)

MSRAM-PLUS is an extension of MSRAM. This methodology adds more capabilities in order to provide a lifecycle decision using the monitoring strategies. MSRAM-PLUS supports a dynamic risk decision technique, which is based on modeling and analysis addressing and interworking with the MSRAM methods, models, software and data.

2.2.4 MAritime RISk Assessment (MARISA)

MARISA is a decision-making system, based in fuzzy logic, that studies safety at sea environmentally and it is used in particular to prevent the pollution. MARISA does not examine ICTs [3].

2.2.5 Comprehensive Maritime Awareness (CMA) System

CMA provides both the methodology and the tool, which analyze and correlate the knowledge from different inputs, such as the PACOM Common Operational Picture (COP), Automated Information System (AIS), Department of Defense systems, Department of Commerce databases, and Department of Homeland Security information. Thus, identifies gaps related to safety threats. CMA studies track maritime movements, including vessels, people, and cargo identifies potential threats and classifies them [23].

2.2.6 Comparison and Evaluation

All the above methodologies are addressing only the safety of the ports and their PICT systems. ICT or cyber threats are a different sector, not covered by these methodologies [15].

2.3 Outcomes

These efforts cover the requirements of current maritime legislation or standardization, but not the IT security of ports. They do not face ports as independent critical infrastructures, which also have IT systems. Thus, there is a need for an approach that will address ICT security concerns in such environments.

3 Enhancing Safety and IT Security Management

3.1 Necessity for a New Approach

As discussed in the previous sections, because the management of information security risk is a major concern of organizations worldwide and especially for CIIs, such as ports, several security management methodologies have been proposed. From the discussion above though, one can easily conclude that none of them satisfies completely the needs of the current demanding ICT systems. Also, almost all of them focus on IT security, and only STORM studies both safety and security, as it is defined on their foundations.

The proposed methodologies don't solve specific problems and threats, which are often a combination between safety and security threats. Even though some of them are quite collaborative, the participating users must have a deep knowledge of the organization and they have to be experts in IT. Also, the users' participation is not catalytic on the computation of the risk because of the lack of effective discussions and exchanges of information, ideas and thoughts.

As it is conceivable, it is necessary to develop a new improved approach in order to analyze and evaluate the security of critical infrastructures taking into account the knowledge of all the personnel of the port [14].

3.2   Objectives of a New Approach

The objective of a new approach will be to enhance the protection of ports. The view of this enforcement must be focused on the physical as well as the cyber assets' environment. These assets could be ships, passengers, crew, cargo, port authorities, IT systems with entire entities, such as servers, workstations, hard disks, U.S.B. drives, including data (personal, economic, etc.) etc., maritime and insurance companies, customs, ship-industry administrators, banks, government ministries, other commercial providers and other critical infrastructures.

First of all, the new methodology will have to identify the possible threats that critical infrastructures may face either in their internal environment, such as interacting entities and infrastructures, or in their external environment, such as ships, travelers, vehicles, etc., or from other correlations with external entities [22]. These threats will be associated with all the types of assets. The major factor of identifying them is the current legislation and standardization, especially on personal and economic data. Thus, the opportunity will be provided to take into account risks and threats from different geographic levels and attack modes as specified in the corresponding legislation and standardization. Using this new methodology, a new tool must be developed whose features must be the collaborativeness, and the involution of the physical and the cyber assets and their interdependencies. This new system will analyze and manage all types of threats, vulnerabilities and risks and, using crisis' scenarios, it must be able to generate and update security documents.

The goal of such a new methodology is to increase the collaboration among all the participants in order to enhance the safety and the security of critical infrastructures based on standards, legislation, best practices and guidelines.

3.3   Desired Features of a New Methodology

The development of a new methodology must be based on features which will cover the gaps of existing methodologies and it must satisfy the demanding and dynamically changing environment of the ports.

One of these features is that new methodology should study all the types of assets, either physical or cyber, about their criticality. Moreover, the new methodology must not separate assets between safety and IT security.

Another feature is the need for collaborativeness. In order for the new methodology to be collaborative, a significant participation of users (personnel) is required. These users will assist in estimating threats and risk levels, and will be in close collaboration with the expert users of the port. The participation and involvement of such a large number of users must be realized in such a way so as not to lead to erroneous results. Because of the participation of an increasing number of users, it is necessary to revise the estimation procedure of the threat, risk and vulnerability levels. The wide spread of the users' knowledge is a major factor which must be taken into account during this estimation. The new estimation procedure must be more reliable and it must depend on the users' knowledge so as to extract results which will lead to enhanced safety and security in ports.

3.4 Desired Results

The first desired result is the development of a new holistic and targeted risk management methodology for ports. The new methodology needs to be set up and the ports' assets need to be identified and classified based on their type (physical or cyber) as well as on their interdependencies. In addition correlations need to be identified between assets and threats as well between the estimation procedures of threats and the risk levels.

The new tool/system, must be able to manage the assets, either physical or cyber, based on the existing legislation, standardization procedures, best practices and industry guidelines.

4 Conclusions

In this paper we presented the need to develop a new approach in order to cover the gaps and the weaknesses of the existing methodologies in order to be able to satisfy the current port environment. The new approach must be a new risk management secure methodology that assesses risk tolerance. Also, it is desired that be compliant with the ISO family of standards for safety and security and be created and parameterized regarding the needs of the environment it is expected to be used [30].

The major features which will differentiate this methodology are the collaborativeness and the computational schemas of the threat and risk levels. Also, it must be a multi-criteria decision technique, where the users must be a catalytic factor in the impact and total risk evaluation.

Such a significant effort to develop a new approach with the desired features is currently realized in a new project, the Collaborative Cyber/Physical Security Management System (CYSM, www.cysm.eu), which focuses on covering the needs and requirements of such a demanding critical infrastructure. In CYSM, the development of the Secure Methodology Assessing Risk Tolerance (S.M.A.R.T.) is envisioned, that will try to provide a holistic approach to security management of Port Information Management systems.

References

1. Adler, R., Fuller, J.: An integrated framework for assessing and mitigating risks to maritime critical infrastructure. In: Proceedings of IEEE Conference on Technologies for Home-land Security, pp. 252–257 (2007)
2. Alberts, C., Dorofee, A.: Operationally critical threat, asset, and vulnerability evaluation (OCTAVE) method implementation guide, v2.0. Software Engineering Institute, Carnegie Mellon University (2001). http://www.cert.org/octave/

3. Balmat, J., Lafont, F., Maifret, R., Pessel, N.: MAritime RISk Assessment (MARISA), a fuzzy approach to define an individual ship risk factor. Ocean Eng. **36**(15–16), 1278–1286 (2009)
4. BSI Standard 100-1: Information Security Management Systems (ISMS) (2005). www.bsi.bund.de
5. BSI Standard 100-2.: IT - Grundszchutz methodology (2005). www.bsi.bund.de
6. BSI Standard 100-3: Risk analysis based on IT–Grundszchutz (2005). www.bsi.bund.de
7. Club de la Securite de L' information Francais Methods Commision: Mehari 2010: Risk analysis and treatment Guide, France, August 2010 (2010). http://www.clusif.asso.fr/fr/production/ouvrages/pdf/MEHARI-2010-Risk-Analysis-and-Treatment-Guide.pdf
8. Crespo, F., Gomez, M., Candau, J., Manas, J.A.: MAGERIT – Version 2, Methodology for Information Systems Risk Analysis and Management, Books I – The Method. Ministerio de Administraciones Publicas, Madrid (2006)
9. Crespo, F., Gomez, M., Candau, J., Manas, J.A.: MAGERIT – Version 2, Methodology for Information Systems Risk Analysis and Management, Book III – Techniques. Ministerio de Administraciones Publicas, Madrid (2006)
10. Crespo, F., Gomez, M., Candau, J., Manas, J.A.: MAGERIT – Version 2, Methodology for Information Systems Risk Analysis and Management, Book II – Catalogue of Elements. Ministerio de Administraciones Publicas, Madrid (2006)
11. Downs, B.: The maritime security risk analysis model. In: USCG Proceedings of the Marine Safety and Security Council (2007). http://www.uscg.mil/proceedings/
12. Ebios: Expression of Needs and Identification of Security Objectives Premier Ministre Secrétariat général de la défense nationale Direction centrale de la sécurité des systèmes d'information Sous-direction des opérations Bureau conseil (2010). www.ssi.gouv.fr
13. El Fray, I.: A comparative study of risk assessment methods, MEHARI & CRAMM with a new formal model of risk assessment (FoMRA) in information systems. In: Cortesi, A., Chaki, N., Saeed, K., Wierzchoń, S. (eds.) CISIM 2012. LNCS, vol. 7564, pp. 428–442. Springer, Heidelberg (2012)
14. Elachgar, H., Regragui, B.: Information Security, new approach. In: Conference on Innovative Computing Technology (INTECH). IEEE (2012)
15. Analysis of cyber security aspects in the maritime sector. ENISA report (2011). http://www.enisa.europa.eu/act/res/other-areas/cyber-security-aspects-in-the-maritime-sector/cyber-security-aspects-in-the-maritime-sector-1. Accessed 4 Mar 2014
16. Insight Consulting: CRAMM User Guide. Issue 5.1, United Kingdom (2005)
17. ISAMM - Information Security Assessment & Monitoring Method (2002). http://www.telindus.com
18. ISO/IEC:17799: Information technology - security techniques - code of practice for information security management (2005). http://www.iso.org
19. ISO/IEC:27002: Information technology - security techniques - code of practice for information security management (2005). http://www.iso.org
20. ISO/IEC:27005: Information technology - Security techniques - Information Security Risk Management (2008). http://www.iso.org
21. ISO/IEC:27001: Information technology - Security techniques - Specification for an Information Security Management System (2005). http://www.iso.org
22. López, D., Pastor, O., García Villalba, L.J.: Dynamic risk assessment in information systems: state-of-the-art. In: ICIT 2013, South Africa (2013)
23. Maritime Domain Awareness Data Sharing Community of Interest (MDA DS COI). Data Management Working Group, Spiral 2, Vocabulary Handbook Version 2.0.2 (2007). http://www.uscg.mil/acquisition/nais/RFP/SectionJ/MDA-COI-vocab.pdf

24. National Institute for Standards and Technology: Risk management guide for information technology systems. NIST Special Publication 800-30, USA (2002)
25. Ntouskas, T., Polemi, N.: A secure, collaborative environment for the security management of port information systems. In: Proceedings of the 5th International Conference on the Internet and Web Applications and Services, pp. 374–379. IEEE Press, Spain (2010a)
26. Ntouskas, T., Polemi, N.: Collaborative security management services for Port Information Systems. In: Proceedings of International Conference on e-Business, pp. 305–308. SciTePress, Italy (2012a)
27. Ntouskas, T., Polemi, N.: STORM-RM: a collaborative and multicriteria risk management methodology. Int. J. Multicriteria Decis. Making 2(2), 159–177 (2012)
28. Ntouskas, T., Polemi, N.: STORM-RA: an implemented, collaborative, multicriteria decision making risk assessment methodology. In: 7th Meeting Multicriteria Decision Analysis, Greece (2010b)
29. OCTAVE Method Implementation Guide Version 2.0. Carnegie Mellon University, June 2001 (2010). http://www.cert.org/octave/
30. Polemi, N.: Security management of the ports' information systems. ENISA project (2013). http://www.enisa.europa.eu. Accessed 4 Mar 2014
31. Polemi, N., Ntouskas, T.: Open issues and proposals in the IT security management of commercial ports: the S-PORT national case. In: Gritzalis, D., Furnell, S., Theoharidou, M. (eds.) SEC 2012. IFIP AICT, vol. 376, pp. 567–572. Springer, Heidelberg (2012)
32. Syalim, A., Hori, Y., Sakurai, K.: Comparison of risk analysis methods: Mehari, Magerit, NIST800-30 and Microsoft's Security Management Guide. In: International Conference on Availability, Reliability and Security (2009)

e-Governance I

Synthesizing a Criterion for SOA Reference Architecture to Sustain eParticipation

Muntazir Mehdi[1,2]([✉]), Arkadiusz Stasiewicz[2], Lukasz Porwol[2], Deirdre Lee[2], and Adegboyega Ojo[2]

[1] Department of Computer Science, Technical University Kaiserslautern, Kaiserslautern, Germany
m_mehdi10@cs.uni-kl.de
[2] Digital Enterprise Research Institute, National University of Ireland, Galway, Ireland
{arkadiusz.stasiewicz,lukasz.porwol,deirdre.lee,adegboyega.ojo}@deri.org

Abstract. With inception of Service-Orientation in research and industry, the need to select a Reference Architecture (RA) that supports Service Orientation in some specific domain has developed into a challenge. Institutionalizing a criterion that helps software designers and developers to properly extend or design an RA for a domain-specific, goal-aware and context-aware implementation of a Service-Oriented Architecture (SOA) system has evolved into a necessity. In this article, a criterion derived from understanding existing standard SOA reference architectures is presented. In following presented work, we focus specifically on the eParticipation domain to validate the proposed criterion. The criterion will not only help improve the process of refining and specialising standard SOA-RA, but also provides a set of key ingredients to sustain SOA-RA definition in the eGovernment domain, specifically to sustain information integration in eParticipation.

Keywords: Software architectures · eGovernment · eParticipation · Service Oriented Architecture · SOA reference architecture

1 Introduction

Service-Oriented Architectures (SOA) have existed in research and industry for 25 years and have been providing an architectural approach to enterprises enabling the reuse of business operations. SOA is an evolving architecture model that gains maturity from its predecessors, while drawing on the concepts of service-orientation [9]. With the widespread acquisition of Information and Communication Technologies (ICT) in multitude of enterprises, skilled software architectures are clearly in-demand to coordinate and manage systems and processes within and between enterprises. Today, the focus of both industry and research revolves round the development of distributed systems with effective and efficient design processes and work-flow integration. Business applications in the past were simple and thus there was no need to define complex architectures.

A.B. Sideridis et al. (Eds.): E-Democracy 2013, CCIS 441, pp. 39–51, 2014.
DOI: 10.1007/978-3-319-11710-2_4

But with the advances of ICT, introduction of technologies involving big data and cloud computing, complex architectures introduced themselves albeit with their respective challenges. In past, with the introduction of multi-tier applications, the biggest challenge was to define a template or an abstract architecture using which concrete architectures could be built or drawn. Even though the template was abstract, its purpose was to define technologies, boundaries, rules, necessities, and design characteristics that apply to the desired solution. These templates or abstract architectures are known as Reference Architectures (RA) [9].

RAs have proved to be very effective for domains involving extensive use of Information and Communication Technologies (ICT). eGovernment domain builds itself based on the use of ICT. eGovernment refers to extensive use of technology in the public sector to support the provision of public services and management of government and public affairs. David McClure, Associate Director of the U.S. General Accounting Office, views eGovernment as [14]:

"Electronic government refers to government's use of technology, particularly web based Internet applications to enhance the access to and delivery of government information and service to citizens, business partners, employees, other agencies, and government entities. It has the potential to help build better relationships between government and the public by making interaction with citizens smoother, easier, and more efficient. Indeed, government agencies report using electronic commerce to improve core business operations and deliver information and services faster, cheaper, and to wider groups of customers".

eParticipation is an increasingly important component of a complete eGovernment strategy, which involves the use of ICT to achieve certain common goals [11]. Blogs, discussion forums, and the use of social media like facebook and twitter have proven to be the most effective eParticipation tools. With the ongoing growth of Internet, there is a growing interest in using social media platforms (facebook, twitter, etc.) for eParticipation [11]. However, with social media becoming mainstream in eParticipation, a new set of information integration and information sharing challenges have arisen.

Service Oriented Computing (SOC), a realisation of Service Oriented Architectures (SOA), has extensive potential of addressing both information integration and information sharing challenges using the power of web-services in different heterogeneous platforms on the Web. But choreographing web-services to address information integration and information sharing challenges is a nontrivial task in social media platforms due to their distributed nature [7]. SOA Reference Architectures (SOA-RAs) are an extension of RA that incorporate and support service orientation. Currently, there are some standard SOA-RAs that support implementation of a SOA system in different domains. However, there is no existing approach on how to extend or customize standard SOA-RAs to any user-required, newly adopted domain-specific implementation.

In addition to this, the confidence of a SOA architect on standard SOA-RA is also a critical consideration while implementing SOA systems. The decision to adapt to the idea of using services or service-orientation in business, the assessment of current situation of the business, and quantification of benefits achieved from implementing SOA, needs to be carried out beforehand. Software Architects thus are responsible for defining reference models at different level of abstractions and derive an RA that extensively merges these reference models [12].

In this article, we propose criterion for SOA-RA for use in eParticipation systems. The criterion enables architects to define an RA based on which SOA implementations can be carried out. In Subsect. 2.1, a brief motivation that drove our work towards determining criterion for SOA-RA is presented. In Subsect. 2.2, a systematic approach of deriving criterion for SOA Reference Architecture (SOA-RA) is described. Section 3, gives a brief insight into general architectures and their importance, and discusses a criterion that is derived from understanding the basic concepts of Reference Architectures (RA). In Sect. 4, a discussion of RA in context of SOA is presented. Specifically, we discuss SOA-RA proposed by The Open Group to develop our understanding of standard SOA-RA [12]. And in Sect. 5, detailed criterion for SOA-RA is presented. Finally in Sect. 6, an eParticipation SOA-RA and detail of some of its components are presented.

2 Motivation and Approach

2.1 Motivation

"Puzzled by Policy" (PbP)[1] is a European Commission project, funded under the Competitiveness and Innovation Framework Programme (CIP) ICT Policy Support Programme (ICT PSP). This large eParticipation project has a consortium consisting of twelve partners from nine European Countries (Greece, Hungary, Ireland, Italy, the Netherlands, Portugal, Slovenia, Spain and United Kingdom) and is led by INSIGHT - Centre for Data Analytics (formerly DERI) at NUI Galway. The main objective of the project is to increase citizens awareness of the current EU and individual member countries immigration policies and to engage citizens directly in policy-making process. Before joining the discussion users are allowed to graphically compare their views on immigration with national and EU immigration policies. After that they are encouraged to join discussions on particular aspects of immigration policy they feel strongly about. The Puzzled by Policy platform is available in five languages, including English, Spanish, Greek, Hungarian and Italian. Additionally, online discussions can be automatically translated into any language. Main topics are separated into threads, which contains posts related to a particular user. This eParticipation tool is hosted at http://join.puzzledbypolicy.eu.

As previously discussed, social media (SM) has a great potential to widen and boost eParticipation. Therefore inclusion of the information retrieved from SM, such as Facebook and Twitter significantly increases the range of discussion on PbP platform. Nevertheless, the inclusion of SM information on PbP platform leads to data retrieval, data sharing and data integration challenges,

---

[1] http://www.puzzledbypolicy.eu/

especially with respect to the volume and heterogeneity of the data. Moreover the integration of the data gathered on PbP platform with the soon new coming deployments or other sister-systems (discussing related topics) demands extra capabilities in regard to data integration and data interchange. In this paper we show an approach that derives specific criterion for defining a SOA-RA for eParticipation addressing the identified, data related challenges.

2.2 Approach

In order to derive a criterion for SOA-RA, we first looked into the definition, importance and criterion for a general RA given in Sect. 3. This provided us with a basic understanding of software architectures, their abstract representations and a criterion based on which they are best judged. Secondly, we investigated RAs in context of SOA. While understanding SOA, its components and one specific standard SOA-RA given in Sect. 4, we formed an observation that lead to the grounds for creating a criterion for SOA-RA. The whole process of deriving the criterion for SOA-RA is shown in Fig. 1. In addition to the grounds or observations extracted from general RA and SOA-RA, we also investigated some industry implementations of SOA-RA to enlist a set of components that are general and serve as basis while defining SOA-RA from scratch. The final outcome of our work is a criterion derived from grounds and observations that we developed while discussing RA, SOA-RA and SOA-RA in industry. The criterion is given in Sect. 5.

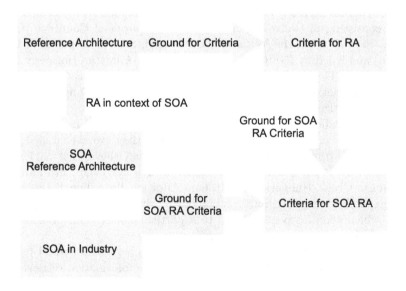

Fig. 1. Process of deriving criterion for SOA RA

3   Reference Architecture

There is no universal, standard or well-accepted definition of RA [6] but to get a basic understanding of it, we found few definitions of RA in literature:

- According to Rational Unified Process (RUP), an RA is, in essence, a prede-fined architectural pattern, or set of patterns, possibly partially or completely instantiated, designed, and proven for use in particular business and technical contexts, together with supporting artifacts to enable their use. Often, these artifacts are harvested from previous projects [6].
- An RA is the generalized architecture of several end systems that share one or more common domains. The RA defines the infrastructure common to the end systems and the interfaces of components that will be included in the end systems. The RA is then instantiated to create the software architecture of a specific system [10].
- According to IBM, an RA provides a blueprint of a to-be-model with a well-defined scope, requirements it satisfies, and architectural decisions it realizes. By delivering best practices in a standardized, methodical way, an RA ensures consistency and quality across development and delivery projects [16].

Thus in simple words it can be concluded that an RA is a diagram/pattern/specification or set of diagrams/patterns/specifications that; (1) depicts the administration of system functions among components in the infrastructure and (2) provides a map for how those functions relate to each other.

After looking at these definitions and drawing our own conclusion about RA, we can say that RA are becoming an integral part of software design and plan-ning, but where did these RA come from and how did they evolve to become a necessity? The answer to these questions is simply the increase in complex-ity of applications that cater with the current business needs in organizations and enterprises. For Instance in classic development approaches where the main focus is to address the functionality on the whole for an individual component. Instead of considering components behavior with respect to entire execution envi-ronment, inclusion of entire functionality within a single component resulted in component dependency within an environment. Based on the needs and neces-sities of businesses to incorporate information technology (IT) as an improving factor, the requirement of making components more independent emerged, so as to achieve high interoperability by creating loosely-coupled components. The development of loosely-coupled components itself has the challenge of design-ing components which encompass the required functionality, support for other components to communicate with it via the same channel, thus making the components reusable, standalone and composite. The increased complexity in development and implementation of distributed systems to achieve high level of interoperability, by creating robust components within the systems is the basis of high involvement of RAs in the software design process. Hence these software RAs can be used as a mechanism for: (1) the development of concrete archi-tectures, (2) standardizing tool that guarantees the interoperability of a system with other systems, (3) standardizing tool that guarantees the interoperability between system components by validating the original purposes and (4) making sure that the basic requirements which were specified during the problem definition phase were addressed [15]. The above scenario fits perfect when we talk about the role of RA in SOA. However, the scope of RA is not limited to this and has a wider audience of architectures to serve. In a nutshell, an RA contains necessary information for project team members; this information provides a set of architectural best practices.

3.1   Importance of Reference Architecture

A Reference Architecture is a combination of Business Architecture, Technical Architecture and Customer context [15]. Therefore, we can infer that an RA ensures that the end users and the participants have the confidence to deploy the technology. Some of the major benefits of RAs are [3]:

1. Reference architecture ensures addressing the core problems and challenges when deploying a technology.
2. Reduces risk of deployment by relying on known and tested solutions.
3. Simplifies decision making.
4. Provides consistent models, capabilities and equipment.
5. Relies on most pragmatic and proven solutions, rather than being adhoc.
6. Helps in bridging cultural gaps between the organizations bringing the expertise and knowledge of each together in a way both can agree upon and provide a common model and set of requirements for everyone by working on design recommendations.

3.2   Criterion for Reference Architecture

After looking at the definitions presented above and noticing the importance, we can say that applications today rely heavily on RAs. However, enough has not been done to support decision making when it comes to selection of RA. During our literature study on RA, we found minimalist criterion for a good RA. The criterion presented in [15] is as follows:

1. Should be understandable for all stakeholders (customers, product managers, project managers, engineers etc).
2. Should be accessible and actually read/seen by majority of the organization.
3. Addresses the key issues of the specific domain.
4. Provides consistent models, capabilities and equipment.
5. Should be of satisfactory quality and acceptable.
6. Should be up-to-date and maintainable.
7. Should add value to the business.

In addition to this, based on the observations made from the definition and importance, we also define the criterion for RA. As we already know that an RA provides a template for architecture of a particular domain i.e. it provides a set of functions with their respective interfaces and interfaces for other domains to communicate with it. Therefore, the level of abstraction at which an RA is selected for a particular domain plays a vital role. While considering the level of abstraction as a pivotal point for RA, the generalization of a system with respect to (1) itself, (2) the subsystems and (3) other domains should also be considered [6]. Context is another consideration that has proved to be vital for an RA [5]. While dealing with Context for RA, the aspects of design and application context which might affect the business goals and design of RA are investigated. The investigation is a result of answers obtained by answering some basic questions like (1) Where will it be used? (2) Who defines it? and (3) When is it defined? Since Context might affect the main goals of RA, therefore Goal should also be selected as a consideration for RA criterion. The Goal consideration is investigated by addressing the main intentions of use for a particular RA i.e. why a particular RA has been defined and does it addresses its major purpose? The Design consideration is the most important consideration for a particular RA in order to encompass the major responsibilities and purposes of its usage. In this particular consideration a specification is formed which contains information regarding the main RA itself, level of concreteness and the way it is represented.

4   SOA Reference Architecture

4.1   Service Oriented Architecture (SOA)

Before we start with SOA-RA we have to completely understand the meaning of Service Oriented Architecture (SOA). There is a wide confusion in understanding a SOA due to the myths and rumors that have come into existence due to its ambiguous definition in different literature. Let us understand it by starting from scratch to get a main viewpoint of SOA itself. The traditional architecture has evolved from mainframe implementation to client-server architecture and then to multi-tier architecture implementations. The application still has remained up to a large extent tightly coupled i.e. the subsystems that executes the major part of application is semantically unaware of its surroundings subsystems but is physically related to them. With SOA, the application's main functionality distribution unit is a service, which is independent and implements the main business logic and contains the associated data. These services interact with each other via message passing for which a specific scheme is already defined, a contract which defines the interface for inter-connectivity and a policy describing the way messages are exchanged [9]. So now, let us conclude the understanding by providing a very basic version of definition: "SOA is a loosely-coupled architecture for addressing all the major business goals of an organization" [13]. For this definition to be correct, it is already known that SOA does not necessarily need Web-Services. Therefore, we come to draw a fine set of facts about SOA that are:

1. Since SOA varies with respect to organizational needs, SOA is independent of vendors, product, technology or industry [13].

2. SOA may be realized using web-services but web-services are not the main need to implement SOA [9,13].
3. SOA should be incremental and should be evolved [9,13].
4. SOA is not a methodology [13].
5. A SOA-RA may not be the best solution for a particular organization [1,13].

The facts stated above give a deep understanding of SOA and their characteristics, and provide solid grounds when describing criterion for SOA-RA. While it can be noted that well implemented SOA can provide organizations with very loosely-coupled distributed application systems, SOA also enables organization to cope with the faster growing market competition by providing effective responsiveness. But not necessarily all implemented SOA provide the desired results and experiences show that most of the implementations have failed [9]. The success of a SOA implementation project is totally dependent upon the organizational needs, business goals and the context. The unawareness of the developers and designers to these factors result into a chaotic implementation of SOA with no business relevance. The main and fundamental objective of SOA is to align IT capabilities with business goals. Since, SOA is not just IT infrastructure nor a business strategy, SOA has to be a perfect combination of both. Therefore, while implementing or planning a SOA, a perfect road-map to SOA and blueprint for its verification is required. The SOA-RA serves as the blueprint of SOA which enables architects to verify that the SOA addresses all the business goals and adheres to the business relevance or it can be said that the RA is a way of making sure that the SOA sticks with the plan of its origin or main cause of its existence [8].

4.2   SOA Reference Architecture (SOA-RA)

As we already discussed in Subsect. 4.1 that RA is like a drawing/blueprint and a set of specification for an organization's business model which is used to verify the concrete version of the architecture, SOA-RA serves as an enterprise business system's reference model which should be defined carefully while defining the SOA road-map phase. For better understanding purposes, let us consider the standard for defining the SOA-RA proposed by The Open Group [12]. Let us first discuss the high-level perspective of the SOA-RA which is shown in Fig. 2. The first five layers depicted in Fig. 2 do not strictly follow the ordering in which they are shown. The main purpose of these layers is to represent the business functionality. The layers and their respective main building blocks are [12]:

- **Operational Systems Layer:** Programs and Data of the operational systems of the enterprise are the main building blocks in this layer.
- **Service Component Layer:** Programs or group of programs that are written to perform service and deliver the service functionality and wrap the programs in the operational systems layer to create services, these wrappers are the main building blocks of this layer.

- **Services Layer:** The central layer of the model containing the portfolio services, conform to a specification defined in the model for the consumers to invoke exposed functions.
- **Business Process Layer:** This layer consists of business processes which may be composition of other business processes or portfolio services.
- **Consumer Layer:** The layer contains users of the system and the programs by which they interface to the portfolio services.

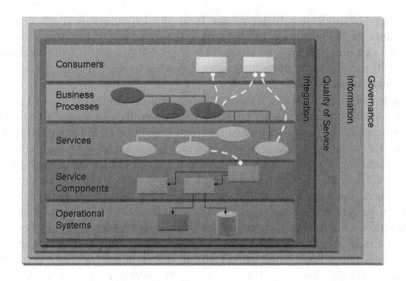

Fig. 2. Layered OASIS SOA-RA [12]

The other four layers depicted in Fig. 2 provide the necessary assistance to the layers supporting the business functionality but does not support each other [12]. They contain building blocks whose purposes relate to:

1. Integration of other building blocks.
2. Quality aspects of system operation.
3. Information.
4. Governance.

Following are the main building blocks which serve as the main constituents for constructing the layers mentioned above of SOA-RA [12]:

1. Composition.
2. Messaging.
3. Service Discovery.
4. Asset wrapping.

5. Virtualization.
6. Event Processing.

These building blocks along with the layers mentioned in OASIS SOA-RA proposed by the Open Group give a solid ground and a set of observations to derive a criterion for defining a SOA-RA.

5 Criterion for SOA Reference Architecture

Observing the understandings we got from the explanations of general RA, importance of RA, criterion for RA, and SOA-RA provided in the above sections, we can now jot down a criterion for a SOA-RA and a list of components which will serve as part of architecture. Following is the derived criterion that we propose for SOA-RA:

While defining SOA-RA, first step is to collect requirements and all the requirements should be clearly understood and an easily understandable requirement specifications has to be made. The requirements should target the specific domain for which the RA is intended. Since we have already highlighted in the explanation of software RA in Subsect. 3.2, even for a SOA-RA, the teams involved in defining the RA should be made very clear about the implementation context, business goals and design strategy for the architecture. All ambiguities in understanding the requirements should be addressed beforehand and the healthy communication between team members for transfer of knowledge should be made. This first step is common and usually followed in almost every software planning phase. Now let us focus on the main goal of this article. After completing the previous step, the second step is to draw a set of principles based on the specified requirements. It is important that the set of principles extracted in this step should be in alignment to the common SOA principles [9]. As it is already very well known that the basic need behind implementing a SOA systems is decoupling the components as much as possible, therefore a set of concepts should be drawn from the requirements collected in first step. These concepts represent the components that will become part of reference model. This reference model will thus serve as a basis for creating an RA. A list of general components that will become part of the reference model and are widely used in standard and industry based implementations of SOA-RA is given below:

1. Business rules and Business process services [1,2,4,8].
2. Data sharing and transformation services [2,4,8].
3. Infrastructure and component services [1,2,4,8].
4. Third party communication and data sharing services [4,8].
5. Identity and security services [4,8].
6. Integration and Event management Services [1,2,4,8].
7. Packaged application access services [1,2,4].
8. Presentation services, Registry and Repository Services [4,8].
9. Messaging, Quality and Governance [1,2,4,8].

These components not necessarily define the concrete and complete criterion for any specific SOA-RA, this means that there might be more components which are further specific to the business needs. However, in this paper we have tried to enlist as much as possible generalized components. The third step is to make sure that the criterion explained in Subsect. 3.2 has been satisfied completely. Fourth and final step is to group together the identified components into layers.

6 eParticipation SOA Reference Architecture

In order to sustain information sharing and integration between PbP and SM (Facebook and Twitter) and presenting the information in an effective manner, we defined a set of reference models to support public participation on PbP platform. Additionally, based on the criterion presented in Sect. 5, we incorporate both reference models to create a SOA-RA that specifically addresses the needs of Service Orientation within eParticipation domain. The SOA-RA is presented in Fig. 3.

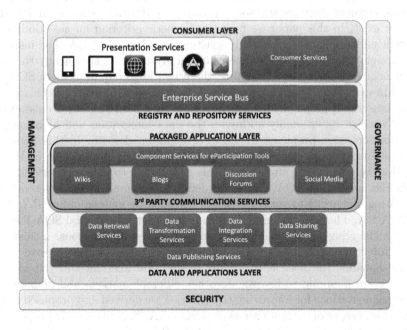

Fig. 3. SOA-RA

In SOA-RA depicted in Fig. 3, most of the services, layers and components are derived from the criterion presented in this paper. Apart from those generic components and layers, we introduced a set of services that are specific to eParticipation domain. Following are the newly introduced services along with their respective responsibilities:

– **Component Services for eParticipation Tools:** These services are integral part of Packaged Application Layer and are used to support 3rd Party communication. The major responsibility of these services is to integrate eParticipation tools like Blogs, Social Networking websites, Discussion Forums and Wikis.
– **Data Publishing Services:** Data integration from different sources and representation of data in homogeneous format is critical to eParticipation. In our scenario: data integration from PbP platform, facebook and twitter facilitates reaching a common goal through active discussion and participation of users. We use Linked Data for representing data extracted from PbP, facebook and twitter.

7   Conclusion

As architectures have evolved, need to refine the business model and incorporate business needs into the architecture as umbrella activity has gained popularity. There are a wide range of SOA-RA existing in market to address different domains, however there are still some unaddressed domains where such SOA-RA does not exist. In this paper we propose a generic criterion for selection, identification and refinement of already existing standard SOA-RA. For instance, with changing nature of eGovernment and eParticipation, specifically the huge involvement of ICT in these domains, there is a huge requirement of SOA-RA that addresses them. So, in order to verify the criterion presented in this paper, we validate this approach by presenting a simplified SOA-RA based on standard SOA-RA which intentionally addresses the data integration and homogeneous data representation problems within eParticipation domain. In this paper we first explained the general software RA along with its importance and criterion. However, the main intention of this article was to define criterion for an RA in the context of SOA. Thus, we defined a general criterion/set of rules for creating blueprints to verify SOA-based system by understanding RA, SOA, and SOA-RA. The criterion given in this paper addresses general SOA-RA, but with the changing nature of business and enterprise applications, inclusion of new architectures into practice and refinement of these architectures to target specific domains, the need is to further extend and abstract this criterion. In future we are planning to investigate other different markets and domain specific implementations for improving the criterion we derived and proposed in this paper. However, as of current situation of SOA-RA, the criterion we propose can serve as good starting point for defining SOA-RA and can also serve as a good blueprint to verify and judge a SOA-RA.

Acknowledgment. This publication has emanated from research supported in part by a research grant from Science Foundation Ireland (SFI) under Grant Number SFI/12/RC/2289 and in part by the European Union under Grant number 256261 (Puzzled by Policy CIP-ICT-PSP-2009-3bis).

References

1. Arsanjani, A., Zhang, L.J., Ellis, M., Allam, A., Channabasavaiah, K.: Design an soa solution using a reference architecture. IBM developerWorks, http://www.ibm. com/developerworks/library/ar-archtemp/ [3], Arsanjani, A., Zhang, L.-J., Allam, A., Ellis, M., et al.: S 3, 10–17 (2007)
2. Arsanjani, A., Zhang, L.J., Ellis, M., Allam, A., Channabasavaiah, K.: S3: a service-oriented reference architecture. IT Prof. **9**(3), 10–17 (2007)
3. Batke, B., Didier, P.: The importance of reference architectures in manufacturing networks. In: CIP Networks Conference (2007)
4. Behara, G.K., Mahajani, P., Palli, P.: Telecom reference architecture, part 2 (2010)
5. Bürkle, A., Müller, W., Pfirrmann, U.: Towards a reference architecture for context-aware services. Advances in Human-Computer Interaction, p. 31
6. Cloutier, R., Muller, G., Verma, D., Nilchiani, R., Hole, E., Bone, M.: The concept of reference architectures. Syst. Eng. **13**(1), 14–27 (2010)
7. Dillon, T.S., Wu, C., Chang, E.: Reference architectural styles for service-oriented computing. In: Li, K., Jesshope, C., Jin, H., Gaudiot, J.-L. (eds.) NPC 2007. LNCS, vol. 4672, pp. 543–555. Springer, Heidelberg (2007)
8. Durvasula, S., Guttmann, M., Kumar, A., Lamb, J., Mitchell, T., Oral, B., Pai, Y., Sedlack, T., Sharma, H., Sundaresan, S.: Soa practitioners guide, part 2, soa reference architecture. Combined Effort, pp. 1–52 (2006)
9. Erl, T.: Service-oriented Architecture: Concepts, Technology, and Desing. Pearson Education India (2006)
10. Gallagher, B.P.: Using the architecture tradeoff analysis methodsm to evaluate a reference architecture: a case study. Technical report, DTIC Document (2000)
11. Gerhardt, G.: e-participation (2009)
12. The Open Group: Soa Source Book. Van Haren Publishing (2009)
13. Linthicum, D.: Reader roi. Service Oriented Architecture (SOA) in the Real World (2008)
14. McClure, D.L.: Statement of david l. mcclure, us general accounting office, before the subcommittee on government management, information and technology, committee on government reform, house of representatives. Committee on Government Reform (2000)
15. Muller, G.: A reference architecture primer. Eindhoven Univ. of Techn., Eindhoven, White paper (2008)
16. Schmidt-Wesche, B., Snitzer, B., Breiter, G., Widmayer, G., Whitmore, J., Villareal, J., Behrendt, M., Caponigro, R., Chang, R., Pappe, S., et al.: Ibm cloud computing & common cloud management platform reference architecture (cc & ccmp ra) 1.0 (2010)

E-ekklesia: The Challenge of Direct Democracy and the Ancient Athenian Model

Ioannis Mpoitsis and Nikos Koutsoupias(⊠)

Department of Balkan, Oriental and Slavic Studies, University of Macedonia,
156 Egnatia str., 54636 Thessaloniki, Greece
impoitsis@uom.edu.gr, nk@uom.gr

Abstract. In the present work we will examine the new possibilities Internet use can offer to Democracy to become more direct and give citizens the opportunity for more and direct participation in policy making. We will discuss the possibility of the creation of what we will call E-ekklesia, an electronic framework on the model of ancient Athens, where every citizen will be able to express his views and suggestions. We will also note the meaning and importance of the responsibility of citizens in a democracy and will examine whether the average citizen feels responsible for the current political situation and what this means for the present democracy.

Keywords: E-democracy · E-participation · E-ekklesia

1 Introduction

2,500 years ago Democracy was born in Athens. It was a transcendental regime in terms of its inspiration as nowhere in nature could be found a corresponding example that people could imitate; a regime with high values and demands. It was the regime that put all citizens, regardless of their economic status and origin (if they were from a wealthy aristocratic family or they were poor workers) as equals. It gave the right to all citizens of "*eklegein*", electing and "*eklegesthai*", be elected. It was the time when at least 6000 people were gathering onto the hill of Pnyx or in the "agora", every nine days to discuss all the political issues. That was the *ekklesia* [32]. In ekklesia every citizen had the right to express his views freely and to report any law or act, he believed to be unfair. He could also denounce a member of an aristocratic family, without being afraid of his power [Athenian's polity, XLIII). This ability was ensured by the concept of *equality*. That meant that no citizen was above another one for any reason. They all had the same rights and chances to become a public officer [1]. That was ensured by the lottery's (the draw) institution, by which were elected all the public's officers (Athenian's polity, XLIII). All citizens could participate in the draw and that meant that everyone could be elected. According to estimations any citizen had many chances to be elected to a critical public position, at least one time at his life [9]. That meant that all citizens were considered to be capable of serving their city as a public officer. The draw represented the possibility and the ability of each citizen to serve his city from a crucial public position [21]. It "forced" a citizen to feel ready and capable of political

© Springer International Publishing Switzerland 2014
A.B. Sideridis et al. (Eds.): E-Democracy 2013, CCIS 441, pp. 52–63, 2014.
DOI: 10.1007/978-3-319-11710-2_5

action. It was politicizing him. Democracy did not require specialized public officers and technocrats but conscious and active citizens. It was a civil polity by the people and for the people [5].

Freedom, equality and *dignity* have been and are the cornerstones of democracy [20]. The rights and the obligations of the democratic regime, were forcing citizens to develop and formulate a political consciousness that contained all these three values. The concept of equality gives citizen a special value, which he feels obliged to defend, while protecting the equality of the other. It produces justice and ensures political harmony [18]. On the other hand, the injustice which is produced by the inequality eliminates these three values and undermines democracy itself. When a citizen doesn't feel equal to the fellow citizen or the one who is a public officer, he loses the feeling of freedom and his dignity. Then he loses his interest to exercise his political rights and his political obligations. The concept of *"epaion"* the one who knows, the expert or the worthy, doesn't fit in with the concept of democracy, at least as it was defined when it was created. Democracy brings balance by giving power to the lower classes and "subtracting" from the uppers and not by keeping the upper class as a guarantor of stability and justice [18]. The argument of the special one who has the proper knowledge and can serve as a public officer more accurately, instead of an ignorant citizen, is the main oligarchic argument. This argument is in complete opposition to democracy and its roots and essence [10]. I'm not equal to someone when I don't have the same opportunities as him to occupy a public office. In ancient Athens this equality was ensured by the draw. According to Aristotle *"democraticon men to klerotas einai tas arxas to de airetas oligarhikon"*, which means that a regime can be called democracy when it elects its princes by the draw, whilst a regime that elects them by vote, is called an oligarchy. Democracy doesn't elect among the highly qualified, but considers all citizens qualified to be elected.

During the last two centuries, after a long period spent in oblivion, democracy regained the western world and continues to spread to the rest of it. Democracy's principles, freedom, equality and dignity earned citizen's appreciation and their preference to them. The right to vote and stand for election "captivated" the people, who were oppressed by despotic kingdoms and dictatorships. The decisive importance of individual voting in the election of public officers and further the use of referendum in some cases, gave people back their sense of power when it came to determining the electoral outcomes. The common people now had the power and also the way to express it. Of course, the models of western democracies were far from that of ancient Athens's, but this was entirely justified. Due to the enormous size of modern states, the regular meeting of all citizens in a place would be practically impossible [9]. The conditions for such a direct democracy are very specific and as Aristotle, Rousseau and Montesquieu pointed out, if it is to work a more direct model of democracy similar to that of ancient Athens's, the cities should not to exceed 30.000 inhabitants. For this reason (the enormous size of the modern states) the ekklesia replaced by parliaments where the elected representatives of citizens, meet on regular bases and make decisions about the future of their countries. Also the institution of the draw was repealed because today's challenges require more qualified public servants and officers. This argument as a point is correct but it would be unfair to underestimate the weight of the challenges that the citizens elected through the lottery system, had to face in antiquity.

Finally it was defined that every four or five years, citizens practice their right to vote and elect their statesmen.

At first glance, the current regimes have been rightly named as democracies as they seem to promote and protect its basic principles. Besides, according to studies and researches the first answer to the question "what do you perceive as democracy?" has to do with the freedom of speech and expression. That is generally the concept of freedom and the right of all citizens to participate with equality in free elections [25]. In short, citizens of democratic states and societies evaluate democracy based on freedom and the right to vote, that today's democracies defend. But is this the definition of democracy as it was defined in the bud? And if until now, there were practical difficulties to implement a model similar to ancient Athens's, with direct participation of citizens, is it possible today, with the evolution of technologies and especially the Internet (web 2.0), to create and to implement such a model?

2   E-participation and E-ekklesia

The current political and economic conditions have created a constantly growing number of dissatisfied citizens for the present situation. Besides, not a few scholars (like Powers [24] and Scharpf [26]) are linking economy with democracy, considering that the basic factor of instability of democracy is the economic deprivation. Additionally we are tempted to say that economic poverty is a factor of instability for any polity and as an example we can site the French revolution. The fact is that the current data generated by the global economic crisis, coupled with the high educational level of western societies and the spread of internet use, makes the question of how could the present republic of technocrats and specialized staffs develop into a direct democracy of citizens.

The rates of internet use in Greece show (Fig. 1) that especially in ages between 17–34 there is a significant familiarity with the Internet.

Of course when it comes to the total population the rates of internet use are different. According to Eurostat's measurements in 2012 [12] Greece had one of the biggest percentages of individuals who had never used the Internet (42 %) in the EU and only one out of two (52 %) had access to the Internet. A classic argument against e-democracy is that those who do not have internet access will be excluded from the political process. We believe that this is a fair assessment and that at any case, e-voting and e-participation should be an alternative and not the only choice [18]. By that way we can protect those who don't have access to internet from social and political isolation and also we can introduce e-democracy to those who are familiar with the internet use. Looking at the rates of the Internet use at the younger ages we can say that the future of democracy is e-democracy. Based on this data we propose the creation of a web site/portal framework that we will name *E-ekklesia*, and which we believe that could be feasible and also could bypass the classiest argument against direct democracy, which refers to the huge population of the existing states and the inability to concentrate all citizens in a particular place. In our model of *E-ekklesia* all the citizens will have the opportunity to be involved in the politics [8], by using a personal code which might be, even the number of their identity card. Following the model of ancient

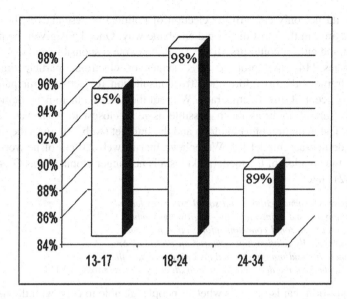

Fig. 1. Internet usage by age range in Greece. (Source: Bari-Focus, November-December 2010)

Athens, all citizens could be informed about the state's issues and could be able to watch the various suggestions on these issues. Also they will be able to vote on the proposal that they find as the most reliable, influencing and defining with the most emphatic way, the political decisions. Each individual citizen, regardless of his geographical location and his economic situation, will be able to consider and decide on issues of political life. We have to note here that we don't expect every single citizen to participate but to beckon those who are interested in politics and to create in the distant future a political culture of direct participation. There are already websites like Our-Space (n.d.) with a political object, where citizens are invited to express their views on the political agenda and to participate in polls that are asking their opinion about a particular topic [22]. At this point it should be noted that the government of PASOK made a fair effort in this direction by creating OpenGov [31] (n.d.). This was a website where citizens could express their opinion and be informed about political issues [20]. This wasn't a very successful effort as there was not too much participation on the part of citizens. We believe that the low participation was not due the indifference of the people, but because they were not convinced that their participation would have any special significance in policy decisions making. If such a model is to work and to win people's trust it should guarantee that their participation will be indispensable precondition for influencing political decisions.

These modern ekklesias defuse the need of citizens for political expression but in an informal form. The views that are expressed there and the results of the votes, have no impact on the formal political decisions. But the creation of those informal ekklesias expresses a need, the need for further political expression on the part of citizens. The creation of an official website for political expression could bring the citizens closer to political power. In the modern ekklesia, the voice of the citizen could be heard directly.

His vote could not only concern the election of political representatives, but political decision making, in the most direct and emphatic way. Once he is given the necessary information, the citizen could first discuss and then vote responsibly and determine the political issues [14]. We propose three stages of electronic participation in our *E-ekklesia* framework: (a) information (b) consultation (c) active participation [28]. This is the concept of direct democracy. Without the ekklesia there is no democracy at all, but an effort to apply as much possible as it is, closest to what was defined as democracy. The evolution of technology and the Internet (web 2.0) gives the possibility of a direct democracy model [8]. We believe that in web 2.0 era of networked communication the creation of the modern ekklesia is no longer utopia and as Giglietto and Roosi (2012) state:

> «*Contemporary communications and social processes leave -
> both intentionally and unintentionally - a growing number
> of digital traces: personal communication shared in social
> network sites, family relationships declared on Facebook or
> political thoughts and opinions posted on Twitter are just the
> top of the iceberg of the dataset available to digital social researchers.*» [14]

The main question that is raised is whether people are able to cope with the demand of such a democracy model, which requires continuous and direct involvement [11].

In regards to the classic argument regarding the inability of the majority of citizens to decide and determine critical political issues, we may initially quote the response of Barber (1984) who notes:

> «*Give people some significant power and they quickly appreciate
> the need for knowledge, but foist knowledge on them without
> giving them responsibility and they will display indifference.*» [2]

As discussed above, democracy requires citizens with conscience and responsibility [27]. Citizens who are ready at any moment to decide and determine, an issue for the society and the state. Who are educated on exercising political action and expressing political opinion. The argument that says that the majority of the citizens do not possess the necessary knowledge for some specific posts and some specific decisions, is correct to some extent, but flirts with oligarchic mentality and culture. No one argues that the majority opinion of citizens is foolproof but also, it can't be argued that the opinion of technocrats is foolproof also [6]. Besides, the recent experience of the present economic situation of Western states which is a result of the technocrat's and "professional politicians" policies, shows the truth. Even an error can provide education and through it the citizen gains experience. It is perfectly natural and expected from people that have never been asked to make a major decision, beyond the practice of voting, to express an embarrassment, the first few times that they will be called to decide on major issues, and of course it's perfectly natural to make mistakes. Democracy, moreover, doesn't promise infallibility and perfection, but the isomer and at the fairest possible.

When something seems distant and detached from the citizen's own opinion and judgment, tends to be ignored or to be watched from afar [6]. We believe that in Greece this can be confirmed by examining (Fig. 2) the abstention rates during the last six election years.

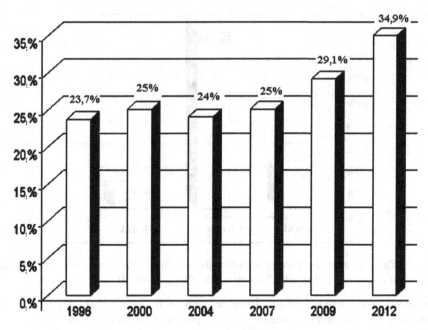

Fig. 2. Abstention rates from Election in Greece by Election Year (Source: Bari-Focus, November-December 2010)

Citizens feel that they are disconnected from their representatives and that the decisions that they make, make things worse. In a METRISIS's research 76, 7 % of the Greek citizens (Fig. 3) believe that the politicians are driving the country in the wrong direction.

As a result there is a general disinterest in politics, which is expressed by the constantly increasing rates of abstention from elections [23]. Of course, in many cases, abstention from elections does not necessarily mean indifference and lack of responsibility, but a political statement and attitude. As Beard and Schultz wrote (1912):

«The smallness of the vote in many instances indicates not a lack
of interest but a high degree of intelligence on the part of the voters.
It often shows that the voters are aware of the fact that they do not know
enough about some particular or local matter to warrant their expressing
an opinion one way or another.» [3]

The sure thing is that, whether citizens feel inadequate in terms of knowledge and information regarding issues of policy, or they feel that they are not interested in politics since their opinion has no real effect on polity decisions making, there is a question of democracy. And there is a question of democracy, because democracy without participation is not feasible. It should be noted here that according to *Economist* [29] Greece is deficient in Democracy.

The difficulties of the past can now be overcome with the help of the Internet (Web 2.0). Participation and information, two issues that are directly linked to the concept of democracy can be more directly and more freely practiced through the Internet.

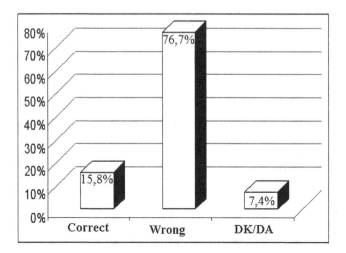

Fig. 3. Relative frequencies of greeks answering the question: *"In your opinion Greece is going in the right or the wrong direction?"* (Source: METRISIS 18-10-13)

The speed of information and updating as well as its intersection, take on greater dimensions on the Internet where there is pluralism of opinion and freedom of expression. This reminds of the ancient ekklesia, where all the citizens were gathering together to agora to learn and talk about the city's issues. And we make reference to the convenience of the Internet to information, because the issue of information and the role played by the media is a question of democracy [16]. At first, because if freedom is a fundamental principle of democracy then citizens should have the right for full access in information, that has to be completely free and independent of any considerations and secondly because information is directly linked to participation. Citizens have the right to direct and freely distributed information and mass media are obliged to provide it [25]. It is obvious that there is a distance between citizens and political decision making and the only ones that can play the role of the intermediate are the mass media. The only way to maintain a link between citizen and government is information. According to AGB'S stats, in 2009 83,3 % of the Internet users used the Internet to be informed for any kind of news. It is obvious that the Internet is gaining the trust of citizens, who seem to believe (according to Pulse's stats 32 %) that it is the most independent mass media. This becomes even clearer in countries where freedom of expression is not obvious, such as China, where citizens consider that only in the Internet can freely express their political views [17].

All these show the power that the Internet is gaining to the citizen's conscience. It is perhaps the only mass media that seems capable to bring back the citizens in touch with politics [7]. The information and the ability to e-direct involvement would strengthen the political consciousness and give new perspectives. Whereas previously, if we were talking about direct democracy, first we had to provide solutions to practical problems that would be faced during it's execution, now, that these problems seem they could be easily overcome, the new challenge concerns the awakening of the political consciousness of citizens. MRB's research shows (Table 1) that 64,4 % of citizens feel that they are not interested in politics.

Table 1. Answers to the question "Are you interested in politics?"

Answer	YES	NO
Rel. Frequency	35,6 %	64,4 %

(Source: MRB 12-12-12)

The majority of citizens have lost their political interest. They feel pessimistic about the future and don't trust their politicians, since 76,5 % of them (Fig. 4), feel that nothing can change and that there is nothing they can do about it.

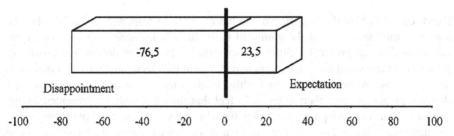

Fig. 4. "Optimism and pessimism rate about the political situation in Greece" (Source: MRB 12-12-12)

This has to do with the decommissioning of the dynamics of society in recent decades, where political activity was expressed and defused only by voting or by action in a labor organization. The only way to recover the dynamics of citizens is to give them the opportunity for more direct participation. Only when they will be given the right and the substantive force to determine the political things, they will regain their political culture. As Welzel and Inglehart say (2008):

«Human empowerment is becoming an increasingly important driving
force behind democratization.»

The empowerment of the citizen is the only way to create and develop political consciousness. The *E-ekklesia* and regular presence in it, along with the correct and prompt information [15], can give the citizen the lost confidence. It is perfectly normal to feel inadequate when someone has never been asked to make a serious political decision. It is also normal to feel you have no political power when he knows that he will never exercise it and that he will never have any real effect on it. All these years, people were convinced that the citizen is insufficient and that only «professional» politicians are able to exercise political action, forgetting that nobody has a monopoly on good judgment [4]. As a result, a culture developed where the citizen and society in general, understood democracy in a way that is far removed from true democracy. We shouldn't forget that the elitist argument of weakness and failure of citizens is the main oligarchic argument [30]. The burden of responsibility will push the need for obtaining sufficient information [2] and the further development of capacity. Besides a few decades ago, women were not allowed to vote in elections, considered by the theorists of this attitude, as insufficient [6]. There isn't too much difference between the argument that is against the participation of citizens in making political decisions and the argument that is against women's participation in elections. In fact, the premise is exactly the same. A group of "experts" consider another group as inadequate and prohibits political participation [6]. Perhaps this paternalistic reasoning is based on some logic, but this logic is certainly not democratic. When now we are in an era where technology can give us the tools we need for the direct involvement of citizens, the issue is not whether we can, but if we want to have a direct democracy.

3 The Concept of Responsibility

The discussion about the importance and the meaning of responsibility dovetails with what was said above, about the ability of individuals to exercise their political rights and strengthening political culture consciousness. In the model of representative democracy, the elected parties, express and represent the electorate that voted them into office. If those parties will remain faithful to the observance of ideology and their electoral programs, then their voters will feel that they have been represented by the right way. But when people feel that they have been deceived, that the party they voted for, departed from its campaign promises and ideological bases, then the concept of responsibility is transferred. How can a citizen be judged for a policy that he didn't actually vote for? For a totally different attitude from that which he was promised by the parties [5]? Democracy is a regime that requires a sense of responsibility and accountability of citizens. But how can we develop it when the citizen feels cheated and decommissioned? Of Course here is a matter of honesty on the part of parties, because honesty is a matter of responsibility, but the interest in this case is about people. MRB's research shows (Fig. 5) that the majority of the citizens have the worst opinion about the leaders of the political parties.

The majority of citizens feel that they are not responsible for the current political situation and that they were deceived by the political parties and their promises. We believe that the concept of responsibility dovetails with the concept of participation. I have responsibility to something when I participate to its function. Therefore, the shorter my participation is, the less my responsibility will be. If citizens could decide on crucial issues through regularly referendums or if direct democracy was put into practice and citizen's participation was immediate, then the feeling of responsibility would be significantly larger. We believe that the participation – liability ratio is proportionate. The greater the participation in a decision is or the more a citizen participates, why not, into the functioning of the state, the greater is the sense of responsibility that he has. In one possible implementation of direct democracy and the creation of our proposal, the formal *E-ekklesia* where Citizens would have a substantial and direct involvement, sense of responsibility would be nurtured immediately. As a point, the rate of growth of consciousness of responsibility underlies the rate of democracy. We shouldn't forget that democracy is "a polity for the people and by the people", which means that when in this citizen's regime, citizens feel uninvolved and without responsibility on the political situation, they don't actually participate in the democratic system of government and a democracy without the participation of citizens, by definition, ceases to be a democracy. In a democracy, citizens should be and

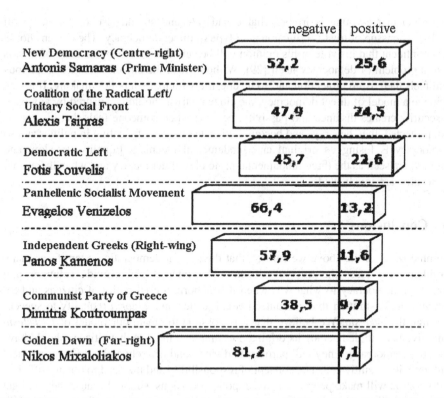

Fig. 5. "What is your opinion about the leaders of the political parties?" (Source: Alco 17-10-13)

feel responsible for its course, but for this to happen, meaningful participation in it should be ensured.

An important index of democracy is whether the parties have distinct ideological differentiation so that all the citizen's political preferences can be expressed. According to MRB's estimations 48,6 % of the citizens, voted with scepticism because they don't feel that the party that they supported express their ideological preferences but they vote it because they feel that there isn't any other alternative. Where an individual's opinion cannot be expressed ideologically by the party that he chose to represent him in parliament, the concept of representation loses its meaning. When a citizen feels that he is not represented by any political party, that is a problem for the democracy. He feels that he is not responsible for the situation, because he doesn't participate in it through the party that he voted. For this reason we believe, that e-participation through *E-ekklesia*, can give to people, the sense of responsibility that democracy requires.

4 The Significance of Trust

To achieve all this, a prerequisite is to ensure public confidence in the voting procedure and generally in the operation of electronic participation in politics [13]. The citizen must feel that e-voting is irreproachable and safe and should also be familiar with it [19]. The issue of trust is critical in an e-type of direct democracy. The citizen should feel confident that his vote or his opinion will be submitted unchanged. Lack of trust is also a problem of democracy itself [29]. Without trust, the citizen becomes suspicious and feels there is no protection and so he doesn't participate in policy-making. If it is to achieve a model of direct democracy, the citizen's trust should be ensured by any way. Insecurity creates distance and passivity, because when someone feels that his vote is not protected, then he strays and becomes alienated from participating in politics and so democracy is losing its original and fundamental meaning. Equality, freedom and dignity, are seen as the three fundamental principles of democracy and when there is no trust, they are invalidated.

5 Conclusions

Summarizing all the above we can say that the present democratic system faces many problems and loses the trust of citizens. The Internet can provide solutions and transform democracy to what was when it was born, a civil polity of citizens and for citizens, a constitution that guaranteed equal justice and *isigoria* (equality to speech) through the *ekklesia*. We believe that it is possible to create our model of *E-ekklesia* and give back to democracy its original meaning and the role that citizens should have in a real democracy. They will participate directly and actively and a different political culture will be cultivated. The concept of responsibility and the need to obtain sufficient information will make people able to set policy decisions, simply because they will get them themselves. It will lead citizens to understand their significance and their importance in regards to the function of the democratic government. The concept of professional politicians is not a democratic one. If we speak about democracy we should understand that there is no democracy without the active involvement of the citizen. *E-ekklesia* will give us this opportunity. The concept of citizenship will regain its true meaning. Every citizen will participate actively in democracy and will feel totally responsible for it. We believe that the Internet is the greatest ally of direct democracy and that if there is a way to ensure full confidence in regards to electronic participation then direct democracy will win the preference of citizens. Through electronic participation we can learn again the true meaning of democracy. In our *E-ekklesia* framework, the concept of representation will lose its meaning, as each citizen will directly represent himself. The fact is that all the means to implement direct democracy exist; the question is whether there is the will to implement it.

References

1. Apostolakis, J., Loukis, E., Halaris, J.: E-Administration, Organization and Implementation. Papazisis, Athens (2008)
2. Barber, B.: Strong Democracy. University of California Press, Berkeley (1984)
3. Beard, C.A., Schultz, B.E.: Documents on the State-wide Initiative, Referendum and Recall, vol. 39, pp. 390–412. Macmillan, New York (1912)

4. Behrouzi, M.: Democracy as the Political Empowerment of the Citizen. Lexington Books, Oxford (2008)
5. Brennan, G., Lomasky, L.: Democracy and Decision. Cambridge University Press, Cambridge (1993)
6. Budge, I.: The New Challenge of Direct Democracy. Polity Press, Cambridge (1996)
7. Burger, R.H.: Information Policy: A Framework for Evaluation and Policy Research. Ablex Publishing Company, Norwood (1993)
8. Clift, S.: Public Strategies for the Online World. Publicus, Minneapolis (2007). http://www.publicus.net. Accessed 12 Nov 2013
9. Dahl, R.: On Democracy. Yale University Press, London (2000)
10. Dalton, R.: Citizen Politics: Public Opinion and Political Parties in Advanced Industrial Democracies. Chatham, New York (2002)
11. Dalton, R., Sin, T.C., Bou, W.: Understanding democracy: data from unlikely press. J. Democr. 18(4), 142–156 (2007)
12. Eurostat, Internet use in households (2012). http://epp.eurostat.ec.europa.eu/cache/ITY_OFFPUB/KS-SF-12-050/EN/KS-SF-12-050-EN.PDF
13. Evans, A.J.: Voters & Voting. SAGE Publications, London (2007)
14. Giglietto, F., Rossi, L.: Ethics and interdisciplinarity in computational social science. Methodolo. Innovations Online 7(1), 25–36 (2012)
15. Hagen, M.: A typology of electronic democracy (1997). http://www.unigiessen.de/fb03/vinci/labore/netz/hagen.htm
16. Hutchings, V.L.: Public Opinion and Democratic Accountability. Princeton University Press, Princeton and Oxford (2003)
17. Link, P., Qiang, X.: From "Fart People" to citizens. J. Democr. 24(1), 77–99 (2013)
18. Lombardini, J.: Isonomia and the public sphere in democratic athens. Hist. Political Thought. 34(3), 393–419 (2013)
19. Mitrou, L., Gritzalis, D., Katsikas, S.: Revisiting legal and regulatory requirements for source e-voting. Secur. Inf. Soc. 86, 469–480 (2002)
20. Ober, J.: Democracy's dignity. Am. Polit. Sci. Rev. 106(4), 827–846 (2012)
21. OpenGov. http://www.opengov.gr
22. OurSpace. http://www.joinourspace.eu
23. Peabody, W.: Direct legislation. Polit. Sci. Q. 20(3), 443–445 (1905)
24. Powers, N.: Grassroots Expectations of Democracy and Economy: Argentina in Comparative Perspective. University of Pittsburgh Press, Pittsburgh (2001)
25. Rowlands, I.: Understanding information policy: concepts, frameworks and research tools. J. Inf. Sci. 22(1), 13–25 (1996)
26. Dalton, R.J., Shin, D.C., Jou, W.: Understanding democracy: data from unlikely places. J. Democr. 18(4), 142–156 (2007)
27. Scharpf, W.: Crisis and Choice in European Social Democracy: Cornel Studies in Political Economy. Lavoisier, Paris (1991)
28. Spirakis, J., Spiraki, C.: From E-Government to E-Democracy. Athens (2008)
29. The Economist, Democracy's Index (2012)
30. Yu, E., Liu, L.: Modelling trust for system design using the i^* strategic actors framework. In: Falcone, R., Singh, M., Tan, Y.-H. (eds.) AA-WS 2000. LNCS (LNAI), vol. 2246, pp. 175–194. Springer, Heidelberg (2001)
31. Vlahos, A.: Building Democracy. Papadima, Athens (1999)
32. Vlahos, A.: Athenian Polity and Elder-Oligarch. Hestia, Athens (2010)

Generic Services for Cross Domain
Use in e-Government

Antonios Stasis$^{(\boxtimes)}$, Victoria Kalogirou, and Stergios Tsiafoulis

Hellenic Ministry of Administration Reform and E-Governance,
Electronic Data Processing Directorate, Vassilisis Sofias 15,
10674 Athens, Greece
{a.stasis,v.kalogirou,s.tsiafoulis}@ydmed.gov.gr

Abstract. The economic crisis was a catalyst in the evolution of the cloud computing and the rationalization of the IT systems that offer e-Government services. The reusability of software and services is a mandatory requirement in the new systems that are being designed and developed. Despite of the differences in use cases that different domains such as e-Health, e-Procurement, e-Business, e-Justice, e-Learning utilize, the core services that are necessary can be summarized in eID, e-signature, e-delivery, e-documents and semantics under a secure and trusted environment. This paper aims to present the main actions in the European Union such as the Connecting Europe Facility program, the principles of the next program after the Interoperable Solutions for Public Administration and large scale pilots such as STORK2 and E-SENS. The sustainability of all these solutions is a challenging issue that should be tackled.

Keywords: e-gov services · e-Documents · Electronic e-Identification · e-Signatures · Privacy · Trust · Authentication · e-Delivery · Large scale pilot projects · LSPs · PEPPOL · SPOCS · eCODEX · STORK · e-SENS · CEF · ISA

1 Introduction

During the last decade a significant boost on E-Government services was reported in Europe mainly based on European initiatives and action plans (e.g. i2010 eGovernment Action Plan [1], eGovernment Action Plan 2011–2015 [2]) and on the structural funds (e.g. European Social Fund [3], European Regional Development Fund [4]).

The public online e-governments services focused among others on [5]:

- **User Empowerment:** by supporting citizen digital inclusion, re-use of public sector information and online collaboration,
- **Increasing the efficiency and effectiveness of public administration** by facilitating the reduction of administrative burdens to businesses and the mobility through Pan-European online cross border services

The IT systems that supported these e-Government services were developed under the supervision of specific public administration bodies that according to their responsibilities identified different operational needs, different business processes, different

© Springer International Publishing Switzerland 2014
A.B. Sideridis et al. (Eds.): E-Democracy 2013, CCIS 441, pp. 64–72, 2014.
DOI: 10.1007/978-3-319-11710-2_6

requirements, different specifications, and consequently different technical solutions and implementations.

Each of these Domain Specific IT systems has to be sustainable; therefore the operational cost and cost related to the evolvement of the IT systems should be included in the budget of the public bodies that were responsible for the operation of the IT systems. The sustainability discussions raised issues related on the return on investment and the cost sharing among different public bodies that have similar needs.

Interoperability, reusability and service oriented approach revealed as the main direction for cost reduction [6]. Service oriented architecture has been adopted by the conceptual model for public service delivery in the European Interoperability framework [7]. The economic crisis in Europe significantly accelerated the results of these discussions and acted as a driving force that facilitated the launching of a rationalization process of the existing IT systems. Moreover the new Connecting Europe Facility Program [8] that is under the final approval process by the European Parliament aims to digital service infrastructure i.e. an infrastructure that connects public administration across Europe, facilitates the cross border e-government service delivery, enhances the access to the public sector information using multilingual services in a secure and safe environment.

Digital Services Infrastructure will offer services for cross domain use. In the following paragraphs of this paper the potential generic services will be reported. Additionally, the goals of the Large Scale Pilot projects of STORK2.0 [9] and E-SENS [10] towards this direction will be presented and the potential future work in this aspect will be proposed.

The paper is organized as follows. Section 2 presents the most significant Domain Use Cases supported by e-Government Services. Section 3 describes the Generic Services from cross domain use and further work on this field. Finally, the paper ends with some conclusions.

2 Significant Domain Use Cases Supported by e-Government Services

Currently public administration is handling a lot of different business domains such as e-Procurement, e-Business, e-Health, e-Justice, e-Social Security and others. Moreover the collaboration among different public authorities at European level is inevitable in order to implement the European policies on the specific domains. Different use cases must be supported by the IT systems. Some important needs and use cases at European level that have been identified by large scale pilot projects that have been funded under the Policy Support Programme of the Competitive and Innovation Framework Programme - CIP/PSP (decision 1639/2006/EC on the establishment of an Competitiveness and Innovation Framework Programme (2007 to 2013) or the and the European Commission Services [21]. The next paragraphs highlight some of these important use cases.

2.1   e-Business Domain

The work on the business domain at European level was initially facilitated by the Services Directive in the internal market (directive 2006/123/EC) that aimed to provide the ability to a business person to start offering services in another Member State of the European Union or the European Economic Area by fulfilling all the administrative procedures and formalities using electronic means, through a Single Point of Contact. In 2008 a large scale pilot project was launched in order to facilitate the implementation of the Services Directive i.e. Simple Procedures Online for Cross-border Services (SPOCS) [11]. The use case that was mainly supported was the activity registration of a business person that required electronic documents signed by the business person, evidence during the electronic transactions among the business person and the Point of Single Contact, the reuse of electronic documents from a source of authentic documents and semantic interpretation of the required supporting documents that the business person should submit in order to get the appropriate licence for offering services. The SPOCS project ended on 2012 and the solutions that were implemented are available through a starter kit that was implemented to help the interested person to reuse the solutions (http://www.eu-spocs-starterkit.eu/).

The work at European level on the business domain is being further developed and now is focusing on the interoperability of Business Registries that according to the Directive 2012/17/EU for the interconnection of the central, commercial and companies' registries will enhance the services that will be offered by the European Justice Portal [13]. Therefore, the large scale pilot project e-CODEX [12] that was launched for handling use cases related to e-justice on 2010 is examining the support of European use cases related to the transfer of the seat of a company that requires interoperability among business registries, and evidence for the transactions. The solutions that are being implemented by e-CODEX are expected to be available to the public during 2015.

2.2   e-Procurement Domain

The discussion for public procurement at European level has started many years ago. An important milestone in this discussion was the directive 2004/18/EC on the coordination of procedures for the award of public works contracts, public supply contracts and public service contracts. A lot of remarkable results on public procurement have been achieved the recent years such as the Tenders Electronic Daily, for browsing the public procurements by country, region, business sector [14], the e-CERTIS [15] that has a mapping for different certificates and attestations among European Economic The period from 2008 until 2012 the large scale pilot project Pan-European Public Procurement on Line (PEPPOL) [16], was implemented contributing to solutions supporting use cases for:

- creating the e-Attestation (Virtual Company Dossier - VCD) i.e. the set of the supporting documents and information that must submitted in each procurement by the companies that are interested to participate,

- creating the catalogue of goods and services that are requested by the contracting authorities and are offered by the suppliers,
- submitting e-Orders to the suppliers and handling the lifecycle of the order until a receipt and / or an e-Invoice is received.

The solution provided by the PEPPOL project supported the signature validation whenever it was necessary, the creation and transport of the appropriate evidence for the transactions among the contracting authority and the suppliers, the semantic mapping of the certificates and attestations for creation of the VCD.

Currently the results from the PEPPOL project are maintained by the ISA programme [17]. In the Joinup platform (https://joinup.ec.europa.eu/) one can find the latest advances related to the PEPPOL software. Moreover, the nonprofit association OpenPEPPOL [16] that was established in 2012 will be responsible for the maintenance of PEPPOL specification and building blocks.

2.3   e-Health Domain

The discussion on Social Security Systems and e-Health at European level was a long term procedure that has reached a minimum convergence in 2011 with the directive 2011/24/EU for the Patients' Rights in cross border health care that respecting the national competencies in organising and delivering healthcare, provides rules for facilitating the cross border health care provision [18]. Additionally, in the e-health domain the data privacy is considered as a top priority issue since the data that are being exchanged are regarded in most of the cases as sensitive personal data (directive 1995/46/EC). In 2008 was launched the large scale pilot project, Smart Open Services for European Patients (epSOS) [19], especially for e-Health use cases. This project is still in implementation and the final results are expected to be delivered by the end of the first semester of 2014. The use cases that are supported are mainly focusing on the transfer of the Patient summary (e.g. the general information about a patient, the most important clinical data such as allergies, the current medication, etc.) and the e-prescription. One more important use case that is being discussed in the context of the co-ordination of the Social Security Systems is the e-Confirmation i.e. the process that verifies the citizens' rights and entitlements regarding cross border health care provision and in particular the reimbursement of health care provided in another Member state. The Electronic Exchange of Social Security Information project (EESSI) [20] aims to elaborate this type of use cases. The time plan for EESSI has been extended up to 2018.

2.4   e-Justice Domain

The principles for cross border judicial co-operation at European level derive from the Treaty of Amsterdam in 1999 and Treaty of Lisbon in 2007. The specific actions for supporting the objective of the treaties using information technology are described in the European e-Justice Action Plan for 2009-2013 (2009/C 75/01). As mentioned above the large scale pilot project that support use cases for e-Justice is eCODEX [12]. The main use cases that have been analysed in eCODEX are:

- The European Payment Order that is based on Council Regulation 1896/2006,
- The Small Claims procedure that is based on Council Regulation 861/2007,
- The Mutual Recognition of Financial Penalties that is based on the Council Framework Decision 2005/214/JHA and the Directive 2011/82/EU,
- The Secure cross-border exchange of sensitive judicial data that is based on Council Decision 2005/671/JHA,
- The European Arrest Warrant that is based on the Council Framework Decision 2002/584/JHA.

The solutions that are being implemented by e-CODEX are expected to be available to the public during 2015.

2.5   Collaboration at European Level

Apart from the specific domains that were described in the previous paragraphs there is a also a plethora of systems that aim to exchange reliable information between European Union authorities and Member States [21]. These special systems are focusing on handling alerts, requesting assistance, collecting data, monitoring and reporting. Moreover these systems facilitate collaboration among stakeholders and/or provide access to specific communities. The architecture of these systems can be either centralized or decentralized. Semantic interpretation and semantic interoperability of the exchanged information is crucial in use cases.

3   Generic Services from Cross Domain Use - Future Work

The analysis of the different use cases from the different domains revealed common functionalities that should be supported regardless of the domain that were used. The work in the different domains in many cases tackled similar challenges, following different approaches and technical solutions. The building blocks that were developed to support the technical solutions in each domain must be separately maintained and sustained increasing the relative cost. Considering the rationalization of the existing systems and solutions and the creation of digital service infrastructures one can easily draw the conclusion that the building blocks that support similar functions must converge to one technical solution.

The eSENS project [10] was launched in 2012 for this purpose i.e. to identify the common building blocks and be converged to one solution that can meet the requirements of the different domains. eSENS aims either to reuse existing solutions or modify them in order to make them suitable for cross domain use.

Furthermore, eSENS will assess the existing solutions and standards using a methodology that will be based on the Common Assessment method proposed by the ISA programme [22]. The solutions-building blocks that will pass successfully this process and be reused in eSENS, will be eligible for further evolvement in the Connecting Europe Facility programme and the basis for the creation of digital service infrastructures.

The detailed analysis of the needs and the above mentioned use cases, in the context of eSENS project, has identified some common generic building blocks and services that could be potentially used at all domains. The most important of them are the following:

3.1 Authentication

Authentication is a generic service that can confirm the identity of a user. This generic service in some cases should also confirm the role or the mandate that a user has. For instance in the case of e-Business and e-Procurement only a user that is legal representative of a company or has the appropriate mandate can act on behalf of a company. Currently the different IT systems can authenticate the users using either the national eID or using special registration procedures. The user registration and management is special function that increases the operational cost of an IT system and consequently the administrative burden to the users. Interoperable eID solutions at European level have been provided by the Large Scale Pilot project STORK1 and STORK2 [9]. The scope of STORK 1 and STORK 2 solutions is IT systems that provide e-government services to be able to identify users based on existing information from identity providers at National level and special registries that are responsible for the provision roles or mandates (delegation of powers). The results of the STORK1 project are available on the joinup platform and the solution is currently being maintained by the ISA programme [25].

3.2 E-Signature

The creation and verification of a digital signature in an electronic document is a horizontal issue that is necessary for an action to have legal effect at e-government services. For Instance in e-Health a doctor should be responsible for the e-prescription, in e- Justice a European Arrest Warrant should be signed by the responsible Judge, in e procurement the business person should be responsible for bid that he/she submits. A lot of solutions for digital signature exist across Europe but most of them use a proprietary format that does not allow the verification from a different system. The solution that has been provided by the European Commission through DG MARKT (Service Directive DSS tool [23] that supports XAdES, PAdES, CAdES standards and is available in the Joinup platform) is compliant to the recent European council decisions for digital signature format. Moreover, in the context of STORK1 project a signature creation solution has been provided (XAdES, PAdES, CAdES). A verification tool has also been developed in the context of PEPPOL (XKMS, Trust Lists) project for e-procurement purposes. In addition, in the context of e-CODEX [12] project the trust library was extended.

3.3 E-Delivery

A secure channel for the electronic exchange of information and exchange of electronic documents is mandatory in order to be able to have the appropriate evidence and proofs that a transaction has been done, especially when the communication has a legal binding with the rights of the Citizens and the Business. The time that a transaction was performed, the systems and users that were involved, the integrity of the content that was exchanged are crucial evidences in e-government services. Solutions at European level for e-delivery infrastructure were proposed by the following Large Scale Pilot Projects: (a) SPOCS [11] implementing the ETSI REM evidence and REM SOAP binding profile, specification for e-Business, (b) PEPPOL [16] implementing specification for Service metadata location and publishing, Secure Asynchronous Reliable Transport, Light weight Message exchange (ebMS3.0), (c) E-Codex [12] trying to converge SPOCS and PEPPOL e-delivery solutions using ebMS3.0 specification, (d) EPSOS [19] and SPOCS [11] have also introduced for e-Health and e-Business a repository (e-Safe) based document exchange i.e. some document initially are stored on a repository and at a later stage are retrieved in the context a specific process.

3.4   Trusted Circle

Trust is a crucial horizontal issue and architecture building block in e-government services. The systems that will be involved in a transaction must fulfil specific security requirements considering mainly data privacy and other provisions of the legal framework e.g. intellectual property rights, and potential threads such as denial of service attack, man in the middle etc. Usually in these solutions one or more national gateways are responsible to register the national systems in the trusted network. These systems are included in a Trust list (ETSI specification for TSL [24] for digital signatures), that has been extended for several purposes by the large scale pilots. SPOCS has introduced an extension to include e-Delivery services, E-Safe Services and service directories for the discovery of e-government services. PEPPOL has used trusts lists for the signature verification services. STORK1 has proposed similar list as gateways for eID services combined with an indicator for the quality of the information (Quality Assurance Level). Finally, also EPSOS has used Trusted lists for National Contact Points.

3.5   Semantics and e-Documents

The interpretation of the information is critical in all e-Government services especially when interoperable services are utilized. Business process must be aligned among different systems that support them. This requirement is more demanding when cross border services are about to be offered. Semantic can be domain independent provided that specific taxonomies, classifications and ontologies will be defined considering generic standards and reusing existing entities. Structured reusable content profiles, schemas, for processes, case folders and documents must be defined. Finally, when comes to cross border services the mapping among services in different Member Sates must be done. Translation service is one of the key generic services that can be used considering semantic mapping in conjunction with heuristic algorithms.

4   Conclusions

The different domains have common functionalities that can be supported by common solutions and building blocks. However, the legal and business aspects at a National and Cross border level are in some cases still a challenge.

So far, e-SENS project will assess the solution proposed by the previous European Initiatives and will try to converge the proposed architectures and building blocks. The outcome of the work that will be done in the context of eSENS project is expected by the end of 2016. e-SENS results will be an input to the Connecting Europe Facility programme.

Therefore, Member States and Public Administrations must be actively involved in these actions. Private sector has also a crucial role in terms of sustainability for designing new products that will be based and/or be interoperable with these solutions. Every aspect must be taken into account so that the offered services can be utilized from citizens and business on a long term basis.

References

1. Information Society, Digital Strategy, i2010 Strategy, eEurope Action Plan. http://europa.eu/ legislation_summaries/information_society/strategies/l24226j_en.htm
2. Digital Agenda for Europe, European eGovernment Action plan 2011–2015. http://ec. europa.eu/digital-agenda/en/european-egovernment-action-plan-2011-2015
3. European Commission, European Social Fund. http://ec.europa.eu/esf/home.jsp?langId=en
4. European Commission, Regional Policy, European Regional Development Fund. http://ec. europa.eu/regional_policy/thefunds/regional/index_en.cfm
5. European Commission communication for the European e-Government Action Plan 2011–2015, COM(2010) 743 final. http://eur-lex.europa.eu/LexUriServ/LexUriServ.do? uri=COM:2010:0743:FIN:EN:PDF
6. European Commission, Interoperability Solutions for European Public Administration. http://ec.europa.eu/isa/
7. European Commission, Communication towards interoperability for European public services, Com (2010) 744 final. http://ec.europa.eu/isa/documents/isa_annex_ii_eif_en.pdf
8. Digital Agenda for Europe, Connecting Europe facility. http://ec.europa.eu/digital-agenda/ en/connecting-europe-facility
9. Secure idenTity acrOss boRders linKed 2.0, co-funded project by INFSO-ICT-PSP-297263. https://www.eid-stork2.eu/
10. e-SENS (Electronic Simple European Networked Services, co-funded project by ICT-PSP-325211. http://www.esens.eu/home/
11. Simple Procedures Online for Cross-border Services (SPOCS), co-funded project by CIP-ICT PSP-2008-2 no238935. http://www.eu-spocs.eu/
12. e-Justice Communication via Online Data Exchange (eCODEX), co-funded project by ICT PSP-270968. http://www.e-codex.eu/home.html
13. European Justice Portal. https://e-justice.europa.eu/home.do?action=home&plang=en
14. Tenders Electronic Daily (TED) a supplement to the Official Journal of the European Union. http://ted.europa.eu/TED/main/HomePage.do

15. European Commission, DG Internal Market and Services, eCERTIS. http://ec.europa.eu/markt/ecertis/login.do?selectedLanguage=en
16. Pan-European Public Procurement on Line (PEPPOL), CIP-ICT PSP no224974. http://www.peppol.eu/
17. ISA Programme, Developing electronic procurement for Europe, PEPPOL sustainability. http://ec.europa.eu/isa/actions/01-trusted-information-exchange/1-6_1-19action_en.htm
18. European Commission, DG Health and Consumers, Public Health, eHealth Network. http://ec.europa.eu/health/ehealth/policy/network/index_en.htm
19. Smart Open Services for European Patients (epSOS), co-funded project CIP-ICT PSP 224991. http://www.epsos.eu/
20. European Commission, Electronic Exchange of Social Security Information (EESSI). http://ec.europa.eu/social/main.jsp?catId=869
21. European Commission, Departments (Directorates-General) and services. http://ec.europa.eu/about/ds_en.htm
22. ISA programme, Achieving a modern ICT standardisation policy, CAMSS – Common Assessment Method Standards and Specifications. http://ec.europa.eu/isa/actions/02-interoperability-architecture/2-2action_en.htm
23. ISA programme, eSignature tools to support cross-border access to eServices for businesses, TSL and eSignature creation/verification tools. http://ec.europa.eu/isa/actions/01-trusted-information-exchange/1-9action_en.htm
24. ETSI TS 102 231, Electronic Signatures and Infrastructures (ESI); Provision of harmonized Trust- service status information. http://www.etsi.org/deliver/etsi_ts/102200_102299/102231/03.01.02_60/ts_102231v030102p.pdf
25. ISA Programme, An interoperable solution for electronic identities (eIDs), STORK sustainability. http://ec.europa.eu/isa/actions/01-trusted-information-exchange/1-5action_en.htm

Building a Logic for a Public Administration Service Transformation Algorithm

Ioannis Savvas[1]([⊠]), Nick Bassiliades[2], Elias Pimenidis[3],
and Alexander B. Sideridis[1]

[1] Agricultural University of Athens, Athens, Greece
{jsav, as}@aua.gr
[2] Aristotle University of Thessaloniki, Thessaloniki, Greece
nbassili@csd.auth.gr
[3] University of the West of England, Frenchay, Bristol BS16 1QY, UK
Elias.Pimenidis@uwe.ac.uk

Abstract. This paper presents a rationale for establishing a Public Administration Service Transformation Algorithm. It introduces an abstract top level reusable model representing how Public Administration (PA) operates in providing services to the citizens, based on an input-output model. The approach adopted here is a goal-oriented one, placing the administrative act at the centre of PA's operation, as act is the means of expressing PA's will. In this way an algorithm which may identify malfunctions, propose services and conceptualize systems to remedy failings in service provision could be built. Using PA's performance, both in effectiveness and efficiency to spot problems, and based on the improvement of these features, suggestions of services and systems could be made.

Keywords: Transformational government · Public Administration operational model · Public Administration effectiveness · Public Administration efficiency

1 Introduction

Transformational government reaches beyond e-government as it aspires to establish dynamic characteristics in the operation of Public Administration (PA), which enable a transformational ability. It can be described as an interdisciplinary domain extending the static nature of e-government to improve the way government serves citizens and businesses, but in an effective and efficient way; Technology, processes and people have to be integrated in its applications. Also, new Public Management and contemporary theories dictate to the State to refocus the operations of PA on stakeholders' goals. Information and Communication Technologies (ICT) are used to achieve and implement these goals in an easy and affordable way.

To address the above challenges to PA, the authors have followed a goal or intention oriented approach that focuses on high level business goals that a PA has to achieve. The *administrative act* (document) is regarded as the central "tool" of operation of the PA. Goals are expressed in terms of the needs of business services and not of technical services. The proposed logic leading to the creation of an algorithm for the Public Administration Service Transformation Algorithm (PASTA), is a useful tool for

A.B. Sideridis et al. (Eds.): E-Democracy 2013, CCIS 441, pp. 73–79, 2014.
DOI: 10.1007/978-3-319-11710-2_7

decision making in PA, supporting improvements in its performance. Furthermore it provides a necessary solution in identifying malfunctions and proposing services to remedy public service failings. The use of PASTA algorithm increases the accuracy of the final specifications of functional requirements of e-government systems that should be introduced.

2 Public Administration Operation

There are many approaches and several criteria for classifying PA's profiles across Europe. References [1, 2] provide a distinction relevant to vision and objectives for e-government (Social state and Market driven models); between increased interest for legal formality ("normative") and result-oriented mechanisms ("operational") model correspondingly. Southern European countries like Greece, Spain, Italy, Portugal, and those of north and central Europe like Belgium, France, Luxembourg, Germany and Austria are grouped together as to the first of the dominant trends identified in both the above works. The PASTA model of the operation of PA is based on and can represent both trends.

To represent PA's operation the authors used an input-output model based on the work proposed in [3], which in turn was based on the conclusions of [4]. This simplified model is depicted in Fig. 1.

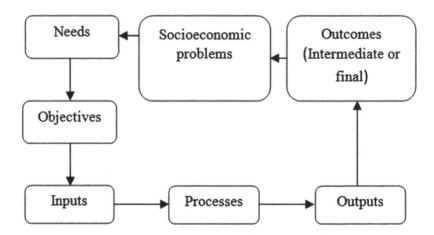

Fig. 1. A simplified input/output model of the role of PA in the socioeconomic environment

In order to provide services, PA issues *administrative acts*. Based on the above input-output model, service is set as effect, *administrative act* as output and finally, as consequence of an administrative action, the long term effect of which is going to be aligned with the aggregation of goals of the stakeholders as set by politicians.

In its daily operation, every PA unit repeats a sequence of activities in order to achieve its mission, which is referring to its external environment concerning the provision of service to citizens and businesses. To issue an *act* a unit has to fill a template, which is a product of a knowledge process and it is incumbent upon the

Administrative Law and the rules for the composition of an administrative document [5]. These rules provide a minimum for issuing of sound *administrative acts* that could sustain to objections for typical reasons. In order to fill the template, a unit needs information which may exist either in its own database or in a database of another administrative entity or in databases of law courts (legal cases), parliament (law) and citizens or businesses (certifications, declarations). To acquire this information, a Public Administration Unit performs either retrieval from one of the databases that it can have access to or communicates with other entities (sending an informative document, which is not an act). As a result the information supplied will be in the form of an *administrative act* or a legal case or a citizen/business document.

The authors consider the *administrative act* as the point where all the knowledge of PA is integrated. Even tacit knowledge of all public servants has to be explicit on an *administrative act*, if provisions of Administrative Processes Code are to be followed.

3   The Algorithm PASTA

To assess the transformational needs of every single service or process, one can start from the effectiveness part. Effectiveness is the measure of achieving goals that are not necessary financial. They could be goals regarding democracy, equity, etc. and in contemporary theories they should reflect stakeholders' needs.

Step 1: The effectiveness part
The ratios of Output over Effect (Output/Effect) and Effect over Consequence (Effect/Consequence) are the two effectiveness measures (vertical axis to the right on Fig. 1).

(i) Effect/Consequence. The ideal situation is to identify consequences of the administrative operation with goals/objectives as set by politicians. These objectives are measurable interpretations of the abstract goals of the stakeholders. Effect is the service. The quotient expresses the ability of a service to achieve or not the goal that the government and the politicians had set. A problem with this ratio reflects for example policy objectives setting and law making problems and to this end is for the time being beyond the scope of this work.

(ii) Output/Effect. This is act/service. It refers to the number of the acts that actually provide the requested service (note that service is also the denial of a request). It concerns number of acts that are invalid due to objections or appeals or even a control process, number of acts that provide service to persons that are not entitled for that and number of acts that provide the service to people who are beneficiaries of a better similar service. Such problems call for changes to the quality of acts (structural and typical matters, matters of interpretation of the legal framework and discretion margins of public servants, matters of dissemination of information).

Step 2: The efficiency part
The quotient of Input over Output (Input/Output) expresses the measure of efficiency (horizontal axis on Fig. 1).

In order to formulate PASTA as a decision tree and if-then-else condition the authors used the attributes from the Application Profile (AP) for Performance

Measurement of a Public Service that the authors have created. The above AP is based on CWA14860 and the other initiatives that CEN reviewed and refines them in sub-elements relative to the purpose of performance measurement. Furthermore it includes elements and sub-elements that are new in order to introduce concepts required for measuring performance of administrative operation. The methodology followed to define the exact elements and sub-elements of the AP was to use the attributes from the ontology of [5] describing the structure and operation of PA, analyzing farther the communicative and resource aspects.

Using the above attributes the authors investigated the different metadata standards (reviewed above) in order to decide on the appropriate elements and sub-elements that are able to describe them. In the majority of these attributes there were elements with similar meaning. Nevertheless, some of the attributes had to be introduced as elements (e.g. objections). On the contrary the majority of sub-elements and their values had to be defined from the scratch.

Services are provided through valid acts. Acts are validated through control procedures, objections and appeals. In turn these could be valid for "typical" and "non-typical" reasons. Typical reasons could be due to template elements which are mis-interpreted and are before or main text elements. When they are main text elements and regard the preamble, they concern the legal framework updating and jurisdiction updating. In such cases there is a clear need for template modeling and legal database support.

In case there are errors due to the before the main text elements, this could be due to the issuing date, a delay in issuing the act.

PASTA translates problematic ratios to problems in the operation of PA. Then it proposes services to remedy the problem. An e-government system that addresses problems like these is finally proposed using established practices. The proposition of the system is indicative as services are defined on a conceptual level (from the business point of view) and no specification of the system and its requirements are considered here. Contextual level analysis including stakeholders' goals will complement this work identifying non-functional requirements of the future system. Then in the "how" part (logical level) further specification of requirements will take place.

4   Application - Validation

To validate the algorithm seven basic processes/services of Greek Regional adminis-tration were selected. These seven processes (process ends to the issuing of an act) concern 4 Directorates and 7 departments of a Region. Fourteen experts' opinions were captured for the purposes of validation; two (the supervisor and an expert employee) of each department responsible for the provision of the services. A first questionnaire was constructed in order to obtain the information needed for the application of the algo-rithm. The questionnaire included questions for the needed metadata. In case there were no exact statistical data the experience of the supervisor and the employees was used to define values. This first set of data was used to feed PASTA in order to have its suggestions for every service. In this first phase the experts were also asked to suggest actions/services for the improvement of the effectiveness and efficiency of their routines. The whole validation activity took part in Region of Central Macedonia (RCM) and lasted for two months (15/6-14/8/2009).

From the above processes/services two are addressed to citizens (naturalization and permission for residence and employment), three to businesses (funding of private investments, pit rending permission, approval of maintenance of environmental conditions), one to another PO (management of Public Investment Program–PIP) and one to public servants and executives (measurement of efficiency and effectiveness).

In parallel the results of a project held in RCM and other seven Greek Public Organizations for the reengineering of the procedures of Greek PA were used. The project was titled "Implementation of reorganization and continuous improvement of the function of Public Organizations" (Ircipo) with a budget of 3.240.000 euros cofunded by EU and the Greek state. The duration of the project was 12 months (2007) and contractors were Deloitte Business Solutions, LDK and Tekmor.

Ircipo used the following methodologies and tools to analyze processes and suggest reorganization and change management: the Program Management Methodology™ - of Deloitte & Touche for project management, the method IDEF, the Industry Print – a software of Deloitte & Touche and the Casewise Corporate Modeller for the impression of processes, the Design™ - methodology of Deloitte & Touche, the Industry Print – a software of Deloitte & Touche and the Casewise Corporate Modeller for the planning of operational procedures, the Change Management Toolkit™ - methodology of Deloitte & Touche for the change management and the Transform™ - methodology of Deloitte & Touche for the organizational and functional reengineering.

Ircipo's team conducted interviews with PA's experts in order to understand the process and the rationale of it. In most of the cases it asked experts to suggest actions for process improvement. The selection of the 7 mentioned services was made in order to be able to compare the results of the two solutions (PASTA and Ircipo) and the processes had to be related to e government solutions. This is the reason for processes having to do with material actions (e.g. demolition of illegal constructions) being excluded.

In the second phase, the experts were asked to assess the results concluded by the application of the algorithm PASTA and the methodology used by Ircipo. In order to maintain bilateralism PASTA's suggestions were limited to high level services for PA, public servants and citizens/businesses. Some general comments/remarks that have arisen for this work are:

- Unlike PASTA, there were very few Ircipo's suggestions concerning effectiveness.
- PASTA's outputs included suggestions for helping public servants composing acts and interpreting legal framework that were not included in Ircipo's suggestion.
- Ircipo's outputs included suggestions like "composition of working committees" that were not included in PASTA's suggestions as they do not interest e-government services. These suggestions were very few though.
- All experts' suggestions were included in PASTA's outputs except from these for the "hiring of experienced personnel" and "use of more resources". PASTA's suggestions did not include "increase of personnel" like two of the 14 experts suggested for their departments as it initially suggests reorganization and automation of processes, in order to decrease workload on public servants and

simplification and reduction of repetitive tasks. PASTA accepts, in the first place, that threshold settings by executives and resource allocations are correct. If problems continue after the proposed reorganization then suggestions for resetting thresholds would follow.

- All other suggestions for services provided to departments to facilitate public service provision were almost similar, though PASTA's suggestions were in most cases more specific.

In the validation questionnaires experts were invited to validate suggested services without knowing the origin of suggestion (if it is Ircipo's or PASTA's suggestion). Services appeared in the questionnaires in random order. Those which were similar were placed only once. If one service was prerequisite for another one it was placed before it or in the same question.

Services were assessed from 1 to 5. 1 being "not useful at all", 2 "rather not useful", 3 "neither", 4 "rather useful" and 5 "very useful". In order to give marks to the suggestions the following occurred: Common services were assessed and graded. An average mark was set on these services. Additional services from "Ircipo" or PASTA were grouped together in order to produce another average mark. If there were not any, no mark was produced. The two marks were added and divided by two in order to produce the final average mark. In the case that there were not any additional services, only the first grade was considered. This was decided because some services suggested either by PASTA or Ircipo could be of no use, but also confusing and costly.

Overall:

- PASTA's results were better than the Ircipo's results in 6 out of 7 cases.
- In no case Ircipo's suggestions were assessed higher than PASTA's suggestions.
- In 6 out of 7 services, experts assess PASTA's suggestions as very useful. They were graded over 4. In the seventh the assessment was that they were useful.
- No important service suggested by experts, was missing from PASTA's suggestions.
- Additional suggestions made by Ircipo were assessed as less important or useful than suggestions made by PASTA. This means that the service mix proposed by PASTA was better than Ircipo's mix, even if there were single services proposed by Ircipo that were marked higher by the experts.

In the field of Decision Support Systems, which provide help for establishing e-gov services, most of the existing systems have been conceived to operate in specific contexts, such as health [6], energy and environmental policy [7–9], public transports [10], agriculture [11] and so on. Systems that are capable of operating on all domains of interest of PA, e.g. [12], do not reflect PA's rationale but they are rather capable for e commerce domain.

PASTA in reverse, is in place to provide general guidelines for process modeling like only limited work has established, to detect problems and suggest services both for effectiveness and efficiency problems and to propose services for helping public servants in expressing PA's will.

5   Conclusions

Process modeling and process reorganization, have been recognized as being of utmost importance for making e-government implementations succeed. Due to the high complexity of governmental processes and organizational structures, appropriate modeling methodologies and tools are, however, not really available yet.

In this paper the authors proposed the algorithm PASTA that can address problems that concern the whole operation of PA and not only specific procedures. It is a generic algorithm that could be applicable for every public service.

The next steps of this work include expansion of the algorithm by the use of stakeholders' requirements and logical level requirements (specification of process requirements) in order to specify e government IT systems.

References

1. Savvas, I., Pimenidis, E., Sideridis, A.B.: A review of e-governance models in the EU. In: Proceedings of Advances in Computing and Technology (AC&T) Conference, University of East London, England, pp. 110–119 (2007)
2. Billiets, M., et al.: D2.2 – Legislative, Institutional and EU Policy Related Requirements. IST STREP PROJECT SemanticGov (2006). http://www.semantic-gov.org/
3. Van Dooren, W.: Performance measurement in the flemish public sector: a supply and demand approach. Ph.D. dissertation, Faculteit Sociale. Wetenschappen - Onderzoekseenheid: Instituut voor de Overheid [IO], K.U. Leuven (2006)
4. Pollit, C., Bouckaert, G.: Public Management Reform: A Comparative Analysis. Oxford University Press, Oxford (2004)
5. Savvas, I., Bassiliades, N.: A process-oriented ontology-based knowledge management system for facilitating operational procedures in public administration. Expert Syst. Appl. **36** (3), 4467–4478 (2009)
6. Homer, J., Milstein, B.: Optimal decision making in a dynamic model of community health. In: Proceedings of the International Conference on System Sciences, Hawaii. IEEE Press (2004)
7. Van Groenendaal, W.J.H.: Group decision support for public policy planning. Inf. Manag. **40**(5), 371–380 (2003)
8. Sokolova, M., Fernández-Caballero, A.: Modeling and implementing an agent-based environmental health impact decision support system. Expert Syst. Appl. **36**(2), 2603–2614 (2009). (Part 2)
9. Morón, A.B., Calvo-Flores, M.D., Ramos, J.M., Almohano, M.P.: AIEIA: software for fuzzy environmental impact assessment. Expert Syst. Appl. **36**(5), 9135–9149 (2009)
10. Fay, A.: A fuzzy knowledge-based system for railway traffic control. Eng. Appl. Artif. Intell. **13**(6), 719–729 (2000)
11. Chaudhary, S., Sorathia, V., Laliwala, Z.: Architecture of sensor based agricultural information system for effective planning of farm activities. In: Proceedings of the IEEE International Conference on Services Computing, Shanghai, pp. 93–100 (2004)
12. De Meo, P., Quattrone, G., Ursino, D.: A decision support system for designing new services tailored to citizen profiles in a complex and distributed e-government scenario. Data Knowl. Eng. **67**, 161–184 (2008)

e-Government Applications, Virtualization

Electronic Government Enactment in a Small Developing Country – the Palestinian Authority's Policy and Practice

Fouad J.F. Shat[1], Amin Mousavi[1], and Elias Pimenidis[2(✉)]

[1] University of East London, London, UK
{u1051068, S.A.Mousavi}@uel.ac.uk
[2] University of the West of England, Frenchay, Bristol BS16 1QY, UK
Elias.Pimenidis@uwe.ac.uk

Abstract. Successful implementation and utilization of electronic government in Palestine has been challenging field for the Palestinian authority, businesses and dispersed citizens. Our research provides an overview of the current policy and practice available to Palestinian institutions for implementing e-government services. It discusses the necessity for e-government services and identifies potential benefits that could be accrued as well as realistic limitations that could be faced in this politically sensitive area. In doing so it identifies the challenges faced due to the dispersed nature of the geographical area that government is exerted by the PA and highlights the required infrastructure for successful enhancement of government offered services to the citizens of Palestine.

Keywords: Electronic government · EGR · Palestine

1 Introduction

The Palestinian Authority (PA) is currently in an early phase of its electronic government implementation and aims at extensive use of ICT to improve services to citizens and to promote economic growth. PA is responsible for serving millions of people in different areas such as cities in the Gaza strip, cities in the West Bank and Palestinian camps in Lebanon. These areas are not connected geographically and which makes implementation of electronic government projects in Palestine comparatively complex and exceptional.

Current literature shows that Palestine has achieved a good level of e-transformation in terms of spirited desire and political will, but it is still in the very early stages of implementing a real e-government project. There are several barriers towards successful electronic governance for Palestinians. The main barriers are Geo-political situation, lack of legislation, decisions making procedures, PA policies and limited users' awareness and readiness to embrace and stimulate the current digital transformation towards true digital government. Any e-government project in Palestine is bound to be affected from a variety of factors such as administrative complexities, interior complexities, and cooperation processes including the exchange of data between government institutions.

Nevertheless, implementing of e-government in Palestine may solve most the problems for accessing public services and communication with government agencies.

A.B. Sideridis et al. (Eds.): E-Democracy 2013, CCIS 441, pp. 83–92, 2014.
DOI: 10.1007/978-3-319-11710-2_8

Considering the exceptional dispersion of the Palestinian population and Israel's control of area, implementing real electronic government may enables government to perform their responsibilities and provide public services electronically to Palestinians and other stakeholders. This also enables citizens to have two ways communicate with their government.

Any successful implementation of e-government services in Palestine will provide a great opportunity to increase the effectiveness and efficiency of the Palestinian Authority's performance in supporting government institutions and serving citizens and businesses. Recent surveys show that the greatest effort for electronic government activities comes from central government in Palestine. However, there are a number of obstacles that could prevent or delay the diffusion of common electronic government promises – such obstacles are political, cultural and technological in nature. This paper has five sections: after this introduction section, the second section reviews the objectives and challenges of electronic governments in developing countries; the third explores the Palestinian Authority current practices in this field; the fourth section propose an initial version of an applicable staged electronic government model; finally, the conclusion discusses and identifies future work of this research.

2 Electronic Government Objectives and Challenges

The term e-government is defined as the use of information and communication technology to transform government by making it more accessible, effective, efficient, transparent and accountable [1]. It is also described as the use of ICT technologies to allow and develop the efficiency with which government services are provided to citizens, employees, businesses and agencies [2]. Pimenidis et al. [3] have further described it as the result of the communications between three different set of powers, each of which has gone through its own evolution: information and communication, management conceptions and government itself.

The key players in the electronic government environment are government agencies, citizens and businesses. Government agencies may consider that the shift from manual processes to IT-enabled processes may increase efficiency in administration and service delivery. Citizens want to learn about this new mode of access in wide-ranging ways. Users of this system are expecting access to an increased amount of information, as well as access to online services from governments in order to enhance their civic, professional and personal lives.

E-government Applications are used to disseminate information and deliver services to citizens and businesses through electronic means and is beneficial in:

- Accountability and efficiency in various governmental processes.
- Transparency and anti-corruption in all transactions.
- Economic and social value.
- Empowering citizens and encouraging them to participate in governance.

Mousavi et al. [4] believe that, after setting up the required infrastructure, the first stage of developing and enhancing electronic government is cataloguing and publishing governmental information. In many countries, such as the US, Australia, New

Zealand and the UK, governments have established special portals for publishing and sharing data [5]. According to Cameron [6], the current prime minister of the UK, "each UK government department should publish the item online if it costs more than £25,000 and from January all government contracts which are worth more than £25,000 will be published". Publishing government data is the first stage to achieving the e-government benefits of such as transparency, accountability and improvements to the public service. However, current research shows that there are a number of challenges in cataloguing and publishing government data; challenges which not limited to technology and policies. Investigating these challenges and identifying tools and techniques to tackle them will improve the quality of electronic government. Looking at similar practices and identifying best practice approach strongly supports identifying the right path for successful implementation of electronic government at the different situations.

The exciting benchmarks of e-government do not provide specific frameworks for assessing, classifying or even making comparisons between different e-government programs in different countries [7]. Some assessment models are focused on the general issues of developing e-government programs. They assess e-government components in different countries while bypassing the fact that different countries have different circumstances. For instance, when looking at some countries, specific factors may need to be taken into consideration but not so for other countries. Some of these models are not including stakeholder's views despite their importance to the success of electronic government projects.

The challenge is how to ascertain what components need to be assessed in small developing countries, and what ICT level these countries need to reach in order to move into the next stage of building an effective e-government project. It is also important to establish a new model for small developing countries in order to guide them to the successful establishment of e-government projects without facing unnecessary and unexpected difficulties.

Before discussing such a model in section four, the next section will look at essential information about the main case study that is used for this research.

3   Palestine Authorities' Current Policy and Practices

The Palestinian territory is located in western Asia, is bordered on the west by the Mediterranean Sea, with a coastline along the east of Syria, with whom it shares a bordered. The west bank also borders with Jordan, whereas the occupied territories in 1948 share border with north Lebanon and Syria. The Palestinian coast extends from Ras Al-Naqura in the north to Rafah in the south. It forms almost a straight line except for the Bay of Acre, the total surface area of Palestine is approximately 27,000 km^2 with population of approx. 11m, after 1948 war the UN recognized Israel as state and because of the hundreds of thousands were forced to move out their cities, towns and villages, The US recognized Palestine as non-member state and its agreed Palestine border as 1967 line, approx. 4 m of the Palestinian living inside the 1967 defined borders (west bank and Gaza strip) and approx. 1.5 million still living inside the historic Palestinian territories, 5.5 millions of Palestinian refugees are still living in temporary camps in different places such as Jordan, Syria, Lebanon, the Gaza strip and the West bank (Fig. 1).

Palestinians in the world

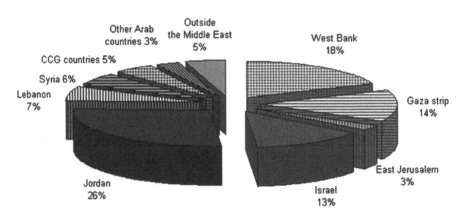

Fig. 1. One Palestinian population spread

The Palestinian Authority (PA) policy over the last a few years has included e-government as one of the top national priorities. President Abbas has assigned a Ministerial Committee for E-Government, this committee has made the first comprehensive E-government strategic Plan in 2005, and this document was part of the PA vision "to provide a better life for our citizens by being a Government that: Empowers citizens to participate in government; Connects citizens, the private sector and institutions to drive economic growth and meet community challenges; and Delivers real public value through citizen-centric government services."

According to OECD the PA's e-government vision and policies in 2010 was including "a public sector that provides citizens with high quality services and value for money". This plan states that the e-government National strategy should, over time, work to increase efficiency and effectiveness of public service delivery; it also states that the Ministry of Telecommunications and Information Technology (MTIT) is main key players in terms of move this initiatives forward, moreover, the 13th government of PA program (Ending the Occupation, Establishing the State and Homestretch to Freedom) has clearly mention that the use of ICT and e-government particular should help public sector reform and this is the most important national priorities.

According to OCED 2011, the Palestinian national plans for e-government policies are well, OCED recommended it as good practices however the 2005 PA e-government plane should be updated to keep pace with new policy priorities.

In order to address the main obstacles of e-government implementation it is essential to pay attentions to the e-government implementation mechanism, and this leads to recognition of the need for a national strategy for implementing real e-government projects.

All Palestinian ministries are widely included the e-government objectives in their organizational strategies. However there is no appropriate policy for the co-ordination between PA governmental institutions and agencies and this lack of co-ordination is identified by researchers as a significant barrier for successful implementation of e-government in Palestine.

According to Saidam [8], Palestine has achieved a good level of e-transformation in terms of the moral will and spirited desire, but is still in the very early stages of implementing a real e-government project due to several barriers such as geo-politics, legislation, decision-making, policies and even an awareness in terms of level of readiness.

The implementing of e-government in Palestine will solve all the problems in terms of accessibility and communication obstacles for Palestinian citizens under Israeli occupation. Currently, the e-government project in Palestine is still suffering from various factors such as administrative complexities, interior complexities, problems of cooperation and data exchange between government institutions and in data accessibility [9].

The ICT and post national strategy in Palestine shows that Palestinian legal framework has some shortcomings as follow:

1. The E-Signature Law;
2. The Electronic Transactions law;
3. The Law of Protection of Individual and Personal Data;
4. The Intellectual Property Protection law;
5. The Electronic Commercial Transactions, and Internet and IT Laws;
6. The Law of Freedom and Confidentiality of Information in Electronic Communications;
7. The Cyber Crimes Law.

According to PA officials, the lack of specific e-signature legislation is one of the main obstacles for implementing an effective e-government; e-signature is often identified as the panacea for e-government implementation. It is indeed a formidable tool that can pave the way to many important and useful e-government services.

The PA already enjoys a robust technological infrastructure; government initiations in Palestine are successfully connected with government computer center and ministry of Finance.

Finally, it's very clear that there is absence of a clear vision in terms of the need of unified technical standards, the need of interoperability frameworks and common culture and practices of data sharing across Palestinian government institutions (PA National ICT strategy), and in other words the need of national strategy of implementing real e-government in Palestine. Furthermore the regional conflict has significant bad impact on ICT infrastructure, and many ministries had to be displaced and this caused a significant delay on e-government implementation. Despite the poor achievements in this field, PA is working to address involved issues and PA e-leaders are well aware of the barriers and they are aiming at overcoming them.

OCED study [10] cites technology issues as one obstacle to smooth development of ICT in the public sector (Fig. 2).

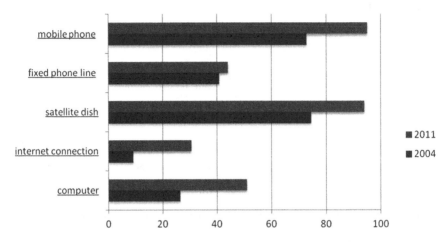

Fig. 2. Percentage of households with IT goods and services in Gaza strip and West bank [10]

It is important to note that the lack of management skills and ICT skills has a significant effect beyond e-government implementation; it prevents the effective application of collaboration frameworks and has an important negative impact on procurement choices. However, skills upgrade is a common topic across OECD and MENA countries, and the PA has made it a top priority in all major policy documents.

These circumstances draw further attention to the critical role of EGR in enabling all e-government stakeholders to benefit from e-government promises. The next section will further discuss EGR as the initial stage which will be followed by reviewing further stages for successful implementation of electronic government.

4   Proposed Staged Electronic Government Model

Electronic government is the measure of willingness for the countries governments to take benefits from information and communication also its defined as the process of measuring the use of information and communication technology for electronic government. The assessment of the electronic government readiness can be used to make comparisons between the governments in the use of the information and communication technology for the electronic government. In the following proposed model, the readiness of the people is based on the acceptance level of both; the citizens and the employees for the electronic government functions and processes (Fig. 3).

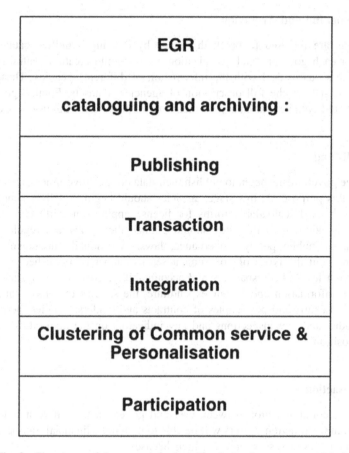

Fig. 3. The stages of the proposed adaptable electronic government Model

4.1   E-Government Readiness (EGR)

The assessing of the electronic government readiness is very important for developing countries. As an example by measuring EGR in Palestine we can work out the current position of this country in this context and can identify required tasks for improving electronic government utilization.

Assessing E-Government Readiness (EGR) dictated the need to investigate e-readiness assessment approaches: since EGR is a main element of a country's overall e-readiness [11]. A country's e-readiness is essentially the degree in which a community is qualified to participate in the Networked World. It is measured by judging the relative advance of the most important areas for the adoption of the ICTs and their most important applications [12].

One of the main aspects of EGR that requires developers' attention is assessing people readiness in order to make sure that people are ready to participate and interact with new systems.

4.2   Cataloguing and Archiving

Governments are required to begin this stage by creating a unified catalogue and interface for each governmental organization. They should create a central catalogue and interface so as to deal with the information of different agencies. These central catalogues must have the full description of agencies' datasets. Finally, government agencies should archive and catalogue their data to prepare for the next stage.

4.3   Publishing

At this stage governments begin to publish their data online, government agencies open portals for this purpose. At this stage, agencies should begin to deliver simple online services, such as downloadable forms for license application, birth certificates, ID forms, etc. In addition to this they should publish their rules and regulations, and information on public policy, governance, laws. Additionally documentation and information about the types of government services must be published. In order to achieve a high level of transparency and accountability, government agencies should also publish information about their expenditure, the salaries of senior staff, budget, organizational charts and pay, copies of contracts and tenders, policies, performance, external audits and key inspections and key indicators on the authorities' fiscal and financial position.

4.4   Transaction

In this stage, communication between user and government is more interactive and includes online transactions. Users will be able to undertake financial transactions such as paying penalties, taxes or renewing their licenses.

4.5   Integration

The government during the integration stage will be able to deliver integrated services across internal and external applications, by offering a single point of contact to their citizens in order to deliver full communication between users and officials.

The transaction stage triggers the transformation stages. This means that, by the time the government fulfils all the requirements of the transaction stage, it can then go to the transformation stage with all the integrated services.

4.6   Clustering of Common Service and Personalization

Citizens at this stage will be able to utilize portals. To enable this to happen, hi-tech web programming is required. Citizens will be able to view the services as a unified group by using these portals. The shape of government structures will transform and take on a new shape, with all services clustered along common lines by government. There will be interactive democracy with public awareness and a range of accountability measures.

In this stage, governments move from a service-delivery model to system-wide political transformation. The governmental websites will start offering hi-tech technology such as emails and electronic subscription, and will allow users to provide feedback, make comments and thereby enhance democracy.

4.7 Participation

In this stage, web-based public services transforms into web-based political activities. Citizens will start participating in political activities such as online voting, online opinion evaluations and online discussions. This stage will also take into account the importance of high levels of privacy and high levels of technology to support it and achieve the targets.

5 Conclusion

This paper revised some of the relevant views on electronic government promises and the level of Palestinians capabilities to utilize potential electronic government services. Following revising current situation, researcher has introduced an abstract of a potential electronic government development model that has capability of serving a small developing country. The future research will focus on finalizing implementation details for each stage of the proposed model.

References

1. Mousavi, S.A., Pimenidis, E., Jahankhani, H.: e-Business models for use in e-Government for developing countries. In: 7th European Conference on e-Government Den Haag, The Netherlands, Haagse Hogeschool (2007)
2. Bélanger, F., Carter, L.: Trust and risk in e-government adoption. J. Strateg. Inf. Syst. 17(2), 165–176 (2008)
3. Pimenidis, E., Iliadis, L.S., Georgiadis, C.K.: Can e-government systems bridge the digital divide? In: Proceedings of the 5th European Conference on Information Management and Evaluation (ECIME 2011), Dipartimento di Informatica e Comunicazione, Università dell'Insubria, Como, Italy, 8–9 September 2011, pp. 403–411 (2011)
4. Mousavi, S.A., Pimenidis, E., Jahankhani, H.: Five stage development framework for electronic government. In:10th European Conference on e-Government. University of Limerick in the National Centre for Taxation Studies, Limerick, Ireland, Academic Conferences International (2010)
5. Shadbolt, N., O'Hara, K., Berners-Lee, T., Gibbins, N., Glaser, H., Hall, W., Schraefel, M.C.: Linked open government data: lessons from Data.gov.uk. IEEE Intell. Syst. 27(3), 16–24 (2012)
6. Cameron, D.: Government to publish new data on health, schools, courts and transport (2013). https://www.gov.uk/government/news/government-to-publish-new-data-on-health-schools-courts-and-transport

7. Hu, Y., Xiao, J., Pang, J., Xie, K.: A research on the appraisal framework of e-government project success. In: Conference Proceedings, ICEC'05, ACM Grant and Chau (2005)
8. Saidam, S.: e-government, the future government (2013). http://www.wafa.ps/arabic/index.php?action=detail&id=133542
9. Chadwick, D.: E-government will solve the accessibility problem with Palestinian government (2013). http://www.wafa.ps/arabic/index.php?action=detail&id=133955
10. The Organisation for Economic Co-operation and Development: Modernising the Public Administration The Case of E-Government in the Palestinian Authority (2011). http://www.oecd.org/mena/governance/50402812.pdf
11. Kovacic, Z.J.: The impact of national culture on worldwide eGovernment readiness. Inf. Sci. J. **8**, 143–158 (2005)
12. Budhiraja, R., Sachdeva, S.: eReadiness assessment. In: Conference Proceedings International Conference on Building Effective eGovernance (2002)

Supporting Lab Courses Using OpenStack

Charalampos Z. Patrikakis[✉], Stefanos A. Kalantzis,
Lazaros Toumanidis, and Fotis Zisimos

TEI of Piraeus, Petrou Ralli & Thivon 250, 12244 Athens, Greece
bpatr@teipir.gr, stefanos.kalantzis@nullstack.eu,
{laztoum,fotis25}@hotmail.com

Abstract. In this paper, an implementation of a versatile laboratory, implemented using virtual machines deployed in a cloud infrastructure is proposed. The idea behind the proposal is to be able to take full advantage of the cloud infrastructure, in order to support multiple laboratory courses on computing and networking, through a single physical infrastructure, consisting of thin clients connecting through a high speed network to the virtualization platform in a computer cluster. The architecture of a prototype implementation over OpenStack at TEI of Piraeus is presented, together with plans for future expansion.

Keywords: Cloud computing · Virtualization · OpenStack · Virtualized laboratories

1 Introduction

Virtualization has changed the way that we view Information Technology in recent years. Instead of using many different systems to perform various tasks, virtualization provide the means towards a unified system with centralized administration for hosting applications and services. Taking into consideration the developments in networking, virtualization is set to become a baseline technology in the near future. Being a foundational element of cloud computing, which in turn has become a powerful (and in many cases necessary) model in higher education, virtualization technologies "provide a way to abstract the workspace environment in such a way as to be able to present educationally valid content on a broad range of devices" [1].

Desktop virtualization introduces the ability to separate the logical desktop from the physical machine [2]. One form of desktop virtualization, virtual desktop infrastructure (VDI), can be thought as a more advanced form of hardware virtualization. Rather than interacting with a host computer directly via a keyboard, mouse, and monitor, the user interacts with the host computer using another desktop computer or a mobile device by means of a network connection, such as a LAN, Wireless LAN or even the Internet. In addition, the host computer in this scenario becomes a server computer capable of hosting multiple virtual machines at the same time for multiple users.

The use of desktop virtualization can prove very useful in cases of laboratories in topics where the necessary infrastructure of the laboratory consists of software tools, since it can introduce many benefits to the setup and management of the computing devices used as hosts [3].

© Springer International Publishing Switzerland 2014
A.B. Sideridis et al. (Eds.): E-Democracy 2013, CCIS 441, pp. 93–102, 2014.
DOI: 10.1007/978-3-319-11710-2_9

In order to support virtualization, the use of a cloud infrastructure is the most efficient solution. Most of the cloud-computing requirements are the same across all industries. However, there are particular issues that are of significant importance in higher education, leading to specific challenges for colleges and universities as regards the deployment and use of e cloud computing infrastructure. In particular [4]:

- **Security and Privacy.** The proliferation BYOD (Bring Your Own Device) programs at many universities have raised the concerns for security and data privacy in higher education, especially in the areas of ICT. As the number of devices used by students in campus has increased, and with the number of courses and teaching material available online (even in the form of streaming), the challenges that ICT and NOC teams have to face have been increased significantly.
- **Private-Public equilibrium.** The vast offer of services to Universities by large IT Corporation, in terms of email, desktop application access and professional tools, has made the need to carefully select and justify this selection of open source vs commercial applications adopted by a University. Keeping the right balance between public and private cloud is equally difficult, and requires the consideration of all relevant legal and security issues.
- **Compliance with University priorities.** As the primary goal of higher level education institutes is education, any strategy adopted should have as a primary goal, the satisfaction of educational goals through the support of cloud technologies, and the improvement of the learning conditions, without introducing extra overhead to the students in order to master specific IT skills.

The rest of the paper is organized as follows: In the next section, the requirements and specifications for the implementation of virtualized laboratories are presented, followed by the description of the architecture of the proposed solution in Sect. 3. In Sect. 4, details on the implementation of the proposed architecture for the support of laboratory courses at the TEI of Piraeus are provided, starting from an evaluation and selection of cloud technologies, and proceeding with the actual deployment of an OpenStack based solution. The paper closes with conclusions and ideas for future extensions of the platform.

2 Requirements and Specifications for the Virtualization Platform

Before we enter the description of requirements of the platform, we need to identify the general idea of the designed system. This can be summarized in the following: The design and implementation of a cloud based, desktop virtualization system that is able to support diverse laboratories on computing and networking issues, allowing for the easy introduction of new laboratory courses, and offering the corresponding framework for time-scheduling of courses. The system should be able to support any type of laboratory that is based on the use of applications and software tools, without the need for specific hardware. Though the paper refers to computing and networking laboratory courses, based on the previous definition, any type of laboratory that can be supported by software tools, should be able to benefit from the use of the proposed platform.

Coming to the requirements for supporting a system for meeting the needs described above, we can identify the following:

- Reduced operating costs.
- Minimization of management and maintenance time.
- High availability and low response times.
- Accessibility from anywhere.
- High levels of security.
- Energy efficiency.
- Simplified user experience.
- Flexibility and minimum deployment time.

The way the above requirements can be met in terms of technology selection and use of tools is listed below.

Reduced Energy and Operating Cost. With the conversion of physical servers to virtual, we can achieve significant cost savings in power for supporting board and peripheral operation, as well as cooling costs. Hosting the servers to a cluster infrastructure as that of a datacenter also introduces extra benefits such as minimization of infrastructure for uninterruptible power supply and physical space for the servers. The same applies for the networking infrastructure.

Minimization of Management and Maintenance Time. The consolidation of resources shortens the time required for server maintenance. Operations such as backup and restore are now easier, as are the operations for introducing a new course topic at the laboratory (installation of software tools, configuration and parameterization, and user management).

High Availability and Low Response times. The ability to immediately (and in some times long term) allocate resources is critical, as it may affect the quality of the lab courses, while in cased of computer based lab tests, availability and response times are even more crucial. The response times in cases of failures or crashes should be minimized, and this is achieved easily through the use of virtualized servers, where substitution of a faulty instance of a server can take place in no time. Of course, the need for a smart management system that is able to quickly substitute a virtual server is obvious here.

Accessibility from Anywhere. Taking into account the need for supporting distance learning, it is important that access to the services of the platform should be provided to students and tutors from everywhere. At the same time, a per user access management, featuring Authentication, Authorization and Accounting is also needed, in order to be able to fully control access to the virtualized laboratories. The inherent abilities of a cloud based implementation fully address this need.

High Levels of Security. The levels of security to be provided by this solution will have to be larger and more effective than the traditional architecture. This requirement should be considered in relation to the previous for a "per user" access management and reporting. Again, security policies applied at the cloud level rather than at host level, simplifies the process and allows for an integrated approach using more powerful security tools.

Flexibility and Minimum Deployment Times. One of the most important advantages that the use of virtual servers on the cloud has to offer is that having the ability to create virtualized laboratories (a set of virtual servers into virtual private network), we can install new technologies and perform tests very fast, while upon successful completion of the evaluation process, direct access to students and educators can be allowed even at a large scale, since cloning a virtual server to many instances requires practically zero time compared to a non-cloud solution. A smart management system here also allows a non-technical user of the platform to easily introduce new servers.

3   Designing the Virtualized Lab

In this section, the general architecture and modules for the implementation of the virtualized laboratory will be presented, following the identification of the general operational framework and needs of the laboratories that could be supported by this virtualized implementation.

3.1   Laboratory Profile

It should be noted that in order to be able to support a laboratory through a virtualized server, the particular needs for training and exercises of the laboratory must allow this virtualization. For example, laboratories that require hands-on access to equipment or devices are not suitable, while laboratories that rely on the use of software tools and simulators are excellent candidates. The vast majority of laboratories on computing and networking issues fall into this category, while in the case of need for large scale simulations, or even interaction between computing/networking nodes, the virtualization offers a greater advantage: the ability to deploy several instances of nodes, and also to give access to computing and network recourses even from thin clients.

Therefore, as regards the laboratory profile that could potentially benefit from virtualization, we would identify it as Computer/Networking related, involving the use of simulators or specialized applications that do not have the need for access to very specialized hardware (i.e. direct connection to a microcontroller board), in need of frequent updates on the operating system, applications and tools used, and potentially needing access to a lot of computational and networking resources. The more a laboratory profile matches the previous list, the more it can benefit from virtualization.

3.2   General Architecture

The general architecture of the virtualized laboratory, is quite simple. In fact, it resembles that of the mainframe computers and terminals architecture, where "dumb" terminals were used to connect and share the resources of a mainframe computer. The difference in our case is that sharing is restricted to the cloud resources offered to support the virtual servers accessed by the user terminals, while the terminals should be able to support the needs of high speed connection to the cloud, as well as rendering capabilities for supporting a rich media environment.

The following picture depicts the general architecture of the solution (Fig. 1).

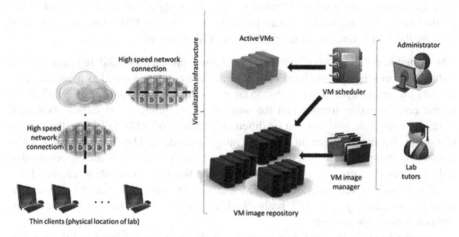

Fig. 1. General architecture

The modules identified in the previous picture are explained in the following paragraphs.

Thin Clients. These are used as terminals and can be located anywhere with a high speed internet connection. Each client is connected to the cloud infrastructure and is capable of supporting high resolution analysis, and also to render high resolution video. Though the networking and image/video support requirements are not that crucial in many cases, the availability of many small size devices capable of supporting high speed connections and rendering high resolution multimedia, makes this requirement easy to meet. On the other hand, the need for high speed connections and enhanced multimedia capabilities may be important for laboratory courses in the area of multimedia and the internet. Thin clients should have the OS installed, and should be preconfigured to connect to a specific VM address. However, the alternative of using a PXE Boot server can also be used. In this case however, there may be a delay in starting up the thin clients (while loading the OS from the PXE Boot server), and in this case, the need for a high speed connection to the PXE Boot server location is very important.

VM Image Repository. This repository holds the VM images for each particular lab. The images are copied to the active VMs space, from where they are accessed by the thin clients. Two cases exist here: In the case that all clients are identical and have the exact same configuration, then one version of the image is stored, while in the case that some configurations of clients differ, several versions of an image are stored and used for the VM instances. Images are managed by the image manager.

VM Image Manager. The image manager is responsible for introducing a new image to the image repository and for creating the necessary entries to the VM directory database, activating access to the VMs and removing a VM. VMs are uploaded by the

Lab tutors, once they have been tested and are made available after the intervention of the administrator of the system. If a particular configuration of a lab exists, where VMs are created using particular configurations (and not being all identical), a manifest file for the setup of the lab is also created and maintained by the VM image manager to be used by the VM scheduler when creating the VM instances.

VM Scheduler. The VM scheduler is managing the creation and removal of VM instances supporting a virtualized lab. Once a VM image is reported as available from the VM image manager, it is possible to create a schedule entry on the time availability of the corresponding images and the way these are going to be created (identical instances using one VM version or different instances of VMs following the configuration at the manifest file of the VM image manager). The VM scheduler while monitoring the virtualized labs time plan, it ensures that no conflicts are encountered in order to create and remove the necessary VMs. At times when no lab is scheduled, the scheduler could revert to a default VM instance in order to make the thin clients capable of operating at a 24/7 basis. Such a case would be that of an internet or computer room for students.

In order to allow the lab tutors to use the platform, a special front end is available, offering them the ability to submit a particular time plan for a lab, describe it in terms of resources, and upload the template images (VMs or other). In the case of a special setup, the lab tutors are able to select specific configurations of thin clients, by assigning different VMs to different thin clients.

The administrator has the supervision of the system, and is responsible for granting the requests for accepting and making available a VM that is entered into the system, creation of a virtualized lab following a lab tutor request, and making it available to the system.

4   Implementation Over the Cloud

In this section of the paper, implementation details of the proposed platform, with references to the cloud computing infrastructure are provided, with a presentation of the considered solutions and reasons for selecting OpenStack [5].

4.1   Presentation of Cloud Technologies

Before we proceed with the description of the implementation and the reference to the cloud computing solution used, a comparative presentation of the available solutions for cloud computing is presented, based on characteristics such as pricing, processing power capabilities, scalability, management and interoperability issues. Using as a reference a detailed analysis of cloud computing solutions available by Virtualizationmatrix [6], the following table presents a comparison between three of the most popular implementations: VMware cloud, Microsoft's Hyper-V and OpenStack (Table 1).

As it can be concluded from the above table, the OpenStack solution, apart from the fact that it is free of charge, is also able to supports high availability of resources, as

Table 1. Comparison of Cloud computing solutions

Characteristics	VMware cloud	Microsoft Hyper-V	OpenStack
Pricing	High	High	Free (Open source)
Hypervisors	esxi	hyper-v	many hypervisors
Maxi host resources (CPU, RAM, etc.)	Medium	High	Unlimited
Maximum VM resources	High	High	Unlimited
VM management	Excellent	Excellent	Excellent
Interoperability	Medium	Low	Excellent
Extendibility	Medium	Medium	Excellent

well as scalability and interoperability. The only drawback is that there is no direct accompanying the installation (as in the case of a paid solution). Instead, support should come from the OpenStack community and volunteers. In the case of an installation at a University however, this is not a problem, as it creates an opportunity for students to learn and work on an emerging technology. In the next section, we will elaborate on the reasons for selecting OpenStack for our pilot implementation.

4.2   Selection of Cloud Technology for the Implementation

There are two main reasons behind the selection of for selecting OpenStack as a cloud computing provider for our pilot implementation.

The first is the importance of this open source project, being close to the one of the Linux kernel. The high number of organizations worldwide that support, use and actively contribute to OpenStack, along with the thousands of active members has played an important role in our selection. By using an open source project, we give the potential for future students to study and see in action such a project, and offer the ground for student thesis and assignments. Closely related to the open source nature of OpenStack is of Couse the free availability, which is also important for reducing the cost of implementation.

The second reason is related to the OpenStack features and extendibility. As the pilot implementation was based on a small installation that should be able to support the full idea of Virtualized laboratories, while on the other hand being able to easily scale up, the features of OpenStack as reported in the previous section of the paper made it the perfect candidate, as it offers scalability in both size and features.

What is very important to mention, is that the platform described in this paper can be considered an OpenStack extension and will be released to the public when ready.

4.3   Implementation Details

The basic OpenStack installation consists of 4 small sized rack servers, a layer 3 managed switch and a pfSense router. Some additional functionality, like OpenVPN and monitoring, is provided via a standard PC with low processing power capabilities.

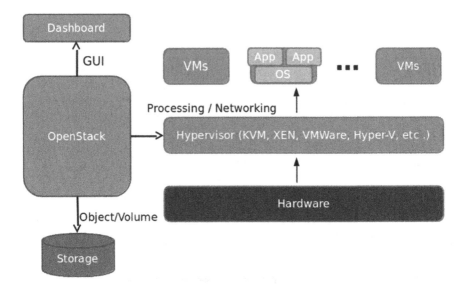

Fig. 2. OpenStack high level architecture

The virtualized laboratory setup is completed with the use of 4 Intel Next Unit of Computing (NUC) computers, connecting to their active VMs via an internet connection.

OpenStack was set up using the Neutron Networking [7] technology. It is the newest and most advanced form of networking available in OpenStack, and provides several plugins for extended functionality. The principal architecture is displayed in Fig. 2.

4.4   Issues to be Addressed

During the implementation and testing of the platform in a University environment, some deployment issues were identified. These are summarized in the following paragraphs.

Connection Speed of the Thin Clients to the Server. The importance of a high speed connection of the thin clients to the server is closely related to the nature of the laboratories supported. In cases where a large volume of information that needs to be rendered to the screen of the client is high (such cases are multimedia labs), then the need of a high speed connection is evident. The parallel use of the infrastructure by many clients amplifies the need for bandwidth. In special cases where downloading of data prior to the use of the virtual desktop connection (this is the case of connection to a PXE boot server), then another important issue is that of loading of the necessary OS and tools. Again, a high speed connection can help minimize the initialization time.

Access Limitations. An issue raised here is the limitation of access to the cloud. In cases where the clients and the cloud infrastructure are on the same LAN, then there is no issue. However, when access is to be provided to clients and laboratories outside the LAN (i.e. other departments), then there is the need for the necessary network setup in the form of VLANs. Going one step further in order to examine access from outside the campus, further issues including network security have to be addressed, as well as user based access and authentication management rather than host based access management.

Storage of User Files. One issue that has been identified through the use of the virtualized laboratories is the need for storage of intermediate results of student exercises during lab courses. As the Virtual Servers of the laboratories are being created and removed, after the completion of a lab, there is the need for storing the results (final and intermediate) of the work of students. Though the use of cloud based storage based on popular solutions such as Dropbox or Skydrive can provide a solution, it would be more efficient to include a personal storage space for each student, within the same cloud infrastructure used for desktop virtualization, so that access to the lab exercises results is always available over one system.

5   Conclusions and Future Work

In this paper, we have presented a proposal for creating virtualized labs based on a cloud infrastructure, and particularly over OpenStack. The proposal can be deployed over a University intranet, and making use of low cost PCs for end terminals, allowing for multiple uses of a PC equipped room with a high speed internet connection. Tests of the implementation of the presented proposal at the Department of electronics Engineering of TEI of Piraeus, have been planned, based on two use cases: Lab courses on Computer Networks and Object Oriented Programming.

As it has been reported earlier in the paper, the platform described in this paper can be considered an OpenStack extension and will be released to the public when ready. Information will be available at http://networklab.teipir.gr.

Enhancements to the platform have also been identified, in order to focus on the students, and allowing them to store and share their lab related work and exercises. For this, the introduction of one more role in the system, that of the user is foreseen, linked with a personal storage space in the cloud for each user, where the intermediate results of exercises can be stored during the lab courses, and accessed from everywhere.

Also, the ability to access the VMs of the labs even outside the lab hours, allowing students to continue working on their lab exercises even after the lab is also in the future plans, where on demand creation of VM instances, and access to them through system-student accounts will be offered.

Acknowledgments. The authors of the paper would like to thank Thanassis Parathyras CEO of www.stackmasters.eu and responsible for the Athens OpenStack User Group who volunteered to assist in the OpenStack configuration.

References

1. IBM Global Education White paper, Virtualization in Education (2007). http://www-07.ibm. com/solutions/in/education/download. Accessed 1 Feb 2014
2. Microsoft Corporation, Strategies for Embracing Consumerization, April 2011. http:// download.microsoft.com/. Accessed 1 Feb 2014
3. Fotis, Z.: Design and Implementation of a desktop virtualization framework using cloud computing and emphasizing of the mobile devices. Diploma Thesis for the Degree of Electronic Engineer of TEI of Piraeus, October 2013
4. Cisco White Paper, Cloud 101: Developing a Cloud-Computing Strategy for Higher Education (2012). http://www.cisco.com. Accessed 25 Feb 2014
5. OpenStack Opensource cloud computing software. http://docs.OpenStack.org/. Accessed 25 Feb 2014
6. Groth, A.: Virtualization matrix: Compare VMware, RedHat, Citrix & Microsoft. http://www. virtualizationmatrix.com/matrix.php#general Accessed 25 Feb 2014
7. OpenStack Newtron project. https://wiki.openstack.org/wiki/Neutron Accessed 25 Feb 2014

Local Government Processes of Small Settlements in the Czech Republic

Vojtěch Merunka[1,2](✉) and Iveta Merunková[3]

[1] Faculty of Economics and Management, Department of Information Engineering,
Czech University of Life Sciences Prague, Prague, Czech Republic
vmerunka@gmail.com
[2] Faculty of Nuclear Sciences and Physical Engineering,
Department of Software Engineering in Economy,
Czech Technical University in Prague, Prague, Czech Republic
[3] Faculty of Agrobiology, Food and Natural Sources,
Department of Landscape Architecture, Czech University of Life Sciences Prague,
Prague, Czech Republic
merunkova@af.czu.cz

Abstract. One of the actual and specific problems in the Czech local government of small settlements is very low level of participation and technophobia of citizens in these small villages. This paper presents the original computer-aided process modeling and visualization as the vital preparative technique being performed before the subsequent business process analysis, design and simulation of country planning and building development processes. We practically experienced, that our computer-based approach saves time and improves the validity and correctness of the decision making process in specific conditions of country planning management in order to improve participation, quality of life and knowledge transfer.

Keywords: Local government · Country planning · Building development · Computer-aided modeling and visualization · Business process · Knowledge transfer · Small settlements

1 Introduction

Nowadays we have to solve many problems related to the small settlement development and expansion, landscape care and over-all efforts to improve the quality of life and the level of democracy while preserving the conditions of the sustainable development (addressing living standard, cultural and historic value, agricultural and industrial production, transport infrastructure construction, tourism potential, etc.). Technophobia of local people is here the significant factor for growing of this problem, because it is strongly contrasting with incoming investors and external people penetrating the rural area using good ICT (especially GIS and project management software) knowledge.

A.B. Sideridis et al. (Eds.): E-Democracy 2013, CCIS 441, pp. 103–112, 2014.
DOI: 10.1007/978-3-319-11710-2_10

Business process models show and animate (when they are simulated) the collaboration of more participants within the solved system. We need this approach for simulation, validation and verification the real world problems. This issue is stressed in specific areas of technical systems analysis and design in area of agriculture, landscape management and country planning. A very important purpose of such a business model is to create and simulate an interconnected complex system where local actors, citizens, regional government, various interested organizations and partners and other participants mutually communicate. In addition to that, business process models are also the foundation of subsequent system modeling activities of software engineering, organizational design and management consulting. Typical way of performing these activities is to start directly with drawing process diagrams just during the initial interviews. But in this paper, we present the idea, that for better modeling, we need to use a specific textual technique, which helps us to recognize, define and refine our initial set of business process participants and their properties before the graphical business process model is assembled.

2   Motivation

There is very low level of knowledge in the area of participation at the processes of country planning and building development. Everybody together with many political declarations by E.U. like Aarhus agreement and European Regional and Spatial Planning Charter by the European Council agree that computer technology can solve the problem of low community participation of people, which decreases the quality of life of these people.

Expected output of business process modeling and simulation activities is presentation of information and data in a form that can be directly used as a tool for knowledge improvement or implementation some system or organizational change in the spirit of management consulting. However, this is not the easy case; there are following issues described by [1,5]:

1. *oversimplification* - while trying to at least finish business and organizational model we are forced simplify the problem being modeled and
2. *inability* - some important details cannot be expressed because of the method being poorly used.

The practical impact of this wrong inequality between people is the urban sprawl as it is stressed by Frumkin in [4].

Urban sprawl is a phenomenon that emerged in the last decades in the advanced industrial countries (USA, France and Great Britain) and recently also in our country. Inhabitants of affected settlements usually perceive the urban sprawl positively at first, mainly because of the lobbying. It can be described as an uncontrolled expansion of certain kind of urban build-up into the free landscape caused by favourable land prices, demand for cheap but modern estates, etc. Duany [3] writes about harmful absorption of original small settlement structures, which causes following negative effects:

1. Pawning of infrastructure development of the original settlement. New inhabitants fulfill themselves and shop only at the place of their work in a metropolis and the settlements are just a kind of sleeping accommodation for them. New inhabitants' lack of interest in contributing to the settlement development leads to misusing of democratic principles of the self-administration against the original local inhabitants and inevitably to the rise of social segregation between the original and the new inhabitants.
2. Urban sprawl causes disruption of the cultural and historical value of the settlement, disruption of the ecological stability of the area, deconstruction of the transport infrastructure, loss of touristic attractiveness etc.
3. Loss of the quality agricultural soil.

The cause of the urban sprawl in the small settlement development is the fact that the elected technophobic members of local administrations (e.g. mayors and clerks) are not aware in all the details of GIS, law, state and local administration agenda and their effects on living in the settlements. They don't know how to use fully the technology in favor of the settlements and usually depend on a misleading interpretation provided by their governing bodies and more often by another subjects (usually privately involved in the process in question and thus biased).

3   Our Project

One of the actual and specific problems of technophobia in the Czech landscape is very low level of participation of citizens from small settlements in rural areas. Our project was about mapping process-based knowledge in area of urban planning and building development. This project was about the organizational modeling and simulation as a tool for improvement the decision-making on the level of mayors and local administrations. It offers the possibility to model and simulate real life situations in small settlements. The project activities were for modeling, simulation and reengineering processes related to the regional government processes of small towns and villages, and the subsequent development of supporting information systems addressing life situations of local people.

We analyzed the legislation and local officials' knowledge related to the processes and agendas of the urban planning of the landscape areas and small settlements with regards to the new housing and building law and regional management trends in the European Union. Or project consisted from two individual parts:

1. Statistical survey from 463 people (e.g. 8 % of the total population) in 13 small settlements in the Central Bohemian area mapping the knowledge and related participation at the processes of country planning and building development.
2. Subsequent implementation and testing of proposed new method with 57 people from these villages.

4   Method Used

Our approach is improved and modified Business Object Relation Modeling (BORM), which is an approach to both process modeling and the subsequent development of information systems. It provides an approach that facilitates the description of how real business systems evolve, change and behave. BORM - Business Object Relation Modeling was originally developed in 1993 and was intended to provide seamless support for the building of object oriented software systems based on pure object-oriented languages, databases and distributed environments. Subsequently, it has been realized that this method has significant potential in business process modeling and other related business issues [6]. Our extension of this method for better modeling of local processes was firstly published at the HAICTA 2013 conference and used in the E.U. research workshop: Grundtvig project - Citizens of Mountainous Regions and Technophobia in Athens 2013.

Our approach using process models and their visual simulation helps the officials (especially in the smallest settlements) to clarify the legislation and shows them possible ways of its usage. Our models and their visual simulation show how it can be used to improve the process of decision-making on the level of mayors and local administrations. It offers the possibility to model and simulate real life situations in small settlements. The example at the Fig. 1 shows our business object diagram of a process of starting urban plan. Our modeling software shows the concrete simulation step. A diagram is a visual representation of object associations and communications in a particular process. Our notation is the re-used UML notation from the state diagram, activity diagram and sequence diagram UML but combined and simplified into the only one new diagram that shows the process as object-oriented participants in the form of mutually communicating Finite-State-Machines. Moreover, we can use a visual simulator in order to animate these processes and evaluate them. Our simulator has included the communication module inspired by Facebook-like chatting them within a group of users (Fig. 2).

Our BORM innovation is based on the reuse of old thoughts from the beginning of 1990s regarding the description of object properties and behavior using finite state machines (FSM) and modeling the process-based knowledge as the communication of FSM, each representing a process participant. In this approach, states and situations are stressed in contrast to activities as it is in standard process diagrams. The first work expressing the possible merge of OOP (Object-Oriented Paradigm) and FSM was the Shaler's and Mellor's book in 1992 [7]. One of the first best books speaking about the applicability of OOP to the business modeling was written by Taylor in 1995 [8]. These works together with our practical experience is why we believe that the business requirement modeling and simulation and software modeling could be unified on the platform of OOP and FSM, where objects (e.g. process participants described as Mealy-type FSMs) are interconnected via messages (as it is in OOP) together in order to realize some business process. Furthermore, we introduced two textual tools, which we call modeling cards and scenarios.

Each modeled process participant has its own modeling card. It is a special kind of small structured textual table describing in boxes participant's name, related legislation, documentation and responsibilities.

Scenario is also a structured textual table, which refines the process. Scenarios are written in a specific tabular form, that always includes at least following columns:

- Initiating situation, which is a brief and accurate verbal description of the beginning of the scenario and includes any inputs or entry conditions.
- Verbal description of the process itself.
- Set of participants, which is the set of those subjects (e.g. participants) of the system, which are required for the process.
- Result, which is a verbal description of the end and outputs of the scenario.
- Related legislation and documentation.

Once modeling cards and scenarios have been determined, it is good idea to evaluate them via an interview-driven process visualization.

5   Discussion

Our survey collected from 463 people was based on the questionnaire having 40 questions about details of processes in four areas of participation of the public:

1. New urban plan for a village.
2. Change of an old urban plan of a village.
3. Building management of a village.
4. Building permission.

The questions were about the knowledge of particular documentation and internal situations inside of these processes and about existing participation in these situations expressed in an ordinal scale (*good, fair, something, very little, nothing*). For reason of mapping participation of people, we stressed the detail of particular processes. This is about concrete states and situations, where one can comment, ask or consult something in the process. This is very important, because legislation precisely defines situations, where concrete process participants have chance to participate in these processes.

Collected results were very alarming:

1. About 81 % people have no knowledge about these procedures.
2. About 84 % of people never participated in these processes.
3. About 10 % of people participated in these processes only once per more years.
4. In the result, only about 6 % of people participated on these processes at least once per one year.

Based on these alarming results, we tried to apply our method and performed series of method presentations, training and semi-structured questionnaire meetings with 57 people collected by the non-discriminating snow-ball technique.

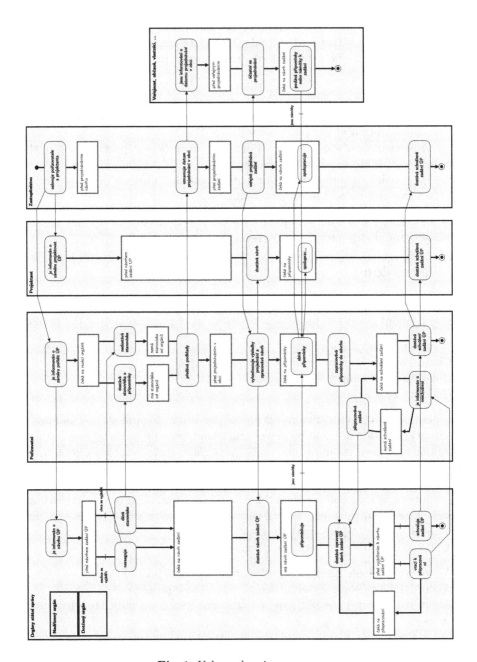

Fig. 1. Urban planning process.

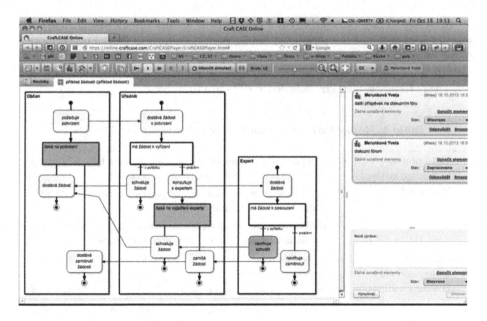

Fig. 2. Social network as communication of users during the process simulation.

participant = *participating person*
POŘIZOVATEL

činnosti = *responsibilities*
Musí mít osvědčení o zvláštní odborné způsobilosti. Vytváří zadání na územní plán a je zodpovědný za jeho odsouhlasení. Předkládá zadání územního plánu dotčeným orgánům. Spolupracuje se zastupitelstvem obce a ve spolupráci s projektantem předkládá zadání na veřejném projednávání na obci.

legislativa = *legislation*	dokumentace = *documents*
zákon 183/2006 Sb. v novele 350/2012 Sb. účinná od 1.1.2013, §44, §46 Zákon 312/2002 Sb. v novele 46/2004 Sb.	• zadání územního plánu

Fig. 3. Modeling card example: country planning participant: acquiring person.

After these workshops, 95 % of people evaluated our approach as a useful tool for breaking technophobia barriers of local officials in order to improve quality of local life via making better opportunities for local people to negotiate with outside interests, which often misused their low knowledge for private interests having the negative urban-sprawl impact on the countryside and rural landscape (Fig. 3).

In higher detail, the contingency between the answer about the efficiency of our new method and the estimated better participation was 0.64. Furthermore, based on the new knowledge 67 % of tested people expressed the fact, that they were manipulated by external investors and lobbyists in the past due to their low level of knowledge. The detailed results are in Table 1.

Table 1. Reduced results of semi-structured survey from 57 people.

Previous process knowledge at the level 1 of CMM [2]	We performed processes in ad-hoc manner, were led by clerks, we did not manage our processes	39	68 %
	We have one (or more) experienced person in our village, who knows and can help us	7	12 %
	Regardless our municipal representatives try hard, we do not expect better situation to the future	34	60 %
Method testing, understanding, process visualization	It is possible to understand the process visualization in about 5–20 min	49	86 %
	Method is interesting and useful	54	95 %
	Based on my new knowledge, I remember one or more events in the past, when I behaved wrong	39	68 %
	I would like to add new features into the visualization software. e.g. concrete doc tracking, personalized workflow, ...	26	46 %
	These processes are very complicated. Who does not know them, that one has a significant disadvantage to participate	55	96 %
Improved process knowledge after usage the visualization method at the level between 2 and 3 of CMM [2]	Method is beneficial, I want to use it, I have better knowledge	54	95 %
	I will participate and forecast these processes better, I can better plan my activities	51	89 %
	In the past, I was informed in a misleading way by clerks, lobbyists or other people	38	67 %
	I want more and more frequently participate in these processes for my benefit and also for benefit of my community	35	61 %

Of course, when introducing our approach, the target staff is typically not educated in any computer science-related techniques. (Even if they are people from small settlements) On the other hand, the process-mapping phase must be performed quickly. This is why the analysis team does not have any time for detailed modeling courses such as the explanation of all aspects of used method with consequences into software engineering. Courses on any CASE tool are also inappropriate here. There is time only for a very little introductory session about subset of used tools and techniques. In our experience, one of big advantages of our technique is fact that it requires only 20 min introductory session. After this very short introduction we are able to start the workshops.

Workshops that put together teams and experts are the best tools how to facilitate and speed up the modeling. Consulting team members should precisely perform three independent roles:

1. Problem domain expert, who is responsible for querying and best practices knowledge.
2. Methodology expert, who is responsible for functions, scenarios and diagram consistency because of problem domain people often tend to confuse modeling concepts, do not respect the scenario borders and cross from one process to another.
3. Project-Relationship Manager, who knows personal names and personalities of all target staff team members, who watches them, who is able to initiate the particular discussions or countdown some debates, for example.

Finally, we recognized that the ICT equipment is not a big barrier for introducing our method. Prepared models in process visualization are prepared in non-commercial free software and are fully accessible via Web 2.0 internet connection, which is almost standard in the Czech Republic. Our approach can also initiate subsequent development of software solutions integrating this process-based knowledge into miscellaneous work-flow applications, public information systems etc.

6 Conclusion

In this paper we presented our original approach to computer-aided modeling and visualization of process-based knowledge in order to meet specific requirements of law-based socio-technical processes of country planning and improve the participation ad quality of life in small settlements in the Czech Republic. Our project described in this paper was about the organizational modeling and simulation as a tool for improvement the decision-making on the level of mayors and local administrations. It offers the possibility to model and simulate real life situations in small settlements. The project activities were for modeling, simulation and reengineering processes related to the regional government processes of small towns and villages, and the subsequent development of supporting information systems addressing better life situations of local people.

To the future work we are preparing the collaborative grant project of the Technological Research Agency in the Czech Republic. Also we initiated cooperation with the Czech-Greece Chamber of Commerce in order to use our approach in development projects in the area of Levadia from Boiotian region in Greece.

Acknowledgement. The authors would like to acknowledge the support of the research grant SGS14/209/OHK4/3T/14 and NAKI MK-S-3421/2011 OVV.

References

1. van der Aalst, W.: Business Process Simulation Revisited, keynote speech at the EOMAS workshop 2010 (2010). http://www.eomas.org. 10 April 2011
2. Christiansson, M.T.: A Common Process Model to Improve eService Solutions - the Municipality Case. In: Proceedings of the 11th European Conference on eGovernment – ECEG 2011, Ljubljana, Slovenia (2011)
3. Dualny, A.: Suburban Nation The Rise of Sprawl and the Decline of the American Dream. North Point Press, New York (2001). ISBN: 978-0865476066
4. Frumkin, H., et al.: Urban Sprawl and Public Health: Designing, Planning, and Building for Healthy Communities. Island Press, Washington, DC (2004). ISBN: 978-1559633055
5. Igen, D., Hulin, C.L.: Computational Modeling of Behavior in Organizations - The Third Scientific Discipline. American Psychological Association, Washington, DC (2000). ISBN: 1-55798-639-8
6. Knott, R.P., Merunka, V., Polak, J.: The BORM methodology: a third-generation fully object-oriented methodology. In: Knowledge-Based Systems Elsevier Science International, New York (2003). ISSN: 0950–7051
7. Shlaer, S., Mellor, S.: Object Lifecycles: Modeling the World in States. Yourdon Press, Upper Saddle River (1992). ISBN: 0136299407
8. Taylor, D.A.: Business Engineering with Object Technology. Wiley, New York (1995). ISBN: 0471045217

Electronic Voting Systems – From Theory to Implementation

Nikos Chondros, Alex Delis, Dina Gavatha, Aggelos Kiayias,
Charalampos Koutalakis, Ilias Nicolacopoulos, Lampros Paschos,
Mema Roussopoulou, Giorge Sotirelis, Panos Stathopoulos,
Pavlos Vasilopoulos[✉], Thomas Zacharias, Bingsheng Zhang,
and Fotis Zygoulis

University of Athens, Athens, Greece
pavlos.vasilopoulos@sciencespo.fr

Abstract. Electronic voting for local, regional and national elections and referenda is developing rapidly at a global scale as an efficient and low cost alternative to conventional methods of voting, with a positive impact on the quality of democratic representation. Still, despite the growing international experience, the harmonization of electronic voting systems with the legal and statutory frameworks poses a number of major legal, social and implementation challenges, subject to the national environment. This paper presents an overview of legal and social aspects of an electronic voting system focusing on the case of Greece.

Keywords: E-Democracy · Electronic voting

1 Introduction

During the last decade, the issue of electronic voting has gained prominence in academic and public discourse. A broad definition describes electronic voting as a system "where the recording, casting or counting of votes in political elections and referendums involves information and communication technologies" [1]. The basic distinction in electronic voting systems is between *on-site* and *remote* electronic voting. The first describes a system where the physical presence of the voter in the polling booth is required, while in the second case voters can secretly cast her ballot without the restriction to be present at an electoral center. Remote electronic voting has been implemented in a large number of countries (Estonia, France, the Netherlands, Switzerland and the UK are some examples). It has been argued that remote electronic voting has significant potential for increasing the quality of democratic representation of mass publics, by increasing political participation and representation among traditionally underrepresented groups such as the youth and disabled [2, 3, 4] (but see [5]) as well as lowering the costs of becoming politically informed [5]. On top of these, it has been argued that remote electronic voting, compared to conventional voting, can lead to cost-effective and better administered elections [3].

© Springer International Publishing Switzerland 2014
A.B. Sideridis et al. (Eds.): E-Democracy 2013, CCIS 441, pp. 113–122, 2014.
DOI: 10.1007/978-3-319-11710-2_11

Despite the merits of adopting remote e-voting technologies, the transition to the new technology comes with a set of challenges from a social, legal and technical standpoint. This paper presents an overview of implementation issues of an electronic voting system for the case of Greece. The article has two aims: The first is to clarify the fundamental principles of election systems as codified in the literature of conventional and electronic voting systems, such as suffrage and the free expression of the will of the voters as well as issues of equality, universality and secrecy of the vote by taking into account the problems of implementation. To this direction, we compare the conventional system using paper ballot as is the case in Greece with a remote electronic voting system. The main argument we develop is that despite broad acceptance of the conventional voting method in the Western world [6], or the "illusion of transparency" as Gueniffey has put it (cited in [7], p. 233), traditional paper ballot voting has significant disadvantages compared to electronic voting systems when it comes to the most common types of election fraud such as vote buying and coercion). Furthermore, it poses barriers to the equality of access to polling stations. On the other hand, while remote electronic voting is promising in addressing these issues, it comes with an important number of challenges. The second aim of the paper is to juxtapose the cryptographic and computational mechanisms that achieve the properties of the ideal voting system of an electronic system, in comparison to the respective mechanisms in conventional systems.

The rest of the article goes as follows: We set and discuss thirteen normative standards regarding the transparency and fairness of a voting system focusing on the potential of conventional and electronic voting systems in meeting them. In the second part of the paper we make a direct comparison of the implementation of these standards between conventional and electronic voting systems as well as a presentation of electronic voting technical characteristics. Finally, we draw some conclusions on the merit and feasibility of remote electronic voting for organizing secret and transparent elections.

2   Normative Standards of Fair and Transparent Elections

In this section we set thirteen normative standards on what constitutes an ideal election in regard to fairness and transparency. These are: equal access to electoral centers, secrecy, vote encoding verifiability, vote tallying verifiability, universal verifiability, voter eligibility, one-voter-one-vote, fault tolerance, fairness, receipt-freeness and coercion resistance. We compare their implementation between conventional and electronic voting systems.

2.1   Equal Access to Electoral Centers

An initial normative standard is that an ideal voting system should ensure unrestricted and equal access of all eligible voters to electoral centers [8]. It must be also noted, that for the case of Greece, the constitutionally fortified principle of universality is perceived as requiring the State's motivation to take all the necessary steps towards the enlargement of the electorate, including the adoption of appropriate measures that facilitate electors in exercising their right and that prevent their exclusion from voting on the grounds of practical or technical reasons. This in the case of conventional on-site voting systems includes the transportation of voters at the polling station as well the equal access of population groups which have difficulty accessing the stations, such as the elderly, the disabled and voters with health problems. Although this standard is recognized as an international prerequisite of electoral integrity [8] its implementation in conventional voting systems is often compromised as the costs of electoral partic-ipation in time and effort for some groups are significantly greater than it is for others. For example, a recent comparative study [9] finds a substantial gap in electoral turnout between those of good and poor health, even after controlling for a large number of socioeconomic status and social integration variables. Apart from the accessibility of those with poor health, it is reasonable to expect that the large number of voters who are registered in a different district than the one they reside creates important obstacles for the implementation of equal accessibility to polling stations, especially during the times of an economic crisis.[1] The merit of remote electronic voting for ensuring the equality of accessibility is apparent, as it bears the potential of bridging the electoral representation gap between social groups and especially in people with poor health, a characteristic that is often used for the adoption of internet voting.

2.2 Secrecy

An ideal voting system should be accompanied by the assurance of the secrecy of the votes in the sense that it should be impossible for a party to extract any information about a voter's ballot beyond what can be inferred from the public tally and the party's insider knowledge taking into account the proximity of the party to the (idealized) system infrastructure. The same principle should apply to coalitions of parties. Depending on the setting, certain collusion conditions under which secrecy is preserved may prescribe. It has been found that conventional paper ballot methods are widely accepted by mass publics as ensuring secrecy [6]. On the other hand, in remote elec-tronic voting systems secrecy relies on various technical preconditions that include mathematical assumptions regarding the way the votes are encoded. For the vast majority of people the understanding and verification of the correctness of these techniques is beyond their ability.

2.3 Coercion Resistance

The voting system should not facilitate for any party to coerce voters to vote in a certain way. Vote-buying or coercion by party officials and candidates and is one of the most common types of election fraud [7]. It is significantly higher in societies with clientelistic traditions [10], such as Greece and it is strengthened in cases where parties

---

[1] In fact in regions with a high share of voters who are not residents (such as island Greece) turnout was significantly reduced compared to urban centers during the last twin 2012 elections.

can ensure that ballots have been cast in the agreed way [7]. To use some examples, Schaffer and Schedler refer to cases of party officials in the Philippines providing carbon paper to voters so they can record their voting choices, whereas in Italy there have been reported cases where party officials provide mobile phones with cameras to record the vote choice (Schaffer and Schedler 2007, cited in [10]). What is more, turnout buying (the strategy where party officials bribe voters to turn out and vote) or negative turnout buying (where party officials reward voters for not showing up to the electoral station) is common particularly in settings with strong clientelistic ties such as Southern Italy [10]. While there has not been any research on vote-buying in Greece, news reports of rewards for casting preselected ballots are not uncommon.

Electronic Voting on the other hand offers several improvements to coercion. While perfect resistance to coercion cannot be achieved [11] electronic voting systems may provide electors with the ability to correct their vote multiple times or provide them with fake ballots. In this way coercion becomes difficult to achieve, as the coercer cannot ensure that the recorded vote is the elector's final decision. For example, the coercion scenarios we described earlier (where the voter was using a mobile phone or carbon paper to prove to the coercer her vote decision) cannot be applied in an electronic voting system, as the voter can log into the system and change her decision several times (this clause as been successfully implemented in Estonia) or alternatively can use a fake ballot. What is more, coercers cannot conduct positive or negative turn out buying, as is the case with conventional voting, as the voter can vote from the place of her choice in several time points.

2.4   Cast-as-Intended Verifiability

A third parameter of an ideal voting system is vote encoding verifiability, meaning that the voting system should be accompanied by the assurance to the voter that her vote was cast as intended. This requirement suggests that the election procedure has some built-in auditing mechanisms that enable the voter to ensure herself that the way it accepts the ballot is consistent with the intention of the voter. This can be critical in cases where there is a way to encode the voters' intent and the encoding mechanism is electronically assisted. In such cases any adversarial deviation of the encoding mechanism from the prescribed encoding procedure can result in, e.g., switching the voters' choices and violating her intend. In this domain, public trust in traditional paper ballot voting systems is very high: Alvarez and his colleagues report that the vast majority of the American public appeared confident that their vote had been cast as intended, while confidence in elections conducted with the use of punch cards is significantly lower [12].

2.5   Recorded-as-Cast Verifiability

This property requires that the voter can verify that the ballot that was casted was indeed recorded by the system. In paper-based systems this may be achieved by having the voter herself enter the sealed ballot in a ballot-box which is transparent so it is reasonably ensured that the voter's envelope ends up in the common pile. Electronic (or mechanical) voting systems require more complex auditing mechanisms to ensure recorded-as-cast verifiability.

2.6 Tallied-as-Recorded Verifiability

The fifth parameter of an ideal election is tallied-as-recorded, or the assumption that the voting system should enable the voter to challenge the procedure in the post-election stage and verify that recorded ballots were included in the tally (presumably also her own). This complements the previous types of verifiability and addresses to the setting where the voter wishes to ensure that the vote she submitted was actually included in the tally computation of the election results.

2.7 Universal Verifiability

The voting system should enable any party, including an outsider, to be convinced that a well defined set of votes has been collected and they have been included in the final tally according to the election system. This differs from the voter and tally verifiability property as it refers to external observers and is not concerned with the fate of any individual vote in particular. Universal verifiability has the benefit of delegating the task of verifying certain aspects of the election procedure to interested third parties. In fact, when combined with the previous two properties it may be feasible for a group of voters to delegate the complete audit of the election to an external entity. We note that the universal verifiability property refers to a setting where no privately owned information by the voter is needed for verifying the correct tallying. In conventional voting systems a weak form of universal verifiability is ensured by the presence of party delegates in the vote count.

2.8 End-to-End Verifiability

In many settings the combination of the verifiability properties has been termed as *end-to-end* verifiability. In some systems it is possible for voters to pass or outsource auditing information to a third party thus enabling a single external entity to ensure all levels of verifiability (including capturing the voter intent). It is worth noting that universal verifiability by itself is insufficient for end-to-end verifiability as there is no guarantee that the complete election transcript is not "cooked up" (in this way the election result will be well-defined and properly computed however it will be incongruent with true voter intent).

2.9 Voter Eligibility

The voting system should only permit eligible voters as listed on the electoral roll to cast a ballot. The importance of eligibility cannot be understated. For each district or precinct, it is critical that the eligible voters can be identified. This cuts both ways: ineligible voters should not be capable of submitting a ballot while eligible voters should not be disenfranchised. These issues become particularly complex when an election spans multiple districts and the electoral rolls in separate districts have to deal with duplicate registrations (due to instances of relocation for example). At the same time, the need for identification poses threat to eligible voters that for various reasons may be incapable of acquiring the proper credentials or may be discouraged from participating in elections by lengthy verification procedures [13]. In the case of Greece, voters' addition in electoral poll does not require any action on the part of the citizens. In cases where by mistake an eligible voter has not been included in the electoral records, she can participate in elections with an attestation from local authorities, which is issued on the same day of the election.

2.10   One-Voter-One-Vote

The voting system should not permit voters to vote twice. While voter eligibility deals with the identification of voters, it is also very critical to ensure that eligible voters are participating in the process as specified: in most election procedure instances this coincides with restricting voters to a single vote. We already noted that for various reasons (some of them in fact security related) a system may allow voters to submit their vote multiple times and only a single instance of such ballot submission will be assumed as the valid submission for the election. This enables voters to change their mind throughout the time the election still takes place and has been proposed as a mechanism in some systems to deal with issues of coercion (see below).

Conventional paper ballot in Greece is subject to fraud resulting from voters voting twice because they are eligible to vote in more than one electoral district. In fact this became a serious political issue ahead of the 2002 local and municipal elections, when the opposition directly accused the government of attempting electoral fraud by using 50.000 voters who had registered in more than one electoral district. Although the Ministry of Interior Affairs cleaned up electoral catalogues with the cooperation of local municipal authorities the problem has not yet been fully resolved.

2.11   Fault Tolerance

The voting system should be resilient to the faulty behavior of possibly up to a number of components or parts. We note that some reliance to the correct operation of electronic equipment can be expected for the proper operation of an e-voting system. Nevertheless, a certain degree of equipment faults should be easy to recover from and should be incapable of disrupting the election process. Alternatively widespread equipment faults should be at least detectable (if not recoverable from). We note that fault resilience should be interpreted in the form of the ability of the voting system to report the correct election results.

2.12 Fairness

The voting system should ensure that no partial results become known prior to the end of the election procedure. We note that in some cases this property may be violated by the way an election is managed. As before we state that we are concerned with failures of the electronic equipment and not with procedural failures of a large scale electoral process. For example when running an election process in a large geographic region it might be possible to have districts finalizing their tallies and publishing them prior to the termination of the election in other districts. This is common in the United States for example and it is even considered legitimate to capitalize its advantages in election procedures that seek to elect the presidential nominees of political parties. Fairness is an important concern as it may induce what is known as the *bandwagon effect* where a certain candidate gains momentum by winning on a handful of districts and subsequently capitalizes on this momentum by either having more voters previously undecided turning to her side or having voters supportive of other candidates opting out from participating in the election process [14].

2.13 Receipt-Freeness

The voting system should not facilitate any way for voters to prove the way they voted. The ability of a voter to obtain a receipt of the way she voted opens the possibility for a voter to sell or auction her vote (see previous section). Receipt-freeness specifically refers to the apparent lack of any receipt produced by the voting system, or at least of a receipt that cannot be easily falsified by a voter.

3 Comparison of Generic Traditional and E-Voting Systems

Table 1 extends the comparison between generic conventional and electronic voting systems presented in Sect. 2 by discussing practical implementation differences between the two systems and presenting an overview of the basic mechanisms used in

Table 1. Comparison of Generic Traditional and E-Voting Systems

Property	Generic Traditional Voting	Generic E-voting System
Equal access to electoral centers	In a small scale, traditional voting operates ideally in terms of accessibility. However, large scale deployments have high potential to cause significant problems in terms of accessibility given that voters may be assigned to remote districts and the update of the electoral roll per district can be cumbersome	Remote e-voting provides a very high level of accessibility among voters familiar with the use of digital equipment in general. On the other hand, onsite e-voting exhibits a similar accessibility pattern with traditional voting however it can be possible to perform substantially better through the automation of the voter registration system

(Continued)

Table 1. *(Continued)*

Property	Generic Traditional Voting	Generic E-voting System
Secrecy	Secrecy relies on physical assumptions about the configuration of the voting environment (e.g., private voting booths). These mechanisms are intuitive and their proper operation can – in principle – be easily verified by the voter	Secrecy relies on various technical preconditions that include mathematical assumptions regarding the way the votes are encoded. For the vast majority of people the understanding and verification of the correctness of these techniques is beyond their ability
Vote encoding verifiability	In the paper-ballot setting the voter can follow simple rules to ensure her choices are properly encoded (e.g., only a specific number of "crosses" are allowed – the cross signs have to be non-ambiguous etc.) The ability of the voter to cast a "spoiled" ballot can be in some cases significant as a form of political expression	The voter choice is either encrypted or cast via the submission of a specially prepared code. The verification of the proper encoding is impossible without trusting the underlying equipment or requiring from the voter to perform additional verification steps beyond ballot-casting (however it may possible that such actions can be delegated). Typically there is no way for the voter to cast a "spoiled" ballot
One-voter one-vote	It is ensured by the election officials committee. For instance, the name of the voter is crossed out from the list and no second vote is allowed to be submitted	It is ensured via the proper interoperation of the voter registration system and the ballot casting system
Fault-tolerance	The election relies on the election officials' ability to execute the election protocol properly. Deviations, intentional or not, pose a significant threat to the election process	Tolerating faults is achieved via the distribution of the state of the various sub-systems that comprise the election. Distributed systems provide resistance to faults however they are much harder to analyze and maintain than "monolithic" single server systems. The latter is unfortunately the norm for the vast majority of e-voting implementations
Fairness	The tallying of the results is revealed after the end of the election. This relies on the election officials' adherence on the proper timing of the tallying process. For instance in a multi-precinct election, no ballot box should be "opened" prior to the termination of the ballot-casting process	The tallying system is supposed to provide output only after the termination of ballot-casting. This property can be violated if the system is subverted by an attacker. The ability to distribute the vote collection system state is essential for preventing the violation of fairness (cf. fault-tolerance)

(Continued)

Table 1. *(Continued)*

Property	Generic Traditional Voting	Generic E-voting System
Receipt-freeness	Some forms of receipt are feasible, e.g., via the photographing or videotaping of the ballot casting procedure (e.g., a video shot by the voter, as she seals an envelope with a visible vote choice). Such techniques may not necessarily offer conclusive proof however they may be used as a form of a weak receipt. The collection of uncast paper ballots may also form a weak receipt	Systems that publicly reveal the casted ballot in an encoding form can be prone to receipt generation via digital means. Encryption schemes require randomness that, if accessible to a malicious voter, can be used to prove a certain voter choice depending on the system configuration
Coercion resistance	Private voting booths are congruent with coercion resistance, however the extraction of a receipt as described above may leave the voter vulnerable to coercion	In the case of onsite voting the coercion aspects of e-voting are similar to the conventional case with the additional potential of digital attacks (e.g., against the ballot casting system or the ballot encoding scheme). Remove e-voting on the other hand provides a number of clauses that improve voters' resistance to coercion efforts

electronic voting systems. Overall, despite the significant potential of remote electronic systems, some fundamental challenges remain especially in regard to voters' level of internet literacy and trust.

4   Conclusion

Electoral integrity is a strong prerequisite of effective democratic representation. Contemporary democratic theory posits that elections should be characterized by transparency, fairness and equality of access and these imperatives constitute an integral element of the constitutions of liberal democracies around the world. This paper compared the potential of the Greek conventional paper ballot system with a remote electronic system in the implementation of fundamental aspects of free and fair democratic elections. The main conclusion is that despite broad public trust in electoral systems, conventional paper ballot systems come with significant drawbacks in security especially on ensuring resistance from coercion, double-voting and the equality of accessibility across the electorate. Electronic voting systems are potentially efficient in resolving core deficiencies of traditional paper ballot systems in these domains, yet face a number of significant legal and technical challenges especially on issues of secrecy and vote verifiability.

References

1. IDEA: Introducing Electronic Voting, p. 2 (2011)
2. Trechsel, A., Schwerdt, G., Breuer, F., Alvarez, M., Hall, T.: Report for the Council of Europe: Internet Voting in the March 2007 Parliamentary Elections in Estonia, Robert Schuman Centre for Advanced Studies, EUI (2007)
3. Alvarez, M.R., Hall, T.E., Trechsel, A.H.: Internet voting in comparative perspective: the case of estonia. PS: Polit. Sci. Polit. **42**(3), 497–505 (2009)
4. Alvarez, M.R., Hall, T.E.: Controlling democracy: the principal-agent problems in election administration. Policy Stud. J. **34**(4), 491–510 (2006)
5. Norris, P.: Will new technology boost turnout?. Electronic Voting and Democracy (2003)
6. Birch, S.: Electoral institutions and popular confidence in electoral processes: a cross-national analysis. Electoral. Stud. **27**(2), 305–320 (2008)
7. Lehoucq, F.: Electoral fraud: causes, types and consequences. Ann. Rev. Polit. Sci. **6**, 233–256 (2003)
8. López-Pintor, R.: Assessing Electoral Fraud in New Democracies. A Basic Conceptual Framework. International Foundation for Electoral Systems, Washington DC (2010). White Paper Series Electoral Fraud
9. Matilla, M., Soderlund, P., Wass, H., Rapelli, L.: Healthy voting: the effect of self-reported health on turnout in 30 countries. Electoral Studies, (in press)
10. Morse, J.G., Mazzuca, S., Nichter, S.: Who Gets Bought? Vote Buying, Turnout Buying and Other Strategies. Weatherland Center for International Affairs, Harvard, Working Paper (2009)
11. Birch, S., Watt, B.: Remote electronic voting: free, fair and simple? Polit. Q. **75**(1), 60–72 (2004)
12. Alvarez, M.R., Hall, T.E., Llewellyn, M.: Are Americans confident their ballots are being counted? J. Polit. **70**(3), 754–766 (2008)
13. Geys, B.: Explaining voter turnout : a review of aggregate-level research. Elect. Stud. **25**, 637–663 (2006)
14. Nadeau, R., Guay, J.H., Cloutier, E.: New evidence over the existence of a bandwagon effect in the opinion formation process. Int. Polit. Sci. Rev. **14**(2), 203–213 (1993)

Mobile Learning: An Android App Using Certified Content

Sotiris Karetsos[✉], Maria Ntaliani, and Constantina Costopoulou

Department of Agricultural Economics and Rural Development, Agricultural
University of Athens, Iera Odos 75, 11855 Athens, Greece
{karetsos,ntaliani,tina}@aua.gr

Abstract. The rapid evolution of mobile networks and the exceptional
penetration of mobile devices are under examination by the research and
development community for their exploitation by various sectors, such as
agriculture. Towards this direction, this paper presents an m-learning app for
organic agriculture. It is based on the Bio@gro platform, which provides
accurate, certified and multilingual content (i.e. information and services) for
organic agriculture stakeholders from Greece, Germany, Romania and Cyprus.
By providing certified m-learning content, this app can assist organic stakeholders in achieving and improving their knowledge and practices easily and at
low cost. Functionalities and technical details of the app are presented.

Keywords: Smartphones · Mobile devices · m-learning · Android · Organic
agriculture

1 Introduction

The rapid growth of telecommunication networks and the capabilities offered by
mobile devices and related software, have created opportunities for economic growth
and social empowerment in several business sectors around the world, such as health,
entertainment, education and tourism. Indeed, mobile communication devices are easy
to use and their usage is constantly expanding even for computer illiterate people
through the emergence and domination of smartphones featured with simple touch-
screens. Smartphones and tablets are used in everyday life providing a plethora of uses
and advantages. Usually, smartphones are used by one user who becomes familiar with
the device even if it is with advanced capabilities. This is because users always carry
the device and explore its functionalities quite often. Recent devices include (double)
cameras for photographs and videos, GPS capabilities, connectivity through Wi-Fi and
Bluetooth, enough storage memory, FM radio, various display sizes etc. Moreover, the
improvement of mobile networks from 2G to 3G and 4G/LTE is providing faster access
and browsing of information resources.

Popular platforms for smartphones are iPhone, Android, Windows Mobile, Sym-
bian and BlackBerry. There are thousands of applications (apps) for those platforms
that offer hundreds of functionalities. They vary from simple to more complicated.
Games, social networking, news, weather, music, videos and banking and finance are
among the most popular categories of apps. The great majority of apps are offered for

© Springer International Publishing Switzerland 2014
A.B. Sideridis et al. (Eds.): E-Democracy 2013, CCIS 441, pp. 123–131, 2014.
DOI: 10.1007/978-3-319-11710-2_12

free or at a very low cost. Concurrently, with the aforementioned advancements several research topics have been raised focusing on serving specific population groups.

Mobile learning (m-learning) is considered among the most important topics because it can be applied in several sectors. There is no standard definition for m-learning. Various studies define it as place and time independent learning using portable devices [1–3]. Another definition considers m-learning as any activity helping people to enhance their productivity while consuming, interacting with, or creating information, mediating via a digital portable device [4]. It has huge potential for and endless usages both to formal and informal learning. Both instructors and learners are using the mobile technology more and more to access information, educational resources and content, streamline administration and facilitate learning in groundbreaking ways, creating in this way new learning models [5]. In the era of smartphones m-learning apps have been developed mainly for educational/teaching purposes (e.g. universities, colleges) and health issues (e.g. pain management, diabetes management) [6–9].

The agricultural sector is one of the most significant business sectors since it is the main food supplier. However, it is a sector that has been left aside in terms of the application of new technologies [10]. According to a very recent study [11] "an agricultural information system needs to be developed based on the mass communication technology, such as mobile systems. It is also noted that localization and native language of farmers should be incorporated into the systems". The aforementioned study also suggests that although farmers need specialized information for crops and cultivation techniques, it is not always easy to find it. More specifically, agricultural practices need precise and accurate information to be disseminated promptly to farmers so that better decisions such as managing farm fields, making continuous and scientific changes in their production systems and grabbing advantage of market opportunities can be made [11].

Organic farming is considered as the most qualitative agricultural practice and organic producers as the most innovative group of farmers. In many European countries, organic agriculture stakeholders encounter a number of problems (e.g. high production cost, lack of specialized and technical knowledge and information, technical support by specialized agronomists, coordination and organization of the trading network, promotion mechanisms), which notably block the development of organic agriculture [12]. Therefore, helping farmers to improve their methods through innovative and efficient agricultural practices is considered as an important issue.

Therefore, the objective of this paper is to propose a pilot m-learning app for agricultural education on organic agriculture for the Android system. It is based on the Bio@gro platform which provides accurate, certified and multilingual content (i.e. information and services) for organic agriculture and takes into consideration needs of stakeholders from Greece, Germany, Romania and Cyprus. It is estimated that such an app can assist farmers in improving their knowledge on organic agriculture practices easily and with low cost. The structure of the paper is as follows: The second section provides an overview of mobile device penetration and use in the context of m-learning activities. The third section describes the Bio@gro project and its extension for the provision of m-learning services for organic farmers. Functionalities and technical details of the app are presented. The fourth section concludes this work.

2 Background

The International Telecommunication Union (ITU) has estimated that there were 6.8 billion mobile subscriptions worldwide in 2012. This is translated to 96 % of the world population, showing a substantial raise from 6.0 billion mobile subscribers in 2011 and 5.4 billion in 2010. Mobile subscribers' number in the developed world is rapidly reaching saturation point with at least one mobile subscription per person. In developed countries mobile penetration has reached 128 % of the population, and in developing countries reaches about 89 % of the population [13–15]. Moreover, Internet access rates are double from a mobile device than from a computer [1].

The ubiquity and rapid expansion of mobile devices and networks generated a new direction for m-learning, the one that exploits the capabilities of smartphones and tablets [16]. Previously, the m-leaning approach was making use of the Short Message Service (SMS) and the Wireless Application Protocol (WAP) technologies with smaller screens without "touch" features. In [17] it is noted that there is not a completed theoretical basis for m-learning and researchers are currently working on the identification and the exploration of mobile technologies for serving m-learning. For example, UNESCO has seen great potential in the improvement and facilitation of learning, particularly in communities with scarce educational opportunities [1].

The aforementioned new capabilities are explored for several target groups, and farmers are certainly one of them. As [18] suggests, the mobile phone is the most promising platform to disseminate relevant information throughout the farming community. Already there are services up and running regarding weather forecasts and market prices to farmers through text messages. Also, it is noted that the cost of the farming applications for touch screen smartphones has considerably reduced. As applications and services are appearing on the Web and for smartphones and tablets, the research and development community is focusing mainly on the use of mobile devices. Therefore, several researches conducted in different areas of the world are trying to estimate the penetration and the use of mobile devices by farmers and their use for agricultural practices [19, 20]. A research conducted in 2011 in the USA showed that farmers are quickly adopting mobile devices and, in fact, are making greater use of them than the general public. The survey has evinced that farmers are using smartphones mostly for carrying out their work than for entertainment [21]. Another survey in Canada conducted by Farm Credit has shown that nearly 30 % of farmers have smartphones. This occurs in other well developed countries too. Farmers are performing many work-related tasks through their devices, among which are sending/receiving email; checking weather, news, and markets; and sending text messages to cooperatives. More than 70 % of the survey respondents access agriculture information and services on their phones. Farmers are progressively using more their mobile phones than other devices for accessing the Internet. On average, one third of the survey respondents use their mobile phones equally to other devices, e.g. computers, to access the Internet. The same number uses their phones to access the Internet daily. Younger farmers are making greater use of smartphones, since 71 % of respondents under the age of 39 own a smartphone, compared with the overall total of 39 % [22].

Focusing on apps for agriculture, there is a great range–as previously mentioned–concerning weather, agricultural news, market information, inventory levels and innovative farming techniques and machinery. However, there have also been proposed apps and systems for cattle disease diagnosis and first aid action suggestion [23], irrigation decision support and planning [24], alerts and recommendations to improve productivity based on farmer's inputs related to crops being cultivated and location specific information [25]. Australia presents various relevant cases, such as tracking and managing livestock, monitoring calving, managing water points, managing irrigation, talking between machinery, remote performing of roles (e.g. unloading grain), monitoring sensors in crops, marketing produce, estimating and mapping yield, performing as substitute tools (e.g. spirit levels), calculating space, and mapping soil types. However, apps specifically for agriculture are still limited. Up to now, there are apps for record keeping and accessing agricultural news and technical information [26], with the most dominant app the one related to weather [27].

3 M-Learning for Organic Agriculture Farmers

This section presents the Bio@gro electronic services platform and its extension with the m-learning app for educating farmers in organic agriculture.

3.1 The Bio@gro Electronic Services Platform

Bio@gro is an electronic service platform for organic agriculture, serving as a multilingual single point for providing access to accurate electronic business, learning and government content, as well as mobile services for all European stakeholders of the organic agriculture value chain (e.g. organic farmers, traders, processing companies). This platform has been developed in the context of the European e-Content Programme project for information dissemination and public awareness increase regarding organic agriculture. The design of the platform has been based on a thorough analysis of the requirements of organic agriculture stakeholders in four European countries (Greece, Germany, Romania and Cyprus). The organic agriculture stakeholders are:

- Organic farmers (individuals or farmers' groups).
- Traders, who want to find information, buy organic products and distribute them.
- Processing companies, which purchase organic products and use them as raw material for the production of secondary products.
- Buyers, who want to be informed about or buy organic products.
- Administration agencies, which provide all the necessary legislation, support, and coordinate the developing initiatives.
- Certification and inspection agencies, regarding the exclusive bodies for certifying organic farmers and their production.
- Research institutions and universities, such as the laboratories, which are in charge of research, innovation and technological advancements in organic agriculture.
- Agronomists and farm advisors, who can act as consulting agents to organic farmers.

- European agricultural agencies, which are responsible for organic agriculture activities in European countries.

The platform is based on portal technology and mainly supports: (a) access to multilingual content, and particularly in four languages Greek, German, Romanian and English, (b) access to specialized, updated and certified organic agriculture content, and (c) access via different communication channels (i.e. Internet, short message service - SMS). More specifically, in the "educational resources", a specific category of certified organic agriculture content there are, a catalogue of online educational resources, a digital library with OA reports, studies, papers, e-learning courses, best practice guides and frequently asked questions for organic agriculture. More information can be found in [10]. The work presented in the current article focuses mainly on the content included in the "educational resources" section, and termed as e-learning content.

3.2   The Bio@gro m-Learning App

The Bio@gro platform has been extended in order to make available the educational content related to agricultural practices on smartphones and tablets. The extend notion of the Bio@gro is presented in the following Fig. 1. The user (organic agriculture farmer as well as any other involved stakeholder) is able to access the content through the Internet (the Web based access of the system can be found at the following URL: http://www.bioagro.gr), through SMS and also using a smartphone or tablet for the educational content of the platform.

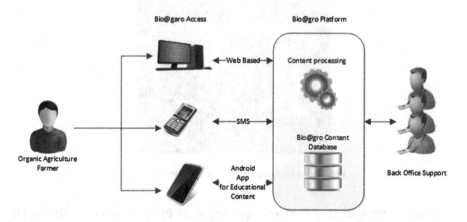

Fig. 1. The extended notion of the Bio@gro platform

The proposed app has been developed using the Android platform for smartphones. This decision has been based on the rationale that the Android OS has greater freedom. The app developed using the Android Developer Tools (ADT) v22.2.1, and tested for displays from 3.2 up to 10.1 inches. The minimum required Android version is 2.2 (Froyo) and the target Android version is 4.3 (Jelly Bean). Initially, the development is targeted to the Greek language and the Greek organic agriculture stakeholders. At present the key functionality includes the home screen which introduces the concept of the Bio@gro app. Then users click the m-learning content categories according to their needs. These categories include crop production, animal production, rules of the organic agriculture practices, organic agriculture for children, and dictionary of basic organic agriculture terms (Fig. 2). For each category, a variety of certified content can be accessed. For instance, by selecting the "animal production" category particular options are revealed, namely fundamental principles of organic livestock, production of organic dairy products, organic beef production, organic apiculture and management of production animal diseases. For instance, the "apiculture" option includes the organic management of *Varoa* disease (Fig. 3).

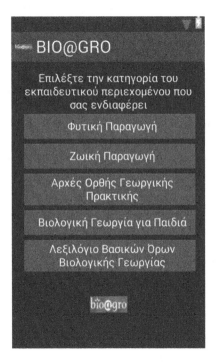

Fig. 2. m-learning categories for Bio@gro app

Based on the taxonomy of mobile apps suggested by Nickerson et al. (2007), the proposed app can be described according to the following dimensions:

- Synchronous: meaning that the user and the app interact in real time;
- Informational and non-transactional: the information is provided only one-way, namely from the app to the user. The user is not able to provide information or purchase services through the app;
- Public: the app can be used by any user who is interested in organic agriculture;

Fig. 3. Organic management of *Varoa* in Apiculture

- Individual: although the app can be used by different users at the same time, each user experiences the app as if is the sole user;
- Non-location based: the app does not use location-based information to function. The provided m-learning services are the same irrespectively of the user's location;
- Non-identity based: the app does not use the user's identity to modify the way the app functions.

4   Conclusions

Farmers, due to the nature of their work, can benefit extensively from the rapid penetration and usage of mobile devices and networks for receiving formal and informal training. Various subjects provided via m-learning, such as agricultural practices and management, electronic government services, exploration and information on markets etc., which can easily be translated to reduced cultivation costs or increased revenues. As new smartphone apps are rapidly emerging (such as in medicine), and the validity and reliability of their content is unknown and in greater question, efforts are made to establish relevant regulation. Obviously, the availability of on time, accurate and validated information and resources is the key success factor of apps. Trying to correspond to that need, in the present paper a pilot m-learning app for organic agriculture has been presented. The app has been developed in Android system. Currently, the app provides in Greek educational content that has been previously used in the context of the Bio@gro platform. Thus, it is certified, validated and reliable. The proposed app can be used complementary to traditional and electronic learning. It is estimated that by using the proposed app the organic agriculture stakeholders can overcome obstacles regarding agricultural practices and improve production quality so as to profit. As future work, the app will be made available via other platforms such as iOS, WindowsPhone and BlackBerry. Moreover, the content will be provided in the rest of the languages of the Bio@gro platform.

References

1. UNESCO: Turning on Mobile Learning: Illustrative Initiatives and Policy Implications in Europe, United Nations Educational, Scientific and Cultural Organization, France (2012)
2. GSMA: mLearning: A Platform for Educational, Opportunities at the Base of the Pyramid, GSMA Development Fund (2010)
3. Wang, M., Shen, R.: Message design for mobile learning: learning theories, human cognition and design principles. Br. J. Educ. Technol. **43**, 561–575 (2012)
4. Fong, W.W.: The trends in mobile learning. In: Cheung, S.K., Fong, J., Fong, W., Wang, F.L., Kwok, L.F. (eds.) ICHL 2013. LNCS, vol. 8038, pp. 301–312. Springer, Heidelberg (2013)
5. UNESCO: Policy guidelines for mobile learning, United Nations Educational, Scientific and Cultural Organization, France (2013)
6. Arsand, E., Tatara, N., Hartvigsen, G.: Wireless and mobile technologies improving diabetes self-management. In: Handbook of Research on Mobility and Computing: Evolving Technologies and Ubiquitous Impacts, pp. 136–156. IGI Global, Hershey (2011)
7. Wu, T.T.: Using smart mobile devices in social-network-based health education practice: A learning behavior analysis: Nurse Education Today online (2014)
8. Fernández-López, A., Rodríguez-Fórtiz, M.J., Rodríguez-Almendros, M.L., Martínez-Segura, M.J.: Mobile learning technology based on iOS devices to support students with special education needs. J. Comput. Educ. **61**, 77–90 (2013)
9. Educause.edu: A Study of Mobile Learning Trends at the U.S. Naval Academy and the Naval Postgraduate School (2013). http://www.educause.edu/ero/article/study-mobile-learning-trends-us-naval-academy-and-naval-postgraduate-school
10. Ntaliani, M., Karetsos, S., Costopoulou, C.: Implementing E-government services for agriculture: the case of Greece. In: Isaias, P., McPherson, M., Bannister, F. (eds.) Proceedings: e-Society 2006, pp.243–249 (2006)
11. Jain, L., Kumar, H., Singla, R.K.: Assessing mobile technology usage for knowledge dissemination among farmers in Punjab. J. Inf. Technol. Dev. (2014) (In press)
12. Karetsos, S., Costopoulou, C., Sideridis, A., Patrikakis, C., Koukouli, M.: Bio@gro – an online multilingual organic agriculture e-services platform. J. Inf. Serv. Use **27**, 123–132 (2007). IOS Press
13. ITU (International Telecommunication Union): Key ICT indicators for developed and developing countries and the world (totals and penetration rates) (2014). http://www.itu.int/en/ITU-D/Statistics/Pages/stat/default.aspx
14. Digby.com: Mobile Industry Statistics (2013). http://digby.com/mobile-statistics/
15. GSMA: Analysis: Scaling Mobile for Development, Harness the opportunity in the developing world. GSMA Mobile for Development (2013)

16. Wimmer, M.A., Grimm, R., Jahn, N., Hampe, J.F.: Mobile participation: exploring mobile tools in e-participation. In: Wimmer, M.A., Tambouris, E., Macintosh, A. (eds.) ePart 2013. LNCS, vol. 8075, pp. 1–13. Springer, Heidelberg (2013)
17. Khaddage, F., Knezek, G.: iLearn via mobile technology: a comparison of mobile learning attitudes among university students in two nations. In: IEEE 13th International Conference on Advanced Learning Technologies, pp. 256–258 (2013)
18. Armstrong, L.J., Gandhi, N., Lanjekar, K.: Use of information and communication technology (ICT) tools by rural farmers in Ratnagiri district of Maharastra, India. In: 2012 International Conference on Communication Systems and Network Technologies (CSNT), pp. 950–955 (2012)
19. Islam, S., Grönlund, A.: Factors influencing the adoption of mobile phones among the farmers in Bangladesh: theories and practices. Int. J. Adv. ICT Emerg. Reg. 4(01), 4–14 (2011)
20. Manige, S., Patil, M., Kumar, P., Kantharaju, V., Prabhu, B.: Impact of mobile phone on agriculture in Gulbarga district of Karnataka. Karnataka J. Agric. Sci. 26(4), 524–527 (2013)
21. Agriculture.com: Smartphones a big trend (2014). http://www.agriculture.com/farm-management/technology/cell-phone-and-smart-phones/smartphones-a-big-trend_325-ar20351
22. USA Today: Farmers growing comfortable with mobile devices (2013). http://www.usatoday.com/story/news/nation/2013/03/03/farming-technology-ipad-apps/1959139/
23. Raj, S.: e-Agriculture prototype for knowledge facilitation among tribal farmers of North-East India: innovations, impact and lessons. J. Agric. Educ. Extension 19(2), 113–131 (2013)
24. Jonoski, A., Alfonso, L., Almoradie, A., Popescu, I., Jan van Andel, S., Vojinovic, Z.: Mobile Phone Applications in the Water Domain. UNESCO-IHE Institute for Water Education, Delft, The Netherlands (2012)
25. Kumar, V., Dave, V., Nagrani, R., Chaudhary, S., Bhise, M.: Crop cultivation information system on mobile devices. In: Global Humanitarian Technology Conference: South Asia Satellite (GHTC-SAS), pp. 196–202. IEEE (2013)
26. Lorimer, S.: Mobile Applications-Helping agriculturalists make better decisions. Horticulture Industry Networks (2012). http://hin.com.au/Resources/Mobile-Applications-in-Agriculture.aspx
27. Roberts, K., McIntosh, G.: Use of mobile devices in extension and agricultural production – a case study. In: Proceedings: 16th Australian Agronomy Conference 2012, Armidale, NSW, Australia (2012). http://www.regional.org.au/au/asa/2012/precision-agriculture/8224_robertsk.htm

Politics - Legislation - European Initiatives

Negotiating the EU Data Protection Reform: Reflections on the Household Exemption

Napoleon Xanthoulis[✉]

Dr. K. Chrysostomides & Co. LLC, Nicosia, Cyprus
napoleon.xanthoulis.09@ucl.ac.uk

Abstract. The re-drafting of the *household exemption* comprises one of the main areas of dispute in the ongoing negotiations for the EU data protection reform. The aim of this paper is twofold: First, we present and critically assess the wording proposals that have been put forward mainly at EU institutional level and identify the particular areas which cause tension. Second, we concomitantly ask which is the most appropriate wording for the exemption in question and in particular, whether the household exemption should comprise a set of decisive criteria or whether it should provide a more general framework. We eventually argue for a broad wording of the Article 2(2)(d) coupled with the addition of further non-determinative criteria at Recital 15, i.e. the non-normative part of the proposed Regulation.

Keywords: Personal data · Household exemption · EU data protection reform · General data protection regulation · Data processing · Data controllers · User-generated content

1 Introduction

The European Commission ('Commission') Vice President Vivian Reding's decision to initiate a review of the current EU data protection legal framework, in January 2012, has as expected dominated the broader legal debate on privacy and personal data protection within the European Union ('EU') and beyond. The proposed General Data Protection Regulation (the 'Proposed Regulation') [1], which aims to replace the existing legal framework, has been the subject of extensive negotiations at EU inter-institutional level and has generated a strong debate between the concerned stakeholders, including Internet Service Providers ('ISPs') and representatives of online users.

In this regard, a major area of dispute comprises a particular issue related to the limitation of the scope of the proposed Regulation, namely the so-called *household exemption*. The said exemption has received a surprisingly lack of scholarly attention, despite its significance, namely that it practically draws the border lines of the application of the proposed Regulation by defining the type of activities which may fall under its provisions, contrary to ones that are considered part of a person's private life.

In the past, the definition and application of the household exemption might have seemed an easy task; in the Web 2.0 era it constitutes a complicated and fragile puzzle. Wong and Savirimuthu [2] argue that today individuals have a range of new

© Springer International Publishing Switzerland 2014
A.B. Sideridis et al. (Eds.): E-Democracy 2013, CCIS 441, pp. 135–152, 2014.
DOI: 10.1007/978-3-319-11710-2_13

technologies for accessing media and sharing information, while at the same time increased connectivity has maximised individuals' exposure and immersion to information. Apparently, as individuals spend more time in the social spaces, we can detect a shift in cultural attitudes towards space, information, identity and privacy. To put it simply, determining when a person acts in his personal or household capacity in the public sphere is much harder to define.

The aim of this paper is twofold: First, to determine the current stage of negotiations at EU level with regard to reforming the household exemption. Here, we focus on presenting and critically assessing the wording proposals made in the course of the negotiation process and identify the particular areas of tension. Second, to ask what is the most appropriate wording for the exemption in question. To achieve this, we analyse the prevailing proposals and categorise them into two general schools of thought. We then re-formulate the main question: What are the benefits and disadvantages of selecting a wording that comprises a set of decisive criteria on the one hand, or provides for a more general framework, leaving more space for flexibility, on the other. Finally, we present our own view which contains, *inter alia,* elements from both of the abovementioned perspectives.

We structure the paper as follows: First, we present an overview of the current stage of negotiations on the data protection reform at EU level. Second, we critically discuss the current application of the household exemption, with reference to the wording of Directive 95/46/EC [3] and the relevant Court of Justice of the European Union ('CJEU') jurisprudence. In this context, we identify the main points of criticism which raised the need to re-draft the household exemption provision. Third, we place the *problematique* of household exemption in the Web 2.0 context to show the interrelation between household exemption and the notion of data controller. We explain how the processing of data within Social Networking Sites ('SNS') and the use of User-Generated Content ('UGC') blur the distinction between *data subjects* and *data controllers* and the consecutive implications. Fourth, we discuss, from a critical perspective, three suggested criteria in determining the application of the household exemption, in the context of the proposed Regulation and identify each one's defects. Finally, we argue for an alternative option, namely, to provide a generally applied framework within the normative part of the proposed Regulation and include additional non-determinative criteria at the respective Recital.

In our paper, we conduct a legal analysis in the course of which we undertake a review of primary sources, such as the proposed legislation, internal EU institutional documents and EU organ's recommendations and reports as well as secondary sources, including the relevant academic literature and proposals published by concerned private undertakings, associations and national competent authorities. We hope that our analysis will contribute to the EU data protection reform literature and assist in explaining why the debate on the household exemption has raised further concerns on the proposed Regulation in terms of controversial wording, potential ineffectiveness, and striking a balance of the affected rights and interests.

2 Negotiating the Reform: Where Do We Stand?

The reform package comprises two legislative proposals based on Article 16 TFEU, the new legal basis for data protection measures introduced by the Lisbon Treaty. The first proposal constitutes the General Data Protection Regulation which aims to replace the existing Data Protection Directive 95/46/EC [4]. The second is a Directive of the European Parliament and the Council on data protection in the field of police and judicial cooperation in criminal matters which intends to replace the Framework Decision 2008/977/JHA. This paper only discusses the application of the Proposed Regulation.

The Draft Regulation is currently debated under the ordinary legislative process, which gives equal weight to both the European Parliament ('EP') and the Council of the European Union (the 'Council') by requiring a broad consensus in order to become law. Since January 2012, when the Commission first published its proposed Regulation, it has been the subject of intense negotiations, re-drafts and controversial criticism. A striking example of the atmosphere that characterises the on-going debate within the EP is that over 3,000 amendments have been put forth by the members of the Civil Liberties, Justice and Home Affairs Committee ('LIBE'). LIBE is currently preparing an amended text for an EP plenary session vote. As a next step, once their respective internal positions are prepared, the EP and the Council will have to engage into inter-institutional negotiations on the finalized text [5].

As far as the Council is concerned, in the middle of December 2013, the Presidency published un updated version of a compromised text of the Commission's original proposal. It is apparent that several Member States, still have reservations on the choice of legal form of the proposed instrument and would perhaps prefer to agree on a Directive. Whilst at the same time acknowledging that substantial progress had been achieved during the negotiations of the Proposed Regulation, the Presidency has considered necessary to note that the Member States' approach is a: "conditional one in the sense that no part of the draft Regulation can at this stage be finally agreed until the whole text of the Regulation is agreed" [6]. Overall, the Council is still to reach a final agreement on several issues including *inter alia* the legal form of the reform, the notion of consent, controllers and processors, the risk-based approach, the extension of the scope to cover EU institutions, agencies and bodies and the EC's potential power to legislate further, in the form of delegated and implemented acts.

The legislative process was initially planned to be concluded by mid-2014 and the Regulation is generally expected to come into force two years after its publication, although significant delays raise doubts on the compliance with such an optimistic schedule. The Council has not yet adopted a common position on the full version or parts of the text and there is currently uncertainty whether the initial timetable will be met [7].

3 The Household Exemption: Current Legal Framework

3.1 Article 3(2) of Directive 95/46/EC

The Directive 95/46/EC (the 'Directive') currently in force contains several exceptions and exemptions, some of them being of general application and others limited to specific parts. The so called *household exemption*, under Article 3(2) of the Directive, to which this paper focuses, comprises an exemption of general application [8] providing that the Directive shall not apply to the processing of personal data: "by a natural person in the course of a purely personal or household activity". In other words, where the exemption applies, the provisions of the Regulation have no effect.

The underlying justification for introducing the household exemption can be approached both from constitutional or human rights protection, and regulatory perspectives. As Wong and Savirimuthu [3] suggest, on the one hand, "any encroachment into the private social spaces would be seen as unjustified and contrary to the prevailing social norms and values" (in other words, as a violation of the right to privacy), while on the other hand, "at a regulatory level, it is not feasible for the State or its enforcement authorities to secure compliance with the obligations".

The Directive's current wording arguably raises more questions rather than providing clear answers. How shall the personal and household activities be defined? Is there an essential conceptual difference between personal and household types of activities? How do we differentiate a purely personal act from a mere personal one? In sum, what criteria shall we apply in deciding whether certain activities of data processing fall under the abovementioned exemption and how are these criteria defined?

Despite its importance and the fact that the said provision, as well as the remaining essential principles of the Directive had been implemented in most of the national laws of the EU Member States, [9] with minor unimportant variations, [10] the application of the household exemption had apparently attracted little or no attention, at least until recently.

In fact, these questions became essential and more topical as the unlimited access to internet and the more functional and sophisticated information and communication technologies ('ICT') opened the way for a range of personal processing activities that the current Directive could not have been expected to anticipate. Individuals today run their own websites and blogs, use social networks, sell items on e-commerce websites, take part in online petition campaigns and share geo-location data with others. Married individuals present digitally recorded data before national courts to obtain a comparative advantage in divorce proceedings. Reference [11] As a result, both adults and minors are now able to make personal data about themselves or others available worldwide, to anyone, instantly [12].

Defining in binary terms, what is personal from what is not, or in essence, what belongs to someone's private life from what extends to the public sphere often seems an impossible task. However, "[t]he amount of everyday activity that until recently took place away from the computer but is now transferred online, legitimizes the need for the law to reflect the variety of online behaviors" [13].

3.2   The *Lindqvist* Judgment

The CJEU has tried to provide some guidance in this regard, in an effort to limit the acknowledged vagueness of Article 3(2) of the Directive and answer the questions surrounding the application of the household exemption.

The leading authority in this respect is the CJEU's judgment in *Lindqvist* [14]. Mrs Lindqvist, a Swedish national, was prosecuted for failing to comply with the data protection laws, following the posting of information relating *inter alia* to her work colleagues on her webpage, without prior obtaining their consent. The national court referred six questions to the CJEU for a preliminary ruling, one of them being whether the act of loading information of this type onto a private home page, which is, nonetheless, accessible to anyone who knows its address, could be regarded as falling outside the scope of the Data Protection Directive on the ground that it is covered by one of the exemptions in Article 3(2). The CJEU held *inter alia*, the following: "[The] exception must therefore be interpreted as relating only to activities which are carried out in the course of private or family life of individuals, which is clearly not the case with the processing of personal data consisting in publication on the internet so that those data are made accessible to an indefinite number of people"(paragraph 47 of the judgment).

Furthermore, the CJEU in this case was of the opinion that the balancing of the concerned interests was a task for the national court. Here, Mrs Lindqvist's freedom of expression had to be "weighted against the protection of the private life of the individuals about whom Mrs Lindqvist has placed data on her Internet site" (paragraph 86 of the judgment).

In this regard, the CJEU seems to be suggesting that, where certain data can be subject to unlimited access, this would result in the act being regarded as falling within the scope of the Directive, thus outside the personal/household sphere. In other words, unlimited access can constitute a criterion towards deciding that the household exemption shall not apply. At the same time, it is noted that the CJEU left open the question how cases, where access is granted to anything close to but less than "access to an indefinite number of people", should be treated.

The *Lindqvist* judgment is indeed an attempt of the CJEU to essentially define what is private in the internet world. As it has been argued, the Court applies the idea of a public/private partition, without, however, indicating where one may draw the line between private and public purposes [3]. In addition, it seems to be placing an onus on the individuals to limit access on their web pages if they wanted to be exempted. In other words, individuals have to show that their web page was intended to be used for private purposes; a requirement which is a harder threshold to prove.

Arguably, the judgment takes a narrow approach to the scope of the exemption by providing that that it will not apply when the processed information is accessible to everyone. On the one hand, it implies that the exemption would perhaps cover situations where information is accessible only to one's family and friends. On the other, "mere acquaintances or like minded contacts (such as within a group that shares recreational or social concerns) would seem to fall within a grey area, not to mention 'friends' on social networking sites who may not, in fact, be 'real' friends or even acquaintances" [15].

The rule applied in *Lindqvist* was further affirmed by the CJEU in *Satamedia* [16], a more recent case where it was also held that the activity fell under the scope of the Directive, given than the purpose of the activities of Markkinapörssi and Satamedia, "was to make the data collected accessible to an unrestricted number of people" (paragraph 44 of the judgment).

Despite the CJEU's genuine efforts to provide clarity to the application of the household exemption, the provision in question was still considered as sufficiently vague and ambiguous and attracted reasonable criticism. First, due to its vagueness, it could not provide any assistance in determining whether an act shall fall under the scope of the exemption. Second, it was argued to be too broad, because it could exempt, in practice, activities that in fact may fall in a person's private sphere, as for example the case might be for part of the activities undertaken within online networks [17, 18].

4   Contextualising the *Problematique*

4.1   Household Exemption and Data Controllers in Web 2.0: Two Sides of the Same Coin?

One way to illustrate the puzzle is to take a closer look at the application of the household exemption in the online world and particularly in relation to activities undertaken within Web 2.0 technologies. Web 2.0 allows users to create and distribute their own UGC, which promotes *inter alia* sharing through mass social networking channels and facilitates users to eventually construct their public profile. References [19, 20] Social networking providers ('SNP') serve as a tool enabling users to create and exchange content and communication [21]. This trend has strong foundations as the use of SNS sustains the misleading impression of the existence of a web "community" [22] or in other words, of a false "intimacy on the web" [23], within which information could be kept private. It is this impression that encourages individuals to increasingly share more information with others.

Therefore the question becomes to what extent are we ready to accept the Directive's application to social networking environments and the use of UGC in online platforms? [24] To answer this question, it is important to illustrate the direct link between the Directive's applicability (and by extension the household exemption's applicability) and the notion of d*ata controller*. This is due to the fact that, if an individual falls under the definition of data controller, then it simultaneously escapes the application of the household exemption and becomes subject to the provisions of the Directive.

Article 2(d) of the Directive provides a broad definition of data controller: "the natural or legal person, public authority, agency or any other body which alone or jointly with others determines the purposes and means of the processing of personal data; where the purposes and means of processing are determined by national or Community laws or regulations, the controller or the specific criteria for his nomination may be designated by national or Community law". Put it more simply, the controller becomes primarily responsible for the compliance with data protection obligations and will also be held liable in case of a breach [21]. The Commission's proposed Regulation endorsed essentially the same definition (see Article 4(5)) and at the time of writing it appears to have also been endorsed by the Council.

Arguably, if the definition of Article 2(d) is applied literally, then its scope would not only cover the SNS but the respective users as well, i.e. individuals who post online information taken by the profiles of other users [22]. Being qualified as data controllers, individual users would be subject to several obligations imposed by the Directive, including *inter alia* ensuring that the processing of the information is done in a fair and lawful manner (Article 6(1)(a) and not be excessive (Article 6(1)(c)) as well as safeguarding specific rights of data subjects under the Directive (see Articles 7, 8 and 10).

In such circumstance, the gateway for escaping the scope of the Directive would be to fall under the scope of other exemptions, such as when the processing is made for journalistic, artistic and literary purposes (Article 9 of the Directive), or for safeguarding public interest values including but not limited to national security, defence and public security, or even when the processing must be considered lawful as being part of a person's right to freedom of expression (see Article 13(1)). In this respect, it would indeed be quite useful to clarify the scope of these exemptions [25], as this exercise would assist in drawing the definitional borders of data controllers and therefore of the household exemption as well. Alternatively, in the event that none of the abovementioned exemptions apply, the only defense available for a user who has undertaken the role of data controller would be to show that the individual to whom the personal data in question relate has provided his consent for their processing (e.g. Articles 7(a) and 8(2)(a) of the Directive). However, showing that such consent has been obtained is not without difficulties [25]. To sum up, even if the household exemption cannot apply in a particular circumstance, users may still rely on the abovementioned specific exemptions to prevent the application of the Directive's provisions.

The analysis shows that it is becoming increasingly easier for individuals (and not merely organizations) to be brought within the scope of the Directive when acting within SNS context [22]. Put differently, in many cases the processing of personal data of other users within SNS (e.g. the posting on information about others on *facebook*) results in individual users assuming the parallel roles of *data subject* and *data controller*.

Limiting the scope of the Directive in social networks environment seems to be a far from an easy task. On the one hand, the granting of a full exemption from data protection requirements to any user who uploads materials on the internet as a private individual would lead to easy circumvention of the rules and, in an age of UGC, would fundamentally undermine data protection and privacy itself. Taking the opposite view, the full imposition of the law to all such individuals would seem excessive and, because of the sheer numbers, would be largely unenforceable [10]. It may also lead to a flood of court actions on behalf of individuals claiming misuse of their private information by other users on SNS [22]. Therefore, where should the line be drawn?

The legislators of the Directive had not anticipated the emerging challenges of Web 2.0 [23]. The new reform builds on the already existing concepts, therefore new conceptualization of old concepts becomes imperative. Not long ago, the Article 29 Data Protection Working Part ('Art. 29WP') suggested the use of certain factors in deciding whether a SNS user does not act in a private context. One of those circumstances would be when the processing information is available to a high number of third party contacts, some of whom the user may not actually know. In other words, if a user takes an informed decision to extend access beyond self-selected *friends*, this would be an indication that the household exception does not apply and thus, data controller responsibilities would come into force. [18] Second, Art. 29WP suggests that if an SNS user (or an individual acting on a different platform using UGC) acts on behalf of a company or association, or uses the Web 2.0 technology mainly as a platform to advance commercial, political or charitable goals, then such activity may extend beyond a purely personal or household activity and thus, the household exemption shall not apply. Here, the user appears to assume the full responsibilities of a data controller who is disclosing personal data to another data controller (SNS) and to other third parties (other SNS users or potentially even other data controllers with access to the data). Reference [18] In view of the above, defining data controllers and the scope of household exemption is likely to be a question of fact. [26].

4.2   Identifying Tensions in a Drafting Exercise

We have shown that in a world where access to Web 2.0 technologies that enable massive data processing is so common, it becomes increasingly more difficult to determine whether processing falls under the household exemption or not. References [27–29] In this light, it is imperative for the law to provide better criteria for deciding whether or not processing is being done for personal or household purposes. Thus, the following questions emerge: (a) which criteria shall we apply in making this decision and (b) how should we incorporate them into a legal text? As it will be suggested below, the answers to both of these questions are equally important and interrelated.

On the one hand, it is argued that maintaining an equally broad exception for personal or household activity (as is currently provided in the Directive) in the proposed Regulation will pose an increasing risk for data protection [30] as there will be no detailed legal instrument to guarantee the private activity of users in the online world. According to this view, to determine in an explicit manner specific criteria that would provide a more solid veil of protection to individuals who, despite being active in the virtual world, should still preserve a limited yet an existing privacy sphere. In the opposite view, composing from the outset a list of set and potentially decisive criteria might result in providing a too narrow or too broad exemption. Such option is criticized for causing the inclusion of more circumstances than actually intended within the household exemption's scope, while also potentially excluding others that should be eligible to trigger the application of the exemption.

Arguably, the level of prescriptiveness should perhaps be higher in a Regulation than a Directive, as the former is directly applicable and needs no further transposition into Member States laws. Reference [31] Although, in principle this is indeed the case, it is in our view precisely the element of direct applicability which makes the selection of wording more challenging. When a rule comes into force in the form of a Regulation, there is limited space for maneuver beyond the literal interpretation.

5   Reforming the Household Exemption

Several wording suggestions focus on limiting the scope of the household exemption by providing one or more determinative criteria in deciding whether it shall apply or not, the main ones being the following: (a) gainful interest, (b) commercial/professional purpose and (c) data accessible to an indefinite number of people. We shall discuss each one in turn.

5.1   The *Gainful Interest* Criterion

The original text of the Commission's proposed Regulation (2012) provided for a household exemption along the lines of the existing Directive, with significant, however, differences. In particular, Article 2(2)(d) of the original text provided that the Regulation shall not apply to the processing of personal data "by a natural person without any gainful interest in the course of its own exclusively personal or household activity".

Two main points should be made here: First, the new wording introduces the concept of *gainful interest*. Second, the Commission considered that the previous term *purely* should be replaced with the word *exclusively* to provide more clarity in this regard.

By introducing the criterion of gainful interest, the Commission seeks to draw a line between those processing activities which are personal and those which are commercial in nature, in line with the Australian and Canadian data protection tradition [15].

Since a definition of *gainful interest* is not available, we seek some guidance from Recital 15 accompanying Article 2(2)(d), where it is mentioned that: "This Regulation should not apply to processing of personal data by a natural person, which are exclusively personal or domestic [...] and without any gainful interest and thus without any connection with a professional or commercial activity." In this regard, Commission seems to treat the notions of *gainful interest* and *professional or commercial activity* as synonymous [32].

The limitation of the household exemption's scope through the introduction of the gainful interest criterion raises certain concerns. First, the reference to gainful interest might give (the wrong in our view) impression that only non-commercial activities can benefit from the exemption. Reference [33] This becomes more obvious in circumstances where, although the processing of personal data is done for gainful interest, the activity itself can still regarded as private, such an example being the setting up of a website to sell unwanted birthday presents. Reference [34] In this light, the inclusion of gainful interest seems to cover unwanted circumstances of data processing which, in our view, should fall within the scope of the household exemption, thus escaping data controllers' obligations.

5.2   The *Commercial/Professional Objective* Criterion

Notwithstanding the Commission's *prima facie* treatment of *gainful interest* and *professional/commercial objective*, as interrelated concepts, it has been argued that the latter serves better as a sole criterion in this respect. Reference [34] When considering the application of this criterion, we note, first, that some non-gainful activities – such as running an online political campaign – would in this case be regarded as non-personal, thus falling under the scope of the Regulation. The paradox is quite obvious as it would be difficult to argue that a political campaign constitutes part of someone's private life. In parallel, we also come across certain cases where, although the processing of personal data on behalf of an individual is done in connection to his or her professional activity, such activity should still be benefited from the exemption. Such is the case of a worker who posts to his blog details of his or her day-to-day work life experiences. Reference [33] In this view, unless the proposed terms are further specified, there is a real risk (similar but broader to the one identified above with regard to *gainful interest*) of narrowing or broadening the household exemption unduly thus, resulting, in certain cases, to unfair treatment and violation of someone's right to freedom of expression respectively.

5.3   The *Access by an Indefinite Number of People* Criterion

As mentioned above in Sect. 3.2, the CJEU decided in *Lindqvist* to use the criterion of *unlimited access* in determining the application of the household exemption. Unsurprisingly, the same criterion has also been suggested to be incorporated into the wording of Article 2(2)(d) of the proposed Regulation.

The main underling rational in this respect is that the Regulation's wording should reflect and be in line with the CJEU's jurisprudence. Reference [35] In deciding whether an activity falls under the public or domestic sector, we should ask whether the information in question can be accessed by an indefinite number of individuals or not. The ultimate aim seems to be simply to prevent individuals who are making data available to several hundreds or even thousands of individuals from automatically falling under the exemption. If no limitation is introduced, then almost all SNS users would fall under the definition of data controller. In the EDPS's own words: "this criterion should be understood as an indication that an indefinite number of contacts shall in principle mean that the household exception does no longer apply" [35]. We note, here, (although it shall be discussed in more detail below) that the said criterion, at least as contained in the EDPS's recommendation, is presented as indicative, rather than determinative. This view found subsequent support in the Opinions of the EP's Committee on Legal Affairs and the Committee on the Internal Market and Consumer Protection, which voiced for the inclusion in Article 2(2)(d) of both the criteria of gainful interest (mentioned above) and access of data to an indefinite number of people [36, 37].

Although it indeed seems reasonable and common practice, both from a normative and practical perspective, to incorporate the CJEU's *ratio decidendi* in the Regulation's wording, it has been suggested that the mere incorporation of the abovementioned broad wording in the normative part of the Proposed Regulation would not assist much in this respect. As it has been characteristically stated: "References to data "made accessible to an indefinite number of individuals" gives rise to questions such as: what circumstances should determine whether the circle of potential recipients of such data is "definite" or "indefinite", in particular whether any significance should be given to the nature of profiles on social networks ("private" or "public" profiles") or to some other circumstances?" [17].

The abovementioned concerns were recently debated extensively within the EP's LIBE Committee, where its members have so far managed to agree on the following worth mentioning wording for the household exemption: "by a natural person (…) in the course of (…) exclusively personal or household activity. This exemption also shall apply to a publication of personal data where it can be reasonably expected that it will be only be accessed by a limited number of persons" [38].

The rational for LIBE's suggested wording is that the proposed Regulation "should not apply to processing of personal data by a natural person, which are exclusively personal, family-related, or domestic, such as correspondence and the holding of addresses or a private sale and without any connection with a professional or commercial activity." Apparently, although LIBE omits from Article 2(2)(d) any specific reference to *gainful interest*, it acknowledges that excluding from its scope activities with *professional/commercial* purpose is in fact the underlying rationale. In addition, it essentially agrees with the idea of incorporating the CJEU's *ratio*, however, it suggests an alternative wording to the ones presented above, the latter focusing on the circumstances where the household exemption would apply, by making reference to access "by a limited number of persons", contrary to the circumstances where it shall not, i.e. when the data is accessible by an indefinite number of people (as *inter alia* EDPS proposed).

Given that LIBE's suggestion is at the time of writing the one to be brought before the EP's plenary session for a final vote, before the inter-institutional negotiations with the Council commence, it worth to pay a closer look. By conducting a literal interpretation of the suggested wording we conclude that it *prima facie* comprises two situations where the household exemption shall apply: The first one refers to the case where an individual's act is conducted in the course of its exclusively personal or household activity. The *second*, appears to be an additional and independent case, in view of the wording "also shall apply"; although, the author's intention could have merely been to explain and analyze the scope of the previous sentence. In any circumstance, what appears to be a *second* case provides for three requirements that must be met in order for it to apply: (a) the personal data must be published, (b) there must be an expectation that there will be limited access to the said personal data ("access by a limited number of persons") and (c) the expectation in question must be reasonable. Here, LIBE introduces an objective reasonableness test by which a court would have to assess the nature and the particular circumstances surrounding the publication of the personal data to conclude whether it provides limited access to third parties. In this regard, to exclude the application of the exemption, there would be no need to provide additional evidence that the said personal data has indeed been accessed by an indefinite number of people. The only thing required to show in this case is that a reasonable person would expect that this would indeed be the case under those circumstances.

In our view, LIBE's wording, although provides some guidance on how the criterion of *unlimited access* shall be applied, it does not resolve the practical difficulties mentioned above at paragraph 3(b) in relation to the *Lindqvist* decision. In fact, it is the inability of such sole criterion to cover all possible situations that has caused for alternative wording options to emerge.

The main alternative view argues for the non-decisiveness of the unlimited access criterion, i.e. that it should not determine *per se* whether the exemption shall apply or not. Instead, such criterion should be treated only as one of the several factors to be considered in assessing a given case, by taking into account the related rights of the concerned parties, in particular the freedom of expression. Reference [17] The following argument made by the Art. 29 WP is in our opinion reflecting the gravity of this view: "making information available to the world at large should be an important consideration when assessing whether or not processing is being done of personal purposes. However, this should not in itself be considered determinative. [...We] need to think through the many consequences – in terms of competing rights as well as logictics – of the possibility of bringing hundreds of millions of social network users – many of whom will have part of their profile open to anyone – and bloggers for example – within the scope of data protection law". Reference [12] In this light, it is submitted that this criterion should only comprise part of the Regulation's Recital 15 and not be included in the strict wording of Article 2(2)(d), as we will discuss below.

5.4   Beyond Normativity: Conciseness and Guidance

The critical presentation of the abovementioned three suggested criteria (otherwise limitations) to the household exemption has shown that each of them suffers alone from specific defects. For each of the proposed wordings, we have been able to: (a) identify situations where a person would be treated unfairly either because the criterion applied is deemed to result in too broad or too narrow application of the exemption and/or (b) identify significant ambiguity in the wording, which results in failing to effectively succeed its purpose, if not creating further complications.

These concerns have led us to consider whether the option of maintaining a rather flexible and broad wording in the normative part of the Regulation, that would capture all instances, without, at the same time, excluding or including more than the ones actually intended, might be of assistance in this respect. We acknowledge that such proposal appears *prima facie* to bring us backwards to the Directive's current wording, which seemingly we have been trying to reform throughout this paper. Indeed, this apparent impression is partly true. However, as it will be shown, any potential deficiency or vagueness caused by the generality of Article 2(2)(d) would be outweighed, in this respect, by the addition of several criteria in the non-normative part, in the form of non-decisive factors that would be taken into account in determining the application of the household exemption in each case.

This approach has so far found strong support in the Art. 29WP's recent opinion earlier this year, where it argued for the preservation of the current wording of Article 3 (2) of the Directive (with a minor replacement of the phrase "of a purely" with the equivalent "of its own exclusively"). Reference [12] Approaching it from another perspective, the Working Party opinioned for omitting the Commission's proposed *gainful interest* criterion and maintaining a flexible but admittedly vague wording as explained above. But that's not all. What could arguably be missing from Article 2(2) (d), the Working Party believes it should be incorporated exclusively in Recital 15 of the proposed Regulation. To put it simply, since it appears that we are unable to provide for a sole criterion within Article 2(2)(d) (or even a small list of those) that would decisively provide a clear cut solution for each case, without causing unjust outcomes, the only realistically practical solution would be to provide a longer list of criteria that would function more as guides rather than switches. Such guides would be considered by a court or national competent authority in a collective manner and not individually, by taking into consideration the particular facts of each case and the potential conflicting rights of the concerned parties.

How such perspective can be applied in practice is illustrated in the Working Party's opinion, which we shall now turn to consider in more detail. First, the Working Party provides in its suggested Recital 15 the general foundation upon which the household exemption shall apply, i.e. "to processing of personal data by a natural person, which is exclusively personal or domestic, such as correspondence, the holding of addresses of personal contacts or the use of social network sites that is outside the pursuit of a commercial or professional objective". Then, having marked the general context, it further proceeds to define four criteria to be used in determining whether a processing falls within the personal/household exemption, namely: (a) potential dissemination of personal data to an indefinite number of persons rather than to a limited community of friends or family members; (b) the nature of the relationship between the person posting certain data and the person to which the posted information refers to; i.e. whether the personal data is about individuals who have no personal or household relationship with the person posting; (c) whether the scale and frequency of the processing of personal data suggests professional or full-time activity and (d) whether there is evidence of a number of individuals acting together in a collective and organised manner.

Remarkably, the negotiations within the Council, at the time of writing, seem to be in favor of partially adopting the above mentioned perspective. Although we are not in a position to conclude whether this outcome is a result of conscious choice or due to the Member States' inability to reach a consensus with regard to including a sole or more criteria in the normative part, we note the Presidency's remarks that Article 2(2)(d) was re-drafted "with a view to reaching a broadly acceptable solution" [39].

More specifically, the latest compromise text published by the Lithuanian Presidency on the Commission's original proposal [40] suggests the following wording for Article 2(2)(d): "by a natural person in the course of a personal or household activity;" We note that the criterion of gainful interest and the reference to "exclusivity" contained in the original Commission's proposal were omitted, which according to the previous Presidency's own words "gave rise to interpretation difficulties and controversy".

Unfortunately, the Council's proposal for the respective Recital 15 is not as rich as the one analysed above by the Art. 29WP, given that it remains to a great extent, along the lines of the Commission's proposal with an addition worth noting, namely a general reference to "social networking and on-line activity". In other words, the Council's current compromising text does not contain specific indicative factors in the non-normative part of the Proposed Regulation, similar to the ones suggested by the Working party outlined above.

Inevitably, a number of questions still remain unanswered, illustrating the challenges of endorsing such approach: When is person considered to use SNS as a platform to advance commercial, political or charitable goals? Concomitantly, when a large number of contacts become too high to be acceptable to the regulator? What does knowing or being in a relationship with someone in the virtual world mean? [10] A preliminary answer to these questions could be that: (a) it might not be useful to provide a theoretical and abstract response which, although it could *prima facie* be easily applied uniformly, however, it would remain unrelated to the specific facts of each case, thus potentially leading to unfair judicial decisions and (b) all the above mentioned criteria should be given collectively proportionate weight in balancing the rights of the concerned parties.

Assuming such perspective comes into force, it would be the initial role of the national courts and competent authorities to conduct the respective assessment, based on the evidence brought before them. Admittedly, the data protection reform in question aims *inter alia* to integrate the differentiated data protection laws currently applied within the EU member states; however, considering the various data protection and privacy traditions among Europe, it not unlikely that this might be a long process. In the event that such proposal becomes law, we would expect that, at least at the early stage, national authorities will give different weight to the provided criteria, which would then perhaps result in a less uniform application of the household exemption between member states. Such controversies caused by the domestic differentiated approaches would, however, be finally solved by the CJEU in the form of preliminary rulings following references from national courts. Eventually, a set of CJEU pilot decisions would provide the appropriate guidance on the interpretation and application of Article 2(2)(d) to which all national court and authorities would have to comply. The possible option to have the Commission or other specialized bodies, such as EDPS and Art. 29WP occasionally, issuing guidelines, recommendations and best practices to ensure consistent application of the Regulation by the national Data Protection authorities would certainly limit any differentiated application of the said provisions among member states. Reference [31] In our view, this admittedly long term but well tested cooperation between the CJEU, Commission and national courts and authorities would provide for an effective application of Article 2(2)(d).

6   Conclusion

The household exemption, as is currently provided in the Directive 95/46/EC, lacks the desired and necessary clarity in determining when and how the processing of certain data on behalf of a person shall fall under its scope, particularly when the processing act takes place in Web 2.0 environment. The CJEU's guidance in this respect, and in particular the *Lindqvist* judgment, does not solve the fundamental defects of Article 3 (2) of the Directive and at the same time leaves a number of questions unanswered.

The processing of personal data within Web 2.0 technologies illustrates the inter-relation between the applicability of household exemption and the definition of data controller. The users' increasing processing of personal data within SNS and the wide use of UGC results in individuals assuming the parallel roles of data controller and data subject, thus blurring the tension between the two concepts.

Reforming the household exemption proves to be a key area of dispute in the course of the ongoing negotiations on the EU data protection reform. The major tension lies on the selection of criteria, if any, which would be expressly mentioned in the normative part of the proposed Regulation. This is due to the fact that they shall in principle determine whether a processing act shall be regarded as belonging to a user's private life or not. At the present stage, the two institutions, equally involved in the legislative process, namely the Council and the EP, have both decided to amend the Commission's original draft, each reaching to different proposals for the wording of what would be Article 2(2)(d) of the proposed Regulation. On the one hand, EP's LIBE committee, seems to be in favor of incorporating the ratio of *Lindqvist* judgment, as a criterion in applying the household exemption which refers to the situations where the processed data can be accessed by an indefinite number of people. The Council, on the other, is, at the time of writing, in favor of adopting a broad wording, equivalent to the one provided by the current Directive, without however containing any further significant guidance, which is in our opinion an essential defect.

Our analysis has shown that the inclusion of one or more determinative criteria in the normative part of the Regulation, although would *prima facie* lead to a more uniform application of the exemption, in fact, it is likely that would eventually cause either too broad or too limited application of the exemption, thus resulting to unjust outcomes. In this light, we argue that perhaps the most appropriate and practically efficient option would be to incorporate a broad wording at the Article 2(2)(d) and add further non-determinative criteria at the non-normative part, namely Recital 15 of the proposed Regulation. The application of the said criteria should be conducted in a collective manner and the balance of the respective interests and rights of the concerned parties would be succeeded by taking into consideration the particular facts of the case. This solution arms a judge or competent authority with a list of non-determinative criteria to be used as a toolbox, in assessing whether certain processing falls under the scope of the proposed Regulation, rather than forcing an abstract ticking-the-box exercise, which would disregard the diversity of cases that can arise in the virtual world and in particular in Web 2.0 environment.

The vast variety of users' online activities, particularly the ones that involve UGC and participation in SNS, prevent the EU legislator from sufficiently providing for a clear-cut definition of *private conduct* (as opposed to activity done in public), thus, leading us to conclude that a fair, efficient and practical solution would only be achieved if the matter is left to be subsequently determined on case by case basis, by national courts and competent authorities and eventually the CJEU. Such long process might result to the initial fragmentation of the interpretation of proposed Regulation's scope, at least in the short term, before a homogenous application of the proposed exemption is achieved.

Acknowledgments. The author is grateful to Dr. K. Chrysostomides & Co. LLC for its invaluable and continuous support as well as to Ms Helen Ayres for her comments on earlier drafts of this paper.

References

1. European Commission: Proposal for a Regulation of the European Parliament and of the Council on the protection of individuals with regard to the processing of personal data and on the free movement of such data (General Data Protection Regulation), Brussels, COM (2012) 11 final, 25 Jan 2012
2. Wong, R., Savirimuthu, J.: All or nothing: this is the question? The application of Art. 3(2) data protection directive 95/46/EC to the internet'. John Marshall J. Comput. Inf. Law **25**, 241–266 (2008)
3. Directive 95/46/EC of the European Parliament and of the Council of 24 October 1995 on the protection of individuals with regard to the processing of personal data and on the free movement of such data, Official Journal L 281, 23 Nov 1995
4. Lostarakou, K.: The new EU Regulation for the protection of private data (in Greek). Media and Communication Law 3. Nomiki Vivliothiki, 353–357 (2013)
5. Hunton & Williams: Council of the European Union Releases Draft Compromise Text on the Proposed EU Data Protection Regulation-Privacy and Information Security Law Blog, 4 Jun 2013
6. Council of the European Union: Presidency Note to the Council. 10227/13. Interinstitutional File: 2012/0011 (COD), Brussels, 31 May 2013
7. Kuner, Ch., Burton, K., Pateraki, A.: The Proposed EU Data Protection Regulation Two Years Later. Bloomberg BNA, Privacy and Security Law Report (2014)
8. Hunton & Williams: Executive Briefing Paper on Proposed General Data Protection Regulation (2012)
9. Mitrou, L.: Privacy challenges and perspectives in Europe. In: Bottis, M. (ed.) An Information Law for the 21st Century. Nomiki Vivliothiki, Athens (2011)
10. European Commission: Comparative Study on Different Approaches to New Privacy Challenges, in particular in the Light of Technological Developments. Working Paper No. 2: Data protection laws in the EU: The difficulties in meeting the challenges posed by global social and technical developments. Douwe Korff, 20 Jan 2010
11. Panagopoulou-Koutnatzi, F.: On personal and household use of personal data (in Greek). Administrative Law Journal 5. Sakkoulas Athens-Thessaloniki, 704-718 (2013)
12. Article 29 Data Protection Working Party: Proposals for Amendments regarding exemption for personal or household activities. Annex 2 to Statement of the Working Party on current discussions regarding the data protection reform package, 27 Feb 2013
13. Warso, Z.: There's more to it than data protection – Fundamental rights, privacy and the personal/household exemption in the digital age. Comput. Secur. Rev. **29**, 491–500 (2013)
14. Case C-101/01 *Bodil Lindqvist* [2003] ECR I-12992, judgment of 06 Nov 2003
15. Roth, P.: Data protection meets 2.0: two ships passing in the night. Univ. New South Wales Law J. **33**(2), 532–561 (2010)
16. C-73/07 *Satamedia* [2008] ECR I-9831
17. European Parliament: DG for Internal Policies, Policy Department A: Economic and Scientific Policy. Reforming the Data Protection Package Study (2012)
18. Article 29 Data Protection Working Party: The Future of Privacy. Joint Contribution to the Consultation of the European Commission on the legal framework for the fundamental right to protection of personal data. WP 168, 1 Dec 2009
19. Mitrou, L.: Privacy in WEB 2.0 (in Greek). Media and Communication Law 3. Nomiki Vivliothiki, 319–327 (2010)
20. Van Alsenoy, B., Ballet L., Kuczerawy, A., Dumortier, J.: Social networks and web 2.0: are users also bound by data protection regulations? Ident. Inf. Soc. 2, 1 (2009)

21. Giannakaki, M.: The EU Data Protection Directive revised: New challenges and perspectives. In: 4th International Conference on Information Law, Thessaloniki, 20–21 May 2011
22. Wong R.: Social Networking: Anybody is a Data Controller (2008), available at: SSRN http://ssrn.com/abstract=1271668
23. International Working Group on Data Protection in Telecommunications. Report and Guidance on Privacy in Social Network Services – "Rome Memorandum". 43rd meeting, Rome, 3–4 March 2008
24. Garrie, D., Wong, R.: Social networking: opening the floodgates to "Personal Data". Comput. Telecommun. Law Rev. **16**(6), 167–176 (2010)
25. Wong, R.: Social networking: a conceptual analysis of a data controller. Commun. Law **14** (5), 142–149 (2009)
26. Article 29 Data Protection Working Party: Opinion 1/2010 on the concepts of "controller" and "processor"'. WP 169, 16 Feb 2010
27. Mitrou, L., Karyda, M.: EU´s data protection reform and the right to be forgotten - A legal response to a technological challenge? In: 5th International Conference of Information Law and Ethics, Corfu-Greece 29–30 June 2012
28. Panagopoulou-Koutnatzi, F.: Social Networks and Identity (in Greek). Media and Communication Law. Nomiki Vivliothiki, 186-195 (2012)
29. Piskopani, A.-M.: The protection of privacy of Facebook Uses (in Greek). Media and Communication Law 3. Nomiki Vivliothiki, 338 (2009)
30. European Digital Rights (EDRi): Position on the Regulation on the protection of individuals with regard to the processing of personal data and on the free movement of such data (General Data Protection Regulation) (2013)
31. Council of the European Union: Presidency Note to the Council. 16525/1/12. REV 1. Interinstitutional File: 2012/0011 (COD), Brussels, 03.12.2012.2
32. BEUC Position Paper: Data Protection, Proposal for a Regulation. X/2012/039, 27 July 2012
33. UK Information Commissioner's Office (ICO): Initial analysis of the European Commission's proposals for a revised data protection legislative framework (2012)
34. UK's Information Commissioner's Office (ICO): Proposed new EU General Data Protection Regulation: Article-by-article analysis paper. V1.0, February 2013
35. Opinion of the European Data Protection Supervisor on the data protection reform package, 07 March 2012
36. Opinion of the Committee on Legal Affairs for the Committee on Civil Liberties, Justice and Home Affairs on the proposal for a regulation of the European Parliament and of the Council on the protection of individuals with regard to the processing of personal data and on the free movement of such data (General Data Protection Regulation) (Rapporteur: Marielle Gallo), 2012/011(COD), 28 Jan 2013
37. Opinion of the Committee on the Internal Market and Consumer Protection for the Committee on Civil Liberties, Justice and Home Affairs on the proposal for a regulation of the European Parliament and of the Council on the protection of individuals with regard to the processing of personal data and on the free movement of such data (General Data Protection Regulation) (Rapporteur: Lara Comi), 2012/0011(COD), 28 Jan 2013
38. Committee on Civil Liberties, Justice and Home Affairs: Draft Report on the proposal for a regulation of the European Parliament and of the Council on the protection of individuals with regard to the processing of personal data and on the free movement of such data (General Data Protection Regulation). COM(2012)0011–C7-0025/2012 – 2012/0011(COD). Rapporteur: Jan Philipp Albrecht, 21.10.2013. Rapporteur: Jan Philipp Albrecht, 16 Jan 2013

39. Council of the European Union: Presidency Note to the Council. 10227/13, Interinstitutional File: 2012/0011 (COD), Brussels, 31 May 2013
40. Council of the European Union: Presidency Note to the Working Party on Information Exchange and Data Protection. 17831/13. Interinstitutional File: 2012/0011 (COD), Brussels, 16 Dec 2013

Legal and Social Aspects of Cyber Crime in Greece

Anastasios Papathanasiou[1]([⊠]), Alexandros Papanikolaou[2],
Vasileios Vlachos[2], Konstantinos Chaikalis[2], Maria Dimou[3],
Magdalini Karadimou[2], and Vaia Katsoula[4]

[1] Cyber Crime Prosecution Subdivision, Financial Police and Cyber Crime Unit,
Hellenic Police, Athens, Greece
a.papathanasiou@cybercrimeunit.gr
[2] Department of Computer Science and Engineering,
Technological Educational Institute of Thessaly, Larissa, Greece
alxpapanikolaou@gmail.com, {vsvlachos,kchaikalis}
@teilar.gr, m_karadimou@hotmail.com
[3] Department of Electrical and Computer Engineering,
University of Thessaly, Volos, Greece
mdimou@uth.gr
[4] Information Technology Lawyer (LLM), Auditors Department (Internship),
Data Protection Authority, Athens, Greece
julie.katsoula.law@gmail.com

Abstract. The increased use of personal computers and other personal devices with the ability to connect to the Internet, as well as the availability of public WiFi hotspots, enabled people to make extensive use of the offered Internet services, thus rendering them a tempting target for cyber criminals. Furthermore, cyber crime has a transnational character and can simultaneously affect individuals at different geographical locations, thus requiring international cooperation in order to be fought effectively. This paper presents the various international efforts against cyber crime that involve Greece, along with the relevant legal framework and some planned developments for the future.

Keywords: Cyber crime · Cyber crime prevention · Cyber crime legislation

1 Introduction

The rapid evolution of technology, the development of information technology and the widespread use of the Internet have brought about revolutionary changes in all daily activities, the production process, trade, education, entertainment and even in the way modern people think and act. Along with these changes, which intend to improve the quality of our lives, new forms of crime are developed and have been introduced. These new forms of crime are committed in the Information and Communications Technology (ICT) environment and are covered by the term *computer crime*, which also includes *cyber crime*. The latter, unlike "traditional" forms of crime, has no geographical limitations. That is, a crime committed by an offender can affect multiple

© Springer International Publishing Switzerland 2014
A.B. Sideridis et al. (Eds.): E-Democracy 2013, CCIS 441, pp. 153–164, 2014.
DOI: 10.1007/978-3-319-11710-2_14

individuals who may be at different locations, either within the same country or not. What is more, under certain circumstances, this can even happen concurrently.

In order for the competent law enforcement authorities to investigate and successfully prosecute a cyber crime that has been reported by a citizen of a specific country, they frequently have to intercept, monitor and process digital traces of information in more than one jurisdiction, since the offence may originate from other countries or simply pass through their communication networks. The vast diversity of legislation and legal frameworks among different countries world-wide can cause significant delays in obtaining the required permits and providing the requested information or can even completely inhibit the criminal procedure, due to the inability of proving direct criminal intent. Therefore, in order for cyber crime to be fought effectively, an international co-operation is necessary, so as to adopt a harmonised legislative framework and appropriate processes that will speed up the transnational cyber crime investigations and prosecutions.

Given the increased cyber crime incidents in Greece, an appropriate subdivision of the Hellenic Police was founded quite recently for handling such incidents effectively. Furthermore, through the actions of this Police Unit, the need for revisions and/or extensions in the national legislation so as to include the various and complex aspects of cyber crime, became very evident.

The paper is organised as follows. Section 2 presents the definitions of cyber crime and computer crime. Section 3 presents some social aspects of cyber crime. Section 4 provides information about the Budapest Convention for combating cyber crime. The relevant departments of the Hellenic Police responsible for dealing with cyber crime are presented in Sect. 5, whereas the relevant Greek legislation is presented in Sect. 6. Finally, the paper concludes in Sect. 7.

2   Definitions of Cyber Crime and Computer Crime

Computer technology has undoubtedly broadened the range of crimes, which require expertise and advanced IT training. There is quite a lot of controversy about the significance of the terms. While every crime can be facilitated by the use of computers or ICT [1], in many cases the use of computers does not change the fundamental character of a crime; a bribery remains a bribery, regardless of whether the money was sent electronically or not. However, the use of a computer may affect the level and punishment of the crime. In any case, the introduction of information and communication systems is a qualitative change, according to the aforementioned reasons.

It is worth mentioning that computer crime precedes chronologically and logically the category of cyber crimes [2]. According to the definition in [3], any violations of criminal law that involve a knowledge of computer technology for their perpetration, investigation, or prosecution can be considered computer-related crimes. This definition encompasses all three main categories: computer crime in the strict sense, any computer-related crime and computer abuse (intentional acts where the perpetrators could have made gain and their victims could have suffered loss).

According to the Organisation for Economic Co-operation and Development (OECD), criminality through computers "regards any illegal, unethical or unapproved behaviour related to the automatic data processing and transfer" [4].

Depending on the way of committing computer crimes, they are divided into:

1. Crimes committed both in the "real" and digital world, e.g. slander is committed also by the use of electronic mail (e-mail mission).
2. Crimes committed only in a computing environment (namely, without the use of the Internet) and
3. "Genuine" cyber crimes where the criminal behaviour is exclusively related to cyberspace [1].

Furthermore, depending on the content, crimes are divided into:

1. Crimes against personality and privacy.
2. Crimes against property.
3. Illegal and unfair/harmful content.

Cyber crime possesses some special features, the most evident of which include:

- A *cross-border character:* Its effects can occur simultaneously in many places, sometimes affecting different countries simultaneously.
- The *"discretion" of committing:* Can be committed by anyone and affect anyone, without requiring the offender's transition to another place. Furthermore, it is quite easy to become organised crime.
- *Difficulty of investigation:* Its investigation is quite difficult, due to the demanding requirements for specialised training and expertise.

3 Social Aspects of Cyber Crime

The extensive use of Information and Communication Technologies (ICT) in our everyday lives has created a strong link between the two. Hence, any kind of cyber crime could potentially be related to our social lives, either directly or indirectly, thus giving birth to new methods for committing cyber crimes with the use of ICT. In what follows, some indicative examples are presented.

The lack of appropriate user awareness and training is possibly one of the most important reasons that allow such cyber crime incidents to take place or become the "fuel" that keeps them going (e.g. for hoax e-mails and chain letters). Users who are not aware of the potential dangers of cyberspace tend to become the most frequent victims. What is more, since they will most probably not be safeguarding their privacy appropriately, combined with their lack of knowledge and experience regarding security-related issues in cyberspace, the impact of such an attack against them may be amplified significantly. The situation can worsen even more in cases where the individual is a computer illiterate. Several such incidents have been recorded that triggered exaggerated reactions from the victim's side, which in some times lead to extremes, such as committing suicide.

Furthermore, the extensive use of personal electronic devices can aid cyber criminals in performing their unlawful acts. Since such devices usually have the ability to connect to the Internet, the attack surface increases dramatically, giving the option for remote attacks as well. For instance, the theft of a mobile phone or a tablet may offer the perpetrator a large collection of personal and private photographs, a long list of e-mail addresses and phone numbers, or even a set of credentials (usernames and passwords) for logging into various on-line web services. Consequently, the offender can exploit the aforementioned information for performing identity theft, threatening and blackmailing the victim in multiple ways.

Perhaps one of the most popular means of user interaction in the cyberspace is the use of electronic social networking platforms (e.g. Facebook, Flickr, Twitter, Google+, hi5, Bebo, Foursquare), mainly in their leisure time. In order to use these platforms, users have to create a profile with some personal information and they can then upload content-rich information consisting of text, images and videos, as well as interact among them in various ways, such as discuss privately or in groups via chat services, tag their friends in photographs, express their preference via e.g. "like" and "+1" functionality, share their current location or activity and so on. In most cases, however, users upload excessive amounts of personal information and due to the absence of appropriate access control policies and/or configuration, they create serious security issues that could lead to privacy violations (their own and/or their contacts').

Finally, cyber crime is also related to the current socio-political circumstances. For instance, during the past few years, Greece is suffering from an economic crisis, which is correlated to some degree to the increase in financial cyber crime incidents. Such examples are fake employment agencies that require a fee in advance and promise to offer jobs, though they never do so; travel agents offering extremely cheap vacation packages that never reach the customers who have paid for them; illegal on-line gambling services advertising particularly tempting payouts.

4   The Budapest Convention on Cyber Crime

The forms of computer crime vary and evolve along with the continuous technological development. To address this peculiarity, an inter-governmental co-operation was necessary, in order to lead to the composition of a comprehensive and effective strategy for combating cyber crime. This objective was met at the Conference on Computer Crime (Convention on Cybercrime), held in Budapest, the conclusions of which were finalised in the Convention signed at the end of the conference on November 23, 2001. In the Convention of Budapest, which essentially is the first international agreement for combating cyber crime, signed by 26 ministers of European countries (including Greece), there are explanations and regulations for all kinds of computer crimes. Although this convention has been signed by Greece, it has not been adopted yet, via the formation of a relevant national law. Such an effort was initiated very recently by the Greek Minster of Justice who ordered the formation of a legislative committee whose objective would be, amongst others, to incorporate the provisions of the Convention in the Greek national law [5].

In this convention the necessity for international and mutual law enforcement assistance among countries for combating cyber crime is emphasised and also the critical question about the courts' competence and jurisdiction of such crimes is raised.

The aims of the Convention were:

1. The harmonisation of internal penal laws of the member states in the field of cybercrime.
2. The adoption of internal procedural criminal law which is necessary, not only for the investigation, prosecution and adjudication of cyber crime (as well as other crimes committed with the use of computer systems), but also to collect evidence which are found in electronic form.
3. The establishment of rapid and effective rules in international cooperation and communication.

The Convention comprises:

1. Substantive criminal law provisions.
2. Criminal procedural law provisions.
3. Provisions on international judicial co-operation.

The need for international legal harmonisation has also been highlighted by Clough [6], who claimed that it is imperative for facilitating international co-operation in order to eliminate "safe havens" for cybercriminals. In his work, taking the Budapest Convention as a starting point, he examines the degree to which harmonisation is achievable and presents the various international and regional legislative amendments that have been added world-wide for dealing with potential issues of cyber crime. Nevertheless, he concludes that due to incompatible and inconsistent national legislations, the harmonisation process has been significantly hindered.

Regarding the ratification of the Convention by the United States, the author in [7] concludes that the benefits for enacting the Convention outweigh any possible threats to the right of privacy that will emerge through the requirement for intercepting and monitoring communications.

As soon as the Budapest Convention is ratified by Greece, various gaps that currently exist in the legal framework will be filled, since the Convention targets three main goals:

- Harmonisation of the Substantive Criminal Law.
- Harmonisation of the Procedural Criminal Law.
- Establishment of rules for an international judicial co-operation.

The various Substantive Criminal Law provisions exist in the first section of the second chapter of the Convention and cover the following crime categories:

1. Crimes against the confidentiality, integrity and availability of data and systems (articles 2–6).
2. Crimes related to computers (articles 7–8).
3. Crimes related to the content of data (article 9).
4. Crimes against intellectual property and related rights (article 10).

5 Bodies for Fighting Cyber Crime in Greece

5.1 The Greek Cyber Crime Prosecution Subdivision

According to the Presidential Decree 100/2004, within the Police Division of Attica, Subdivision of Financial Crimes Antiquities and Ethics, the 5th Department of Cyber Crime was founded and put into operation, which was responsible for the prosecution of crimes committed over the Internet. On January 3, 2005 the respective department within the jurisdiction of the Police Division of Thessaloniki was founded and was made operational.

Subsequently, the structure of these cyber crime departments was re-organised, improved and specialised. Hence, with the Presidential Decree 9/2011 [8] the Financial and Cyber Crime Police Unit (FCCPU) was founded and came into operation in July 2011, as an independent Central Office subjected to the Hellenic Police and supervised/controlled by the Chief of the Hellenic Police.

Almost one year after its establishment, the Greek Cyber Crime Prosecution Subdivision (GCCPS) has significant results to exhibit for 2012. More specifically, a total of 458 people were accused for committing various cyber crimes and a total of 104 people were arrested. As far as flagrant crimes are concerned, the vast majority of them were related to child pornography (55.77 %), followed by copyright infringement (11.54 %), satellite piracy (5.77 %), various Internet frauds (5.77 %), violations of privacy in telecommunications (3.85 %), violations of privacy (2.88 %), violation of computer systems (0.96 %) and the remaining uncategorised flagrant crimes added up to 13.46 %. Another very important achievement was the prevention of suicide attempts that were detected, either because individuals wanted to commit suicide for unspecified personal reasons and were publicising their intentions through social networking sites (mainly Facebook), or because they had become victims of other kinds of cyber crimes, where the perpetrator had exerted unbearable psychological pressure on them. In particular, the GCCPS managed to prevent a total of 265 suicide attempts, ranging from 11 to 32 cases per month. It is worth pointing out that the number of cases related to financial cyber crime accounted for 87 % of the total recorded ones. By using the data of an e-mail help service, the authors in [9] estimated that between the years 2007 and 2009 the number of cyber crime cases related to financial fraud were 49.4 % of the 491 total cases. The observed increase in financial cyber crime is therefore a strong indicator of a possible correlation with the Greek economic crisis that started around mid 2010.

5.2 The Financial and Cyber Crime Police Unit (FPCCU)

The Financial Police and the Cyber Crime Unit were established as an independent central Service, of Police Directorate level, that is under the authority of the Hellenic Police Headquarters and is supervised and controlled by the Chief of the Hellenic Police. The aforementioned Unit resides in Attica, exercises its competencies to the whole of the Hellenic territory (except the areas where the Coast Guard is responsible for), as established by special provisions and its mission is to prevent and suppress economic crimes, as well as crimes committed via the Internet or other means of electronic communication. The FPCCU, apart from its own staff, it also contains the Financial Police Sub-Division and the Cyber Crime Prosecution Sub-Division [8].

5.3 The Subdivision for Cyber Crime

An independent department of the FPCCU is also the Subdivision of Cyber Crime Prosecution (SCCP), having its headquarters in Athens, with nation-wide reach.

The Subdivision for Cyber Crime is further divided into:

1. *The Department of General Affairs and Personal Data Protection*, which is entrusted with the continuous quest across the Internet and other means of electronic communication and digital storage, aiming at the detection, investigation and prosecution of criminal acts committed via them throughout the country, apart from those defined in case (2) below.
2. *The Department for Child Protection*, which is entrusted with the investigation and prosecution of crimes committed against minors, through the use of the internet and other means of electronic or digital communication and storage.
3. *The Department of Intellectual Property Rights Protection*, which is entrusted with the handling of cases concerning illegal penetration in computing systems, theft, destruction or illegal distribution of software, digital data and audio-visual material, committed throughout the country, as well as for rendering assistance to other competent services investigating such cases, as defined in the legislation in force.
4. *The Department of Telecommunications Security*, which operates as defined in provisions of the decision 7001/2/1261 and the Common Ministerial Decision (B' 1879) of the Ministers of Internal Affairs, Economy and Finance, Justice on August 28, 2009 [8].

In order to fulfil its mission, the Subdivision for Cyber Crime, co-operates with the local Hellenic Police Services, as well as with other competent Services, authorities and bodies and it is equipped with the necessary resources. Moreover, within the scope of its mission, it co-operates with competent Services, organisations and bodies of European Union, in accordance with the provisions in force and the international agreements and conventions. The provisions of Law 2472/1997 regarding the protection of individuals with regard to the processing of personal data, shall apply during the processing and exchange of information and data accomplished within in the scope of the Unit mission. The personnel of the Subdivision receives extensive training, both locally and abroad, for the effective accomplishment of its mission [8].

For dealing with the ever-growing and changing forms of computer crime and to fulfil its purpose and mission, the Subdivision of Cyber Crime Prosecution features a highly-technological infrastructure and it is staffed by highly-qualified young scientists, who are in possession of masters and doctorate degrees in the wider field of Informatics. Furthermore, they have a high level of both theoretical and empirical expertise in telecommunications, networks and on the examination of digital evidence.

5.4 The Greek Cybercrime Center (GCC)

The Foundation for Research & Technology – Hellas (FORTH) in collaboration with the Hellenic Self-Regulatory Body for Internet Content (Safenet), the Faculty of Law, Economic & Political Sciences of the Aristotle University of Thessaloniki (AUTh) and the Center for Security Studies (KEMEA) have joined forces to form the Greek Cybercrime Center (GCC), a co-ordinated European effort aiming at improving education and research in the area of cyber crime. Its objectives are to [10]:

- Advance cyber crime training and University education in Greece.
- Improve research in focused areas of cyber crime such as botnets and cyber attacks.
- Mobilise the Greek constituency in the area of cyber crime.
- Collaborate with similar centres so as to maximise the uptake of the results.

The GCC plans to improve the understanding of cyber crime for the new generations of both scientists and law students through a set of university courses. In addition, via a set of short-term highly-focused training courses, the GCC plans to improve the understanding of the notion of cyber crime for existing Local Education Authorities (LEA) personnel, judicial authorities and industrial employees.

Within the scope of the EU programme "GCC: A CyberCrime Center of Excellence for Training, Research, and Education in Greece", the 1st Advisory Board meeting was held on September 12, 2013 at KEMEA Conference Room premises, with the participation of Project Consortium Partners [11]. In this meeting, the notion of cyber crime was analysed and the exact role of the Advisory Board was addressed. Next, the structure of the project was outlined, the research activities were presented in detail, as well as the future actions of the GCC. It is worth pointing out that significant reference was made to the current legal framework and structures regarding cyber crime, as well as to the project's individual actions. Strong emphasis was given on the need for creating a national strategy for security against cyber crime, according to the latest EU standards.

6 Greek Legislation Related to Cyber Crime

6.1 The Need for Cyber Crime Laws

Undoubtedly, computer crime is a continually increasing form of crime, both at national and international level, which mutates as novel and sophisticated methods for committing offences appear. This is mainly due to the rapid development of technological systems, the use of the Internet by an ever-increasing number of users, the difficulty in detecting/proving (computer and network forensics) and of course the anonymity it can potentially provide to its users. The Unit has often been called to investigate offences, where the offender may be located anywhere in the world and tracking his location requires time-consuming and specialised technical investigations.

Since the Subdivision of Cyber Crime Prosecution was established, the number of crimes and criminal cases that it has been called to investigate, either ex officio through a preliminary investigation under the Article 243 of the Code of Criminal Procedure, or via the public prosecutor's request to conduct a preliminary investigation, have experienced rapid growth, mainly due to the reasons mentioned in the paragraph above. Additional factors that have contributed to this growth are the following:

- *The continually-increasing number of broadband connections in Greece.* According to publicly-available reports by the Hellenic Telecommunications and Post Commission, the broadband connections at the end of December 2012 reached 2,689,428 [12], while at the end of 2010 they were 2,250,000 active broadband connections in Greece [13]. From just 488,000 active connections at the end of 2006 [14], the number almost tripled two years later, reaching 1,400,000 at the end of 2008 [15]. This fact alone gave criminals a growing "digital" field for their unlawful actions.
- *The nature of Cyber Crime Unit's responsibilities.* The fact that its responsibilities are not confined to the local competence of Attica, but spread throughout the entire country.

Moreover, it is worth pointing out that in such cases all necessary investigation acts are performed which are necessary to ascertain the offence and reveal the offender(s); at the same time, a proper digital investigation is performed, which includes a set of actions to identify digital data in computer systems and devices, in order to solve a case. It also includes methods and techniques of computer forensics to maintain the integrity and authenticity of data. Futhermore, due to the competence and subject of the cases under investigation, a large volume of digital or electronic media/exhibits is confiscated and the (digital) evidence of crimes under investigation are mainly found in the memory storage of the aforementioned media/exhibits.

The range of cyber crimes and cases where the Internet was used as a simple platform for committing crimes and solved in Greece from Cyber Crime Unit is quite large. To name a few, it includes fraud and computer-related fraud, computer-related forgery, identity theft, misuse of devices, illegal access (hacking, cracking), data espionage, illegal interception and data and system interference, aggravated burglary and theft, libel and false information, slander, defamation of public limited company (PLC), criminal organisation, cyber-extortion, racism, hate speech and glorification of violence, spamming, phishing, circulation of counterfeit, copyright and trademark-related offences, privacy and private data violations, cyber-laundering, cyber-warfare, cyber-terrorism, intellectual property crimes, child pornography, dissemination of erotic or pornographic material, child soliciting and abuse, cyber-stalking, violating the memory of the dead, drug trafficking, illegal gambling.

6.2   Related Greek Legislation

In Greek legislation, from the scope of the Penal Code, there are no laws referring exclusively to the Internet and the actions of users that use it. Thus, general criminal laws apply, along with the so-called "special criminal laws". In 2005, the Presidential Decree 47/2005 was implemented to clarify the preconditions under which a communication may be intercepted, including communications over the Internet. Tables 1 and 2 present some frequently-used Articles of the Penal Code, Laws and Presidential Decrees regarding cyber crime.

Table 1. Articles of the Penal Code, referring to cyber crime.

Penal Code article no.	Subject
292a	Crimes against the security of telephone communications
348a	Child Pornography
348b	Attracting children for sexual purposes
361	Insult
362	Libel
363	Defamation
370	Unauthorised access to transmissions
370a	Violation of confidentiality of telephone communication and oral conversation
370b	Unauthorised access to secret data
370c	Unlawful access to data
386a	Computer Fraud

Table 2. Laws and Presidential Decrees regarding certain cyber crime categories.

Category	Relevant laws and presidential decrees
Electronic communications and telecommunications	Law 2867/2000 "Organization and operation of the Telecommunications sector"
	Law 3431/2006 "Electronic communication and other issues"
	Law 3783/2009 "Identification of owners and users of mobile telephone services and other issues"
Intellectual property	Law 2121/1993 "Intellectual property, related rights and cultural issues"
Personal data	Law 2472/1997 "Protection against personal data processing"
	Law 3471/2006 "Protection of personal data processing and private life in the sector of telecommunications – Amendment of Law 2472/1997"
Confidentiality of communication	Law 2225/1994 "For the protection of freedom of response and communication" as amended until today
	Law 3674/2008 "Strengthening the institutional framework to protect privacy of telephone communication and other issues"
	Presidential Decree 47/2005 "Procedures and technical and organizational provisions to intercept the secrecy and security of communication"
Data retention	Law 3917/2011 "Retention of telecommunication data and other issues". According to this law, telephone and internet services providers preserve communication data only for 12 months after the date of the communication

(Continued)

Table 2. *(Continued)*

Category	Relevant laws and presidential decrees
Electronic commerce	Presidential Decree 150/2001: "Digital Signatures"
	Presidential Decree 131/2003: "Electronic commerce etc"
Decisions	Decision 592/012 (Official Government Gazette B-593, 14/04/2011): "Regulations on Management and Assignment of Domain Names ending in.gr"

6.3   Difficulties Encountered During the Investigation of Cyber Crimes

Taking into account that the privacy of Internet communications is protected by the Presidential Decree 47/2005, while the procedure for their interception is described in Article 4 of Law 2225/94. This fact alone makes it virtually impossible to trace the misdemeanours committed through the Internet, where the only usable item is the electronic trace of the perpetrator of the act.

When crimes are committed through publicly-available networks, where anyone could obtain access to (such as WiFi hotspots in airports and city centres), identifying the offender is extremely difficult.

There are also many cases where the offender lives abroad, which require police and judicial cooperation in order to proceed with the investigation. However, such a procedure is very time-consuming and not guaranteed to succeed, due to the diversities in cyber crime legislation among different countries.

7   Conclusion

In spite of cyber crime's relatively young age, it is a fast-growing kind of crime with very distinctive features. Its intensity, combined with its transnational character and the diversity in legislation among countries has triggered the need for an international co-operation on this matter, aiming to develop a harmonised international framework for dealing with cyber crime in an effective way. One of the milestones towards this direction was the so-called Budapest Convention, which was signed by several countries, including Greece. Despite the fact that the Hellenic Police has quite recently established a special Unit for dealing with cyber crime, the legal framework needs to be revised and extended, so as to include the various aspects of cyber crime and to incorporate the provisions of the Budapest Convention, thus bringing Greece one step forward towards becoming an active member of the allied global fight against cyber crime.

References

1. Lambrinoudakis, C., Mitrou, L., Gritzalis, S., Katsikas, S.K.: Privacy enhancing technologies: a review. In: Lambrinoudakis, C., Gritzalis, S., Katsikas, S.K. (eds.) Privacy Protection and Information and Communication Technologies: Technical and Legal Issues, pp. 3–47. Papasotiriou Pubs, Athens (2010). (in Greek)

2. Parker, D.B.: Crime by Computers. Charles Scribner's Sons, New York (1976)
3. Parker, D.B.: Computer crime: criminal justice resource manual. Technical report OJP-86-C-002, U.S. Department of Justice, National Institute of Justice, Office of Justice Program, 2nd edn., August 1989
4. Karyda, M., Mitrou, L.: Internet forensics: legal and technical issues. In: 2nd International Workshop on Digital Forensics and Incident Analysis (WDFIA 2007). pp. 3–12. Samos, Greece (2007)
5. Ministerial decision, protocol no. 84280/2013, October 2013. http://static.diavgeia.gov.gr/doc/%CE%92%CE%9B%CE%9E%CE%A7%CE%A9-%CE%A7%CE%A4%CE%A3 (in Greek)
6. Clough, J.: The budapest convention on cybercrime: is harmonisation achievable in a digital world? In: 2nd International Serious and Organised Crime Conference (ISOC 2013). South Bank, Australia (2013)
7. Marler, S.L.: The convention on cyber-crime: should the United States ratify? New Engl. Law Rev. 37(1), 183–219 (2003)
8. Establishment, Organisation and Operation of the Financial Police and Cyber Crime Unit (FPCCU). Presidential Decree 9/2011, Official Government Gazette A-24, 21/02/2011 (2011) (in Greek)
9. Vlachos, V., Minou, M., Assimakoloulos, V., Toska, A.: The landscape of cybercrime in Greece. Inf. Manage. Comput. Secur. 19(2), 113–123 (2011)
10. Greek Cybercrime Center. http://www.cybercc.gr/
11. Greek Cyber Crime Center (GCC): 1st Advisory Board meeting (2013). http://kemea.gr/index.php/en/latest-news/298-gcc1st-advisoryboardmeeting
12. Annual report, Helllenic Telecommunications & Post Commission (2012)
13. Annual report, Helllenic Telecommunications & Post Commission (2010)
14. Annual report, Helllenic Telecommunications & Post Commission (2006)
15. Annual report, Helllenic Telecommunications & Post Commission (2008)

Mixed Reality Through the Internet of Things and Bitcoin: How Laws Affect Them

Anastasia Michailaki$^{(\boxtimes)}$

IHRC Research Team, Corfu, Greece
amichailaki@gmail.com

Abstract. According to Prof. Joshua Fairfield paper «Mixed reality: How the laws of virtual worlds govern everyday life», «Most scholarship to date has assumed that modern society is increasingly virtualized. It is more accurate to note that virtual data is increasingly realized as it becomes tied to realspace features and geography. Yet while virtual experiences are entering real life at an ever-increasing pace, the legal literature on virtualization technologies lags badly. The bulk of virtual worlds research focuses on the impact that real world regulatory regimes have on online spaces and communities [...] As Mixed Reality technologies merge real and cyberspace, the critical question is whether online or offline law will determine consumers' rights over property and data».

Keywords: Mixed reality · Bitcoin · Cryptocurrency · Financial crimes

1 Introduction

We drive off-road and a big rock hits our car deforming its axis. We make a stop, wait for a half an hour and then we continue our trip. The axis healed itself! It may sounds like fiction, but auto-healing and shape-memorizing materials are on their way and will be soon in the market hoping to change our everyday lives.

During his last visit in Greece, Eric Schmidt, Executive Chairman & former CEO of GOOGLE, claimed that "The good thing with science fiction is that it often prepares you for the future". The creation of a smarter world, where buildings sense and predict temperatures outside and adjust heating or air conditioning systems, where you can find driverless cars, where house equipments self-diagnose problems, seem like taken from a futuristic movie. In fact, all of these evolutionary things already exist.

The aforementioned examples help us take a glimpse on how Mixed Reality technology works and how this technology has entered our everyday life trying to make it easier and more efficient.

The law that governs virtual worlds (mostly intellectual property and licensing law), undermine the legal regimes that traditionally govern everyday life. As Prof. Fairfield points out in his article «Mixed Reality: How the Laws of virtual worlds govern everyday life», «What we once owned, we will in the future only license. What was once a simple breach of contract may now be a hacking crime or potential copyright infringement». The application of Mixed Reality technology has raised questions concerning the laws and regulations that should be applied in order to resolve all the newborn, in theory and in practice, conflicts.

© Springer International Publishing Switzerland 2014
A.B. Sideridis et al. (Eds.): E-Democracy 2013, CCIS 441, pp. 165–169, 2014.
DOI: 10.1007/978-3-319-11710-2_15

One of the most controversial proofs of the Mixed Reality technology is the appearance of cryptocurrency, like bitcoin, the digital coin that many people use for their transactions and has raised many arguments in legal theory about its legitimacy.

2   Mixed Reality and the Internet of Things

Mixed (or augmented) reality is the mixing of virtual and actual reality, the technology that augments real places, people and things with rich virtual experiences. It is the merging of the Internet with the physical world around us. The real world is becoming hyperlinked and indexed, though so far the World Wide Web has been linking together, indexing and making the human knowledge searchable [1].

As Mixed Reality took computing into the real world and made it to appear everywhere, a new term has been born, that of the «ubiquitous (ubicomp) or pervasive computing». Unlike older technologies, ubiquitous computing can occur using any device, in any location and in any format. A user interacts with the computer, which exists in many different forms: laptops, tablets, terminals and phones. When primarily concerning the objects involved, it is also known as physical computing, the Internet of Things [2].

The Internet of things concerns many everyday objects, from diapers to driverless cars, that have (or will soon have) the ability to send and receive data via Internet. During 2008, the number of devices connected to the Internet was bigger than the number of people using the Internet. According statistics, today we have over 10 billion connected objects and by 2020 this is predicted to rise to 50 billion. Wearable devices that collect data (for example how many steps we take, how well we have slept, how many calories we have consumed, our geographical location) and will be able to use them for analysis in their synced phones or tablets, pills with sensors, that will take information from our body, submit it to devices like smartphones and alert us about any medical problems, sensors that we place under our baby's mattresses to monitor their health (breathing patterns and heart rate) and alert us if anything goes wrong, are some very realistic expressions of the Internet of things [3].

Personal computer has become even more personal - it is wearable! The concept of wearable communication is not new. People express themselves with tattoos, piercings and jewellery that usually indicate something about them: their personality, their origin or their profession. But today's wearables sense and communicate much more. They are actually "embeddables", like the sensors swallowed or placed under the skin.

The personal computer is also smaller, cheaper and more powerful every day. Computing technology is becoming 100 times smaller each decade. From ENIAC, the first computer in 1956, that filled a whole room, we invented the tiny chip of a musical greeting card we can buy everywhere. A smartphone is more powerful than the PCs we used to have a decade ago. And even more, the smartphones will be soon replaced by smartwatches, which will make phone calls, be connected to the Internet or take pictures, actually everything that a smartphone or a tablet can do [4].

3 Bitcoin [5]

Bitcoin is an expression of Mixed Reality technology and it is based on cryptocurrency. The creation and transfer of bitcoin is based on an open-source cryptographic protocol that is independent of any central authority. It can be transferred through a computer or smartphone, without an intermediate financial institution. Bitcoin transactions are secured by servers called bitcoin miners, which communicate through an internet-based network and confirm transactions by adding them to a ledger, which is updated and archived periodically, using peer-to-peer filesharing technology [2].

The use of bitcoin is being accepted in trade by merchants and individuals all over the world, although it is strongly criticized by experts for its high risk of loss and its questionable legitimacy.

A Bitcoin "wallet" allows people make transactions and gives them ownership of a Bitcoin balance, so that they can send and receive bitcoins. All "wallets" can interoperate with each other, like an e-mail. There are three kinds of bitcoin "wallets":

a) the software wallet, which is installed on the computer,
b) the mobile wallet, which allows users to bring bitcoin with them in their pocket.
   They can exchange coins easily and pay in physical stores by scanning a code, and
c) the web wallet.

The experts claim that the use and the abuse of digital coins and other similar electronic ways of payment may lead to the transfer of illegal funds and help people hide their income from the IRS. It would be important to notice that the transfer of digital coins has made the European Central Bank express its worries about price stability.

On March 18th 2013, the Financial Crimes Enforcement Network (a bureau of the United States Department of the Treasury), issued a report regarding centralized and decentralized "virtual currencies" and their legal status within "money services business" (MSB) and Bank Secrecy Act regulations. It classified digital currencies and other digital payment systems such as bitcoin as "virtual currencies" because they are not legal tender under any sovereign jurisdiction. In summary, FinCEN's decision would require bitcoin exchanges where bitcoins are traded for traditional currencies to disclose large transactions and suspicious activity, comply with money laundering regulations and collect information about their customers as traditional financial institutions are required to do.

On the other hand and according to the United States District Court ruling (Securities and Exchange Commission V. Trendon T. Shavers and Bitcoin Savings and Trust, Case No.4:13-CV-416): «[...] The Court finds that the Bitcoin Savings and Trust (BTCST) investments meet the definition of investment contract and as such, are securities» [6].

In August 2013, bitcoin has been recognized by Germany, as a legal form of private currency and all sales made in bitcoin shall not be excluded from state taxes.

Since December 2013, the citizens of China are not allowed to make transactions in bitcoins. This regulation is based on the fact that bitcoin is virtual and its currency is not guaranteed by any State or Central Authority. In fact, China makes strong efforts to limit money laundry by blocking the bitcoin transactions.

In conclusion, it is too early to have a thorough and clear opinion regarding bitcoin's legitimacy and as we may see, Bitcoin and its questionable way of use will be a major topic of discussions, among theorists and courts, in the next years.

4 Laws' Application

Virtual worlds should be legally treated like the real one, as real world people create experiences, interjecting elements of reality into the virtual reality and creating Mixed Reality analogies. Although the virtual world's literature claims that they are governed by different rules and regulations than the real world, in Mixed Reality this separation does not exist [1].

Intellectual property law and e-commercial contracts should be applied in the software and firmware of the devices. Property and tort law will continue to play a major role in the real world and the everyday lives of the individuals. However, the problem occurs when Intellectual Property Law and e-commercial contracts begin to govern the real world through its virtualization. Without a developed legal theory of Mixed Reality, Intellectual Property Law and e-commercial contracts will overtake property and torts in real world. And then we will have to face the following danger: if the copyright law applies to online transactions, it will govern the actions of the Mixed Reality's users, in the real world. The law governing intangible assets was not designed to apply to the real world. The opposite will produce complicated and confusing results [1].

The tagging of real people with data, the new experience people reach through smartphones and other similar devices, raises legal objections based on the law of reputation. Everyone can easily upload information, without checking the accuracy of the statements and unfortunately these statements are available to everyone has access to a new technology device. No one is interested in the publisher's intensions, whether he tries to spread rumors or to destroy reputations. And since the Internet has become the prior means of getting information about other people – personal, family or professional, the risk of committing a tort has become really high.

Mixed Reality raises issues that are based on Property Law and that are related to top-level domain names, such as cybersqautting, twitterjacking, to GPS-located tags, mirror worlds etc. In these specific areas, Intellectual Property Laws are mostly applied and in some cases seem to be suitable. But what happens if, for example, a neighbour decides to «write» an offensive word on someone's house, which (i.e. the word) can be seen only through a suitable application, such as Google glasses? Should this case be treated as a problem of cybersqautting or twitterjacking, where Intellectual Property law is mostly applied? In that case, the rules of Property or Tort Law seem to be suitable, as it is about a personality or a privacy offence and not a case of digital land. The house is located in the real world, where no avatars live and the fact that the owner of the house cannot see the offence, but through the application, does not mean that the offence doesn't exist.

5   Conclusion

This paper points out that science fiction will soon become reality. We will have the ability to connect, for example, our tablets with our refrigerator to see if there is anything in absence and make an order to the super market, through Internet. Even better, the refrigerator will have the ability to sense if there is anything in absence and make the order by itself. In that case, what happens if the super market delivers the order and we refuse to pay, claiming that we never ordered anything and it was the refrigerator's initiative? Or, in another case, what happens if the refrigerator orders 30lts of milk, instead of 3lts we usually need as family? Which section of Law should be applied? Is this a case of Intellectual Property Law or a breach of e-commercial contract or should we apply tort law rules?

As Mixed Reality tries to merge virtual worlds with the real one, cases like the aforementioned examples will often appear. Legal theory claims so far that Intellectual Property Law and e-commercial contracts should govern the Mixed Reality technology as well, besides the virtual worlds and the intangible assets. This would be a problematic theory, as Mixed Reality appears in the real world, with real people using it. Legal theory should also take into consideration that Mixed Reality should be governed by tort or privacy law, or even financial law as cases like bitcoin.

References

1. Fairfield, J.: Mixed reality: how the laws of virtual worlds govern everyday life. Berkeley Technol. Law J. **27**, 55 (2012)
2. http://en.wikipedia.org. Accessed: 29 August–26 October 2013
3. Marr, B.: What The Heck is... The Internet of Things? LinkedIn (2013). Accessed: 23 October 2013
4. Evans, D.: The Future of Wearable Technology: Smaller, Cheaper, Faster, and Truly Personal Computing. LinkedIn. Accessed: 24 October 2013
5. http://bitcoin.org. Accessed: 28 October 2013
6. http://www.lawnet.gr. Accessed: 08 August–06 December 2013

Open Access to Archeological Data and the Greek Law

Maria Sitara[✉] and Eleni Vouligea[✉]

Ministry of Culture and Sports, 8th Ephorate of Prehistorical
and Classical Antiquities, Armeni Vraila Street 1A, 49100 Corfu, Greece
{ll2sita,ll2voul}@ionio.gr

Abstract. The economic and technological developments of the last decades have promoted new perceptions of the importance and role of culture in an ever-changing society. A key sector, the "backbone" of culture, is archaeology. Over almost a decade, actions and programs implemented by the Ministry of Culture, aim to promote open access to archaeological information.

Is, though, the archaeological material, digitized or not, truly accessible to the public or even to the field researchers? This paper will explain the traits and meaning of the archaeological material, as well as the existing legal situation in Greece on access to that material, and the regulation in countries with different cultural and institutional background. Actions in recent years in Greece on the management of archaeological data will be described. The paper will also include proposals in order to disengage the existing rigidities of the system.

Keywords: Open access · Archaeological data · Freedom of information · Digitized archaeological databases

1 Introduction

The economic and technological developments of the last decades have promoted new perceptions of the importance and role of culture in an ever-changing society, in which the diffusion of information takes one of the leading positions among the collaborators of the economic, social and cultural development of a nation.

A key sector, «the backbone» of culture, is archaeology. In the modern era, in which people participate in globalization and societies cease to be monolingual, monocultural, monophyletic, the educational role of archaeology is further extended. In this context, over almost a decade, the Archaeological Services and the Museums supervised by the Ministry of Culture have implemented actions and programs in an attempt to promote open access to archaeological information, as well as to attract the general public. Large databases comprise digitized archaeological data, invaluable for research.

Maria Sitara and Eleni Vouligea: Archaeologist, Postgraduate student at Ionian University, Department of Archives, Library Science & Museum Studies, Member of the IHRC research team (Information: History, Regulation, Culture).

© Springer International Publishing Switzerland 2014
A.B. Sideridis et al. (Eds.): E-Democracy 2013, CCIS 441, pp. 170–179, 2014.
DOI: 10.1007/978-3-319-11710-2_16

Is, though, the archaeological material, digitized or not, truly accessible to the public or even to the field researchers? Or rather, does the world of archaeology cultivate even today a spirit of rigid conservatism, confirming that access to data and knowledge is accessible only to a chosen few? Tradition would stand for closure: The first museums were created from academic collections and the treasuries of the kings. Invited-only visitors necessarily had the same level of knowledge and appreciation of the collections as the collectors themselves, something that also served to separate the educated (possible visitors) from the uneducated (non-visitors). It seems that especially in the world of archaeology today, in Greece, the rule is still, plainly one: closure.

Today's archaeology is an interdisciplinary field, that combines the study of patterns of human behaviour (eating habits, installations, economy, etc.) with the study of artefacts and other evidence, in order to outline an holistic view of the past.

2 Definitions

In an attempt to define the meaning of archaeological data or plainly material, one might say that it consists of the following main categories:

- First of all the excavational evidence itself, such as:

  I. The artefacts, for example tools, weapons, pottery, statues, household items, coins, and other objects.
  II. The non-movable objects, meaning the architectural remains, such as fortifications, walls, pillars, sanctuaries and in general buildings that cannot be detached from the ground.
  III. In the same category we include the archaeological diary, which records on a daily basis all the stages of the excavation, the separate catalogues that complete the material with geospatial data and further information, and of course the photographs. We should also have in mind that an excavation remains incomplete without the topographic mapping and archaeological design.

- The second category, that follows the completion of the field survey, is the documentation:

  I. It includes mainly the recording of the findings in databases, the thorough study that aims at the dating of the material, and ultimately the transportation and storage of the material in approved storage areas.
  II. The excavation report that describes the methodology which was used to conduct the excavation and presents the first results.
  III. And finally, the publication of the results of the archaeological research or even the study of individual findings in an official scientific journal.

- The third and final category includes the administrative documents and correspondence, which link a property with the corresponding excavation, from the moment the first archaeological traces appear, during the trial digs, up to the reburial or maintenance of the findings, upon decision of the local council of the Regional Committees or the Central Archaeological Council.

3   The Legal Framework

The question that occurs is who can really have access to all this material and under what circumstances? The law is clear when it comes to scientific researchers, but totally vague in the case of citizens. But even in the case of researchers is the material truly accessible for the advancement of research?

We will refer mainly to *Law 3028/2002*, and in particular *Article 39* [1], which adverts to the publication of the results of excavations and other archaeological research and essentially follows the dictates of UNESCO [2]. After the legislator defines the meaning of archaeological excavation, he separates it into three major categories:

- The *systematic or research excavations* carried out by the Ephorates of the Central or Regional Departments of the Ministry of Culture, by scientific educational institutions of the country specialized in the field of archaeological or palaeontological research or by foreign archaeological missions or schools established in Greece, which can last several years.
- The *exploratory excavations*, with limited duration, such as field research and surveys for the detection of new sites.
- The *rescue excavations*, which are carried out in order to rescue monuments revealed by accident, or during building or other works of development, whether public or private, or due to natural phenomenon, or illegal excavations. They constitute the vast majority of modern excavations, which even before the relevant regulation of the 3028/2002 law, were carried out by the Ephorates, in order to facilitate stakeholders [3]. Personnel were financed from these stakeholders, since the available financial resources of many Ephorates did not allow the realization of excavations, a practice which, however, still applies [4].

For each type of excavation the specified qualifications of the director of a systematic excavation, or the conductor of the rescue excavation were given, but without further details regarding the distinction between the director (a supervisor or even the head of the Ephorate?) and the conductor. In the first case, the archaeologist should have at least five years of experience in excavations, after obtaining his/her degree, and two synthetic scientific publications. In the second case, the conductor must have at least three years of experience in excavations, without ever having violated any deadlines concerning annual scientific reports on previous excavations that he/she has conducted. It must be noted that the Presidential Decree of 1927 [5, 6] only mentions that the director of an excavation must have an assistant of a lower grade or if there's none with the required qualifications a student of philosophy or archaeology.

The pre-existing legislation [6–8] did not set precise time limits within which the initial presentation or the final publication of the results of the excavations should be published, which resulted in a multiplicity of unpublished excavations and a subsequent practice of binding the unpublished archaeological material [3, 9].

This administrative practice of binding the unpublished archaeological material is not only illegal, but also in contrast to the Constitution [10], specifically to Article 16 § 1, because it impermissibly restricts the individual freedom of research, including the freedom of choice regarding the subject of research, and impairs the development and promotion of archaeological research and science in general, which is the obligation of the State. Also, it is contrary to Article 5A, since it restricts the right of information and the participation of all citizens in the Information Society. It even recommends violation of Greece's obligations under the Article 4 § 1 of the European Convention of London on the Protection of the Archaeological Heritage [11], to take all practical steps in order to disseminate in a quick and valid way information about the archaeological excavations and findings through scientific publications.

Perhaps the binding of the study and publication of archaeological material from the director of the excavation for a reasonable period of time is based on a kind of customary law and justified not merely as a reward of his/her labour, but also because they are de facto considered to be the most appropriate to interpret the findings.

So, according to Law 3028/2002 [1, 12]:

1. The directors of systematic excavations or other archaeological research and the conductors of rescue excavations are required to publish the results of their research within the time limits set out below, during which they obtain the exclusive right of publication.
2. The directors or conductors must submit to the Ephorates annual scientific reports, the latest in April of every following year, for publication in the journal or online registration.
3. The directors of a systematic excavation shall submit an initial presentation for publication within two (2) years from the commencement of the excavation, which includes also a catalogue of mobile findings and plans of the architectural remains, and a final publication within five (5) years after the completion of the excavation. For excavations with long duration they are also obliged to submit a presentation regarding the course of the excavation every two (2) years, beginning from the completion date of the initial presentation, while the final publication with all the contributions of the members of the research team shall be submitted within five years from its completion.
4. The conductors of a rescue excavation are required to submit a final report, a catalogue of the findings, photographs and plans within nine (9) months from its completion. If they do not wish to publish the results of the excavation they shall declare it in writing, in order for the Ephorate to assign it to someone else. Otherwise, the conductor is required to submit, within six (6) years from the completion of the excavation the final publication, mentioning of course all the contributions of the members of the research team.
5. The conductor of an exploratory or other archaeological research must submit a final publication within two (2) years from its completion.
6. Findings arising during excavation or other field research may constitute a subject for special publications, after authorization from the person who has the exclusive right, within five (5) years from the granting of the license, if it concerns part of the excavation, and within two (2) years, if it concerns the publication of an individual finding.
7. The time limits of the preceding paragraphs are doubled when it comes to underwater archaeological investigations.

8. If the deadline for submission of the final publication of paragraphs 3, 4, 5 and 7 expires, then the exclusive right to publish the results of the excavation ceases. The Ephorate and in general all parties conducting excavations or other archaeological research must facilitate the access to the findings and the available documentation to all interested researchers, if there is no risk of imminent damage.
9. The Minister of Culture regulates issues concerning the submission and publication of studies mentioned in this Article, as well as any other necessary details for its implementation, and also issues concerning the electronic registration of the annual scientific reports or other data.

In 2003 six Archaeological Institutes were established under the Presidential Decree 191/2003 [13] by the Ministry of Culture, each covering an administrative region, i.e. Macedonia - Thrace, Epirus, Thessaly, the Aegean, Crete and the Peloponnese, whose activity "refers to the study and publication of material from excavations already completed or even in progress and for which there is no declaration of interest under the provisions of Law 3028/2002".

Specifically, the Archaeological Institutes are composed of:

1. The research Department, which covers the study and publication of material from old excavations, the organization of programs for creating corpora of monuments, the cooperation with scientific institutions to take up scientific - research programs, the pursuit of European research programs, the organization and operation of the library.
2. The Support Research Department, which covers the maintenance and restoration of the findings from old excavations, as well as their mapping, photography and design.
3. The Department of Administrative and Financial Support.

What do we know regarding the work of these institutes so far? It's difficult to say, since the information on their work is inadequate, as far as it concerns the general public or only known in archaeological circles.

These Institutes, though, can become an opportunity for Greek Archaeology, since their main concern is research, while they complement the work of Ephorates dealing with findings from old excavations, which otherwise would have remained forgotten [14].

Regarding the legal framework governing the archaeological research in Member States of the European Union, we find that most of them are based on the directives of UNESCO and ICOMOS [15]. In particular, Article 7 states that Member States should ensure the provision of accessible reports/files throughout the course of the research (including diagnostic research, monitoring techniques, methods of management, preventive maintenance and repair, etc.). These documents should be kept in permanent records (such as National Libraries), and also be published as soon as possible. Article 9 supplements the excavator's/researcher's obligation to the scientific community and society in general, regarding the validity of the analysis and information provided to the public, based on their data. These instructions are complemented by the directives of various international associations of archaeologists, such as the European Association of Archaeologists [16], who in Article 7 of their code of practice add that the reports should be published electronically as well, within a period of six months. Also the copyright of first publication is granted to the excavator for ten years, during which he should provide information about the material in colleagues upon request, always with the provision that the rights of the first publication are not affected. Over the period of 10 years the material is accessible and available to anyone for analysis and publication. Finally, written consent is required for the use of the material. Also in a possible publication the source should be referred. The Ministry for the Environment, Cultural Heritage and Local Government of Ireland sets narrower time limits [17], according to which the researcher must submit an initial report within four weeks after the completion of the excavation and the final publication within 12 months. Also a synthetic publication should be submitted to the Archaeological Chronicles for the year during which the excavation took place. Finally, we shall refer to the Society for American Archaeology [18], which in its guidelines, and specifically in Article 6, calls for researchers to present the results of their research in an accessible form to as wide a range of interested publics as possible, paying particular attention to the content they publish and its validity. Both publications and reports, as well as other forms of documentation should be kept in a permanent and safe location.

4 Programs and Actions by the Greek Ministry of Culture

In order for the current Ministry of Culture and Sports to follow the contemporary dictates of globalization that promote diffusion of information, and at the same time to reach out and attract the general public, it has developed actions and programs, many of which, however, are still in progress, not allowing us to come to a final evaluation.

One of the most essential actions is the so called *"Information Society"*, a project co-funded by the E.U. [19], which includes three categories:

1. Actions of digitization, promotion and enhancement of cultural assets.
2. Actions of infrastructure, which are implemented by the Hellenic Cultural Organization (HCO), such as digital exhibition of the history of the ancient Olympic Games, portable systems of personal information for museum visitors, production of 15 digital publications, expansion and development of the node ULYSSES, e-commerce infrastructure for the promotion of cultural products and services by Greek cultural organizations on internet.
3. Private projects of digitization and promotion of their cultural inventory.

It should be noted that by 2007 over 200 websites were developed, with digital cultural content from hundreds of thousands of digitized documents, mainly two-dimensional images, but also video, audio, film, three-dimensional objects and monuments.

One of the most important actions is the project *"Digitization and Digital Documentation of the Ministry of Culture Monuments' Collections"*, whose ultimate goal is the implementation of the National Web of Cultural Knowledge, that will link and include all the cultural content of the country and at the same time provide to all citizens the possibility of information, education, knowledge transmission, as well as digital services [20].

As a supplement to this action the *"Digital Convergence"* was created. It is essentially an extension of the already mentioned programs, converting the entire Greek cultural resources in digital form, with the possibility of unified access to all citizens to all the cultural sites in the country, providing information, education, knowledge transmission and digital services [21].

The Ministry of Culture is actively involved in the project *EUROPEANA* [22] that is operating since 2008 and constitutes a portal of open access to over 10 million digitized cultural evidence from across Europe, and is available in all E.U. languages. Initially the Ministry of Culture joined with the project *MICHAEL* (Multilingual Inventory of Cultural Heritage in Europe), which is a directory of digital collections of cultural assets in the country, presenting the first digital collections of cultural institutions in Greece, as well as websites or electronic versions (CD/DVD) from where users can access the digital material [23]. Afterwards follows the project *ATHENA*, which aims to collect the cultural content of European museums and Archives, in order to integrate them into the European Digital Library of EUROPEANA [24]. The collected data, after being correlated and homogenized by a single metadata format, will be made available (in EUROPEANA) through the widespread standard OAI-PMH (Open Archive Initiative – Protocol for Metadata Harvesting), in order to ensure communication and cooperation between the various sources. The ATHENA project will also create a set of software, suggestions and recommended practices, focusing on issues of multilingualism and semantics, metadata and thesauri, on data structures, but also on issues of copyright, for use by the Museums and Archives.

The Ministry of Culture participates in *Linked Heritage* [25], a European project, whose main objectives are:

- The contribution of large amounts of new content to EUROPEANA, from both public and private sector.
- The improvement of quality of the content in terms of metadata, reuse and uniqueness.
- The improvement of search, retrieval and use of the content of EUROPEANA.

The consortium includes representatives from all basic stakeholder groups from 20 E.U. countries, as well as Israel and Russia.

The Ministry of Culture has also been included in the program *"L.E.M. - The Learning Museum"*, which is implemented with co-financing from the European Commission (Lifelong Learning Programme Grundtvig 2010–2013) and aims to create a European network of cooperation and exchange of expertise in the field of Lifelong Learning in Museums [26]. The project is implemented with the participation of 22 partners from 17 European countries and in collaboration with the University of Denver. The main tasks include the establishment and operation of five thematic Working Groups (New trends in Museums in the 21st century, Museum and aging population, Polls, Ways of learning and museum management, The museum as a place of learning, The Museum and Intercultural Dialogue), as well as the production and publication of an equal number of studies, organization of international conferences, the creation of a Portal and the design and implementation of a pilot project of labour mobility in museums. Regarding the Portal, it will be a central source of information to all interested parties on current developments in Europe in the field of lifelong learning in museums, gathering articles, studies, book reviews, news about events, conferences etc.

One of the most important programs carried out by the Directorate of the National Archive of Monuments and Publications in collaboration with the Institute of Computer Science of the Foundation for Research and Technology under the INTERREG II, is the *"Polemon"* [27]. It has the ability to manage a very wide range of information about each monument that comes from the intersection of data for both movable and immovable monuments, not only in archival level but also on maps. It includes a general model of cultural data and a production of specialized data models for thematic scientific documentation of the main categories of items of the collections and their associations (materials, techniques, artists, venues, themes). This model is compatible with, or even exceeds, the data model of the Documentation Committee of the International Council of Museums (CIDOC/ICOM). It must be noted that since October 1999, when the program first started to operate at the 25th Ephorate of Prehistorical and Classical Antiquities, until June 2000, a sufficient number of records of protected monuments and sites was completed. Alongside to Polemon, the Directorate processes an independent program called *"Polydeukis"*, which is a Thesaurus of names of monuments with the purpose of operating a system nationwide without contradictions or misunderstandings as to the used terminology.

Finally, we mustn't fail to mention the so-called *"Archaeological Cadastre"*, which will be the first single and systematic recording of real estate, Regional Protection of Cultural Interest (Archaeological Sites, Protection Zones I and II, Historical Places, Regional Zones and Surroundings Monuments etc.) and data on immovable monuments [28]. It includes the development of an Integrated Information System, which will incorporate descriptive and geospatial data, while make extensive digitization of archival material and spatial localization by integrating descriptive and geospatial data in the information system. One of the most important features of the system is the provision of electronic services to all citizens and interested parties of the public sector, through the Portal. Unfortunately in this case also the work is progressing very slowly, due to the lack of scientific staff that would supply the system with the required information.

5 Conclusions

After presenting in a very concise way the programs in which the Ministry of Culture participates, we should emphasize that all these efforts relate mostly to material and data already published and known to the general public, leaving once again in the dark the archaeological wealth that is piled up in the warehouses of the Ephorates and Museums. This comes as a result of the prevailing mindset of the majority of archaeologists who tend to appropriate the archaeological findings. The denial of granting the material to young researchers in order to study and publish is hampering the progress and development of scientific research.

How can we change this situation? Starting with the faithful implementation of the existing law, which entitles researchers to claim unpublished material, over the allotted time of 5 years. The Ephorates in collaboration with Universities could exploit the unrecorded and unpublished archaeological material which is stacked in warehouses, to offer learning opportunities to students or even allowing the writing of dissertations and theses. But in order for all this to be carried out, and especially to make the material accessible to everyone, universally shared databases should be developed and implemented, as for example the CIDOC Conceptual Reference Model, which is a semantic model that combines information material from museums, archives and libraries, which will record all the data and metadata of the material. In this case of course, there is always the imminent danger of the material being looted without permission, so the appropriate legal framework should be developed in order to protect the Ephorates from such risks.

References

1. Law 3028/2002: Protection of Antiquities and Cultural Heritage in general. Government's Gazette A' 153/ (2002) (in Greek)
2. United Nations Educational, Scientific and Cultural Organisation: Records of The General Conference, Ninth Session, New Delhi (1956)
3. Voudouri, D.: State and Museums: The Institutional Framework of Archaeological Museums. Sakkoulas AE, Athens (2003). (in Greek)
4. Papapetropoulos, D.: Law 3028/2002 on the Protection of Antiquities and of Cultural Heritage in General. Sakkoulas AE, Athens/Thessaloniki (2006). Text – Comments – Interpretation
5. Presidential Decree 1927: Means of implementation of archaeological excavations. Government's Gazette 6/A'/ (1928) (in Greek)
6. Pantos, A.P.: Encoding Legislation on Cultural Heritage. By Topics A, Greek Legislation. Directorate of the National Archive of Monuments and Publications, Athens (2001). (in Greek)
7. Law 5351/1932: On the consolidation of the provisions of the law 5351, as well as on the relevant enforced provisions of the Laws 2646, 2447, 491, 4823 and the Legislative Decree of the 12/16th June of 1926 to a single text law, bearing the number 5351 and the title «About Antiquities». Government's Gazette 275/A'/ (1932) (in Greek)
8. Presidential Decree 99/1992: Design and execution of archaeological projects in general. Government's Gazette A'46 (1992) (in Greek)
9. Maniatis, A.: Archaeological Field Surveys (2008). http://www.nomosphysis.org.gr/articles.php?artid=3561&lang=1&catpid=1 (in Greek)
10. The Constitution of Greece. (1975/1986/2001/2008) (in Greek)
11. Law 1127/1981: European Convention on the Protection of the Archaeological Heritage. Government's Gazette 32/A/ (1981) (in Greek)
12. Pantos, A.P.: The Institutional Framework of Excavations in Greece from the 20th to the 21st century. http://anaskamma.files.wordpress.com/2013/06/06_pantos.pdf (in Greek)
13. Presidential Decree 191/2003: The Organization of the Ministry of Culture. Government's Gazette 146/A/ (2003) (in Greek)
14. In Antis, About Archaeology....and not only.: Archaeological Institutions: Present and Future. http://inantis.blogspot.gr/2009/01/blog-post.html (in Greek)
15. International Council on Monuments and Sites.: Ethical Commitment Statement for ICOMOS Members. http://www.usicomos.org/content/ethical-commitment-statement-icomos-members

16. European Association of Archaeologists: The E.A.A. Code of Practice (1997, 2009). http://www.e-a-a.org/EAA_Code_of_Practice.pdf
17. National Monuments Service.: Code of Practice between the Department of the Environment, Heritage and Local Government and the Irish Concrete Federation (2009). http://www.archaeology.ie/media/archeologyie/PDFS/FileDownload,329,en.pdf
18. Society For American Archaeology.: Principles of Archaeological ethics (1996). http://www.saa.org/AbouttheSociety/PrinciplesofArchaeologicalEthics/tabid/203/Default.aspx
19. Hellenic Ministry of Culture and Sports.: Actions by the Ministry of Culture and Sports under the Operational Program "Information Society" of the Third Community Support Framework. http://www.yppo.gr/4/g411.jsp
20. Hellenic Ministry of Culture and Sports.: Actions by the Ministry of Culture and Sports under the European Union. http://www.yppo.gr/4/g413.jsp
21. Hellenic Ministry of Culture and Sports.: Actions by the Ministry of Culture and Sports under the program "Digital Convergence" of the Fourth Community Support Framework. http://www.yppo.gr/4/g412.jsp
22. EUROPEANA. http://www.europeana.eu/portal/
23. Hellenic Ministry of Culture and Sports.: MICHAEL Plus (Multilingual Inventory of Cultural Heritage in Europe). http://www.yppo.gr/5/g5151.jsp?obj_id=18590
24. Hellenic Ministry of Culture and Sports.: ATHENA: Access to Cultural Heritage Networks across Europe. http://www.yppo.gr/5/g5151.jsp?obj_id=29730
25. Hellenic Ministry of Culture and Sports.: Linked Heritage. http://www.yppo.gr/5/g5151.jsp?obj_id=54453
26. Hellenic Ministry of Culture and Sports.: L.E.M. - The Learning Museum. http://www.yppo.gr/5/g5151.jsp?obj_id=45692
27. Hellenic Ministry of Culture and Sports.: Polemon: Program of Electronic Recordings of the Monuments. http://www.yppo.gr/5/g5151.jsp?obj_id=611
28. Hellenic Ministry of Culture and Sports.: Archaeological Cadastre, http://www.yppo.gr/5/g5151.jsp?obj_id=47752

e-Governance II

Evolution Towards Mobile Government:
The Greek and the Czech Cases

Constantina Costopoulou[1]([⊠]) and Martin Molhanec[2]

[1] Informatics Laboratory, Department of Agricultural Economics
and Rural Development, Agricultural University of Athens, Athens, Greece
tina@aua.gr
[2] Department of e-Technology, Czech Technical University in Prague,
Prague, Czech Republic
molhanec@fel.cvut.cz

Abstract. The velocity in development of mobile and wireless technologies has enabled the transformation from electronic government to mobile government for accomplishing better government. The aim of this research is primarily, to depict the state of the art of mobile government in Greece and in the Czech Republic. These European countries were selected because they have similar population size, have comparable living standards and show a high degree of mobile phone penetration. Moreover, the study describes a common schema for developing mobile government apps. The case of an agricultural mobile app is discussed. Next, a blog for promoting mobile government apps between the two countries is presented. The findings of this study provide guidance to citizens in identifying easily mobile government apps, and new insights for Greek and Czech public agencies for finding and sharing resources and capabilities though a mobile government community.

Keywords: e-Government · m-Government · Mobile apps

1 Introduction

Public administrations throughout the world have been embarking on electronic government (e-government) endeavors for about two decades. E-Government initiatives and projects of varying scope and complexity have been implemented at central and local governments. Even though e-government adoptions are widespread, results have been mixed. A number of e-government endeavors have failed to achieve their objectives such as extensive adoption by citizens. The increasing penetration of mobile communication devices in the world population has created new challenges for e-government. The recent technological developments permit stable Internet access via mobile communication devices such as mobile phones, smart phones, personal digital assistants (PDAs) or tablets. The mobile subscriptions have seen a remarkable growth in the last ten years. There are 6.8 billion mobile subscriptions all over the world in 2013 that is tantamount to 96 % of the world population [1]. The mobile phone has become a necessary tool for communication, recreation, purchasing business applications, gaming, photography, e-mail and Internet access [2]. Furthermore, the mobile

© Springer International Publishing Switzerland 2014
A.B. Sideridis et al. (Eds.): E-Democracy 2013, CCIS 441, pp. 183–191, 2014.
DOI: 10.1007/978-3-319-11710-2_17

phone has also become an interesting channel for providing and accessing e-government services.

Whereas e-government is the utilization of information and communication technologies (ICT) to improve the efficiency of the government services that are provided to citizens, employees, businesses and agencies [3], mobile government (m-government) regards the use of mobile and wireless communication technologies within government administration and its delivery of information and services to citizens and businesses. M-government can be considered as an extension of e-government to mobile platforms. In [4] m-government is defined as "the strategy and its implementation involving the use of all types of wireless and mobile technology, services, applications and devices for improving benefits to the parties involved in e-government comprising dwellers, enterprises and all government units". According to [5], m-government can be considered as an area of practice to improve the effectiveness and efficiency of public services and the responsiveness of government. Nowadays, governments around the world are adopting or investigating m-government solutions to increase the efficiency and effectiveness of public service as well as users' participation. The emergence of mobile and wireless technologies has enabled the government to transform from e-government to m-government. However the way to implement successfully m-government services is unclear [6].

Likewise e-government, there are four primary delivery models of m-government: government-to-citizens (mG2C), government-to-government (mG2G), government-to-business (G2B) and government-to-employees (mG2E) [7, 8]. Up to now, most of the mobile services follow the mG2C delivery model. The mG2C services fall into four categories [8]:

- push services: This category involves distributing information to citizens without any interactions. Examples of this category are mainly comprised of pushing information through SMS or making it available on a Web.
- interactive services: In this category, citizens can send questions, problems, or service requests to specific public agencies and participate in dialogue with governments. They also can access applications and forms. The communication becomes one to one, rather than one to many.
- transactional services: This category refers to two-way interactions between citizens and the government. Citizens can complete their transactions with public agencies electronically and at their convenience.
- governance and citizen engagement: This category contains services such as elections and voting for achieving citizen engagement.

The structure of the paper is as follows: Sect. 2 presents a brief overview of the recent situation of e-government and m-government mG2C services in Greece and in the Czech Republic. Section 3 presents a common schema for developing m-government apps in both countries. Section 4 describes the design of an agricultural m-government apps, the subsidy app. Section 5 presents the development of a blog for promoting m-government apps for citizens and for enhancing the collaboration and sharing of experience among public agencies in Greece and in the Czech Republic. Finally, some conclusions are given.

2 M-government in Greece and in the Czech Republic

The Czech Republic and Greece have similar population size, have comparable living standards and show a high degree of mobile phone penetration (Table 1). The number of mobile subscriptions in Greece was 5.9 million in 2000 and 13.3 million in 2012, and in the Czech Republic it was 4.3 million and 12.9 million, respectively. Also, in 2012 the figure of mobile subscriptions per 100 dwellers was 116.94 % and 122.79 % in Greece and in the Czech Republic, respectively [9]. The mobile penetration rate in Greece rose to 140.5 % in 2012. On the other hand, Greece with low level of structural reforms, very low productivity growth and a relatively very low level of competitiveness, is hit by the global financial crisis. However, the origin of the Greek crisis lies in the government sector. In this direction e-government and m-government initiatives can speed up the administrative reformation of the public sector. The mobile penetration rate in the Czech Republic reached 138 % in 2011. In contrast to Greece, the Czech Republic is one of the emerging democracies in Central and Eastern Europe after 1989 year. As such, it is one of the most prosperous and stable of the post-Communist states of Central and Eastern Europe [10]. In Czech Republic, mobile phones have entered in 95 % of the 10 million people, one of the highest in Europe and probably in the world. Since the penetration of mobile technology is very high, m-government apps can be more helpful and quick. Several m-government apps are launched and tested for informing citizens about crisis and natural disasters. Nevertheless, e-government services are still at very low level due to an unclear government strategy, corruption, as well as frequent changes of government.

Table 1. Country profile: Greek and Czech data.

Basic data	Greece	Czech Republic
Population	11,290,067	10,505,445
GDP per Capital	79	80
Broadband connection in households	51 %	68 %
Broadband connection in enterprises	80 %	91 %
Unemployment rate	27 %	7,5 %

According to an international survey in 2012, the Czech public administration authorities are the best prepared in Europe for the implementation of the IPv6 Internet protocol. The Czech Ministry of the Interior inaugurated in 2012, the new Public Administration Portal (www.portal.gov.cz), a single electronic gateway to the Czech authorities' information and services. It merged three different portals (Public Administration portal; portal of access to data boxes; repository of public authorities) into one. The objective of this portal is to provide a one stop shop for people and organizations to obtain information on, and communicate directly with, the Czech authorities.

M-government projects, in Czech Republic, are also initiated locally. For example, certain city districts or municipalities provide their citizens with information via SMS. A citizen is alerted in advance of the upcoming block cleaning of streets, traffic closures and other events that would not like to miss. Other alerts regard leisure information on interesting cultural, sporting and social events. One of the most successful projects is the provision of timetables of urban and intercity transport. The system not only provides information on all lines of all carriers, but also is able to find the best connection between the two places. This service is not only web based but there are also clients for mobile devices and tablets. With regards to increased share of corruption not only in government, but also at the municipal level, many municipalities today establishes the so-called transparent accounts, where every citizen can see how the municipality spends a local budget.

On the other hand, a number of large public projects were unsuccessful. For instance, the sKarta, a social card project, forced all recipients of social security benefits, unemployment benefits and disability benefits employ one special card account of Česká spořitelna (Czech Savings Bank). But the project was criticized and eventually suspended. As a result, Česká spořitelna asks almost 204 million Czech crowns for the cancellation of the project from the state. The situation is similar with the so-called IZIP project of web based health books. General Health Insurance Company on it spent in the course of ten years about 1.8 billion Czech crowns. Moreover, 49 % of the shares are held by unknown Swiss company at present and therefore General Health Insurance Company is not empowered to manage the project. These two cases are probably typical examples of corruption and tunneling of public finances.

In Greece, the ERMIS portal is attempting the modernization of the public administration providing electronic services to citizens. This portal operates as a one stop shop service provider regarding the transactions with the Greek public administration [11]. It supplies full-field briefing in citizens and businesses with regard to all their transactions with the public administration (natural or electronic), as well as selected services of electronic transactions. According to their subject the ERMIS services are categorized in the following groups: city planning and land registry; civilization and free time; education and research; environment and natural resources; finance and economy; health and social care; information and communication; international affairs and European union; justice, state and public administration; people, communities and way of living; public order and defense; services for companies; transportation means, trips and tourism; and, work, insurance and pension.

3   A Mobile Apps Framework

For the development of mobile apps, a set of capabilities, tools, and resources should be put together to enable mobile apps to be successfully designed, developed, and implemented. In literature several theoretical frameworks has been proposed on this subject such as [12]. According to these, for the successful deployment of apps two main questions should be initially answered, namely whether the app is a good candidate for mobile development and how the app should be delivered. In specific, questions like the following should be also answered: (a) Which is the purpose of the app? (b) Which target audience will use the app? (c) Which devices do the users have? (d) What data will be sent to the device? (e) What are the security requirements for this data? (f) What is the supporting infrastructure for security requirements? (g) What does that mean to the type of application to develop? (i) Who will test the application and how? In addition, for deploying mG2C services, two stages can be identified. The first stage is to provide what is already available in a computer-based application through mobile devices and the second one is to provide those services and applications, which are only possible through wireless and mobile infrastructure.

Given that the development of m-government apps is still immature in both countries, a common scheme has been adopted for deploying m-government apps (Fig. 1). The proposed scheme has four layers, namely the network operator, the access layer, the service enablement layer and the application layer [13]. The operator network is the mobile network that might also has fixed online and cable networks. The access layer regards access technologies, from mobile standards such as EV-DO LTE, 802.11x, WCDMA, and WPAN to fixed-access networks. The service enablement layer has the features enabled by the network such as location, presence, context-awareness, security, payment, authentication, banking, messaging, browsing, billing video and music streaming etc. It includes the most fundamental capabilities that help implement applications modules. Using the aforementioned features, operators and/or service suppliers can then make application modules that can either be operator-specific or can run autonomously. These modules include mobile health, mobile education, mobile entertainment, mobile tourism, mobile agriculture etc. In the following section special emphasis is given to mobile agriculture apps since the agricultural business sector is of significant importance for Greece and Czech.

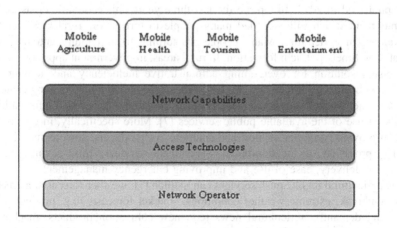

Fig. 1. A scheme for developing m-government apps.

4   Mobile Government Apps in Agriculture

With the development of mobile and wireless technologies, every business sector is changing. The agricultural business sector has the same trend at this time. Nowadays, digital technology and agricultural expertise and knowledge have been merged, thus an assortment of mobile apps according to the farmers' needs has been evolved. There are many agriculture mobile apps on crop prices, weather conditions, inventory levels and innovative farming techniques and machinery. In the case of Australia some tokens incorporate product marketing, managing livestock, managing water, managing irrigation, remote performing of roles such as unloading grain, monitoring sensors in crops, mapping yield, performing as substitute tools (such as spirit levels), calculating area, mapping soil types etc. [14]. However apps specifically for agriculture are still limited. Up to now, the most dominant app is the app related to weather [14]. Other apps are related to record keeping and accessing agricultural news and technical information. The agriculture mobile apps have been classified into six broad categories: agriculture management information apps; agriculture information resource apps; agriculture calculator apps; agriculture news apps, weather apps and m-government apps [15]. However, little interest has been given to m-government apps development by agricultural public agencies.

During periods of economical crisis, a bend towards sectors of primary production is observed and especially towards agricultural sector, as via provisions output first and foremost the survival of humans is reassured, but also the income production. Especially for Greece the rural sector and the sector of provisions alteration have great importance for the return of the country into a viable development. According to researches (e.g. "Greece in 10 years from now" report) in the endeavor of Greece for the recovery of the economy, an important role will play agriculture. Agriculture has a dominant role in the Greek economy. However, the contribution of agriculture to the Greek GDP has shrunk to 4.6 % of GDP from 10 % twenty years ago, while in the Czech Republic it is reported at 2.4 % of GDP in 2010, according to a World Bank report published in 2012. In Greece the last three years, this economic crisis and the unemployment which followed, led many people to turn to the rural areas for their involvement in agriculture. Many people are turning to agriculture and they need accurate and timely public information. In rural areas, m-government apps appear to be a promising solution for overcoming administrative inefficiency and helping rural citizens and businesses. Since they are far off the decision and policy making centers, it is often neither possible nor convenient to travel for gaining the needed information or for making use of the available public services [7]. More specifically, m-government apps can provide particular support and solutions for producers, such as mobility and ubiquity, provision of location-based government services, time saving, on-time information delivery, ease of use and improving emergency management.

The agricultural mG2C push services can include [7]: weather forecasts; alerts (e.g. disease outbreak, extreme weather conditions); market forecasts (e.g. product prices, supply and demand); agricultural news (e.g. new cultivation products, machinery); agricultural policy (e.g. laws and regulations); funding opportunities (e.g. for purchasing equipment); expert consulting (e.g. regarding cultivation techniques, marketing of products, new production standards); and notifications (e.g. for deadlines, resumption of certificates, subjection of documents, new cultivation products or techniques, confirmations of significant dates, farmer union issues, events). The mG2C interaction services can contain: requests (e.g. license renewal); remote-diagnosis (e.g. plant and animal diseases); calculations (e.g. for subsidy or indemnification); employment market (e.g. job offer and demand in particular area); financial dealings (e.g. loan payments); search engine (e.g. for databases, locating agencies in the surrounding area); polls;

forums; messages to public agencies (e.g. agricultural accident reports, events, inter-rogation, complaints, comments, interventions, opinion stating).

The main objective is to help public agricultural agencies to deploy m-government apps [13]. The example of a pilot m-government app, the subsidy app is discussed. It is a simple application but is very important to the farmers. This app has four main components, namely mobile client, mobile agriculture application server, user authentication database and the subsidy database. The proposed system relies on interactive voice response (IVR) technology. The functionality of the app is as follows: Firstly, the farmer (user) requests information if he/she is eligible for a subsidy via the mobile app or the mobile web site. Second, though the carrier network the request goes to the application server. Third, the application server authenticates the farmer (user) and then prepares the query for subsidy lookup. Fourth, the application server gets the outcomes and packages them for display on the mobile phone of the farmer.

5   A Blog for Promoting M-government

For promoting m-government services in Greece and in the Czech Republic a blog has been proposed. The objectives of this blog are: firstly, to aware citizens of the existence of m-government apps and services in both countries; second, to support the exchange of cross-border experience in m-government initiatives and projects, and third to help agencies discuss the challenge to m-government and design their mobile strategy. The blog entitled "Promoting m-Government Apps" and has been implemented using Google blogger, one of the most popular programs for creating blogs of any subject. The design of the blog is based on the principles of usefulness and accessibility by everyone. The blog can be accessed at http://mobilegovernmentapps.blogspot.gr. In particular the blog has the following categories:

- m-government apps: This category includes a list of mG2C apps. User can be aware of a variety of m-government apps and can find appropriate apps according to their preferences and needs. Some apps need to be downloaded on user's mobile phone while others can be accesses using the mobile phone's web browser.
- cross-border experience: This category aims at building relationships with the agencies in both countries; helping agencies understand and resolve policy issues; finding and sharing resources and capabilities through a mobile-government com-munity of practice, and promoting mobile government efforts.
- assistance to agencies: This category contains a list of initiatives by central or local government, m-government efforts, guidelines, best practices, general mobile news, trends in mobile use, and issues on implementing mobile for the public.

For the Greek case the blog includes mobile apps by the municipality of Thessa-loniki, Thermis, Volos, Gortynia, Milos, Heraklion, Kifissia as well as mobile services by the municipality of Ioannina, Eleusis, Acharnon, Ierapetra, Sitia, Mylopotamos, Rethymno, Kissamos, Platania, Chania, Agrinio and Trikala. For the Czech case the blog includes mobile apps such as Czech sights, Prague trips by public transport, Czech money, Czech spa resorts, metro, crisis and natural disaster and others.

6 Conclusions

The use of mobile technology can play a significant role in the growth, and economic success of any country. It overpasses the borders of time and place, and is becoming the most rapidly adopted technology in the world as well as the most popular and well-know personal technology in history. A growing number of people have adopted mobile communication devices and have changed the way of finding information and using services. Mobile phones subscriptions have exceeded the number of Internet connections globally. In this direction, mobile technology can help government to reach its citizens and businesses. M-government can offer wider access and prolong the access of government information and services to the public. In the current financial crisis, especially in Greece, agriculture can play a significant role. However, few agricultural m-government apps exist. This paper proposes a scheme for developing m-government apps in Greece and in the Czech Republic. Also, a blog is presented operating on the one stop shop concept. It gives to the dwellers the convenience of finding a figure of mobile apps in one location, instead of having to browse different portals. It also provides a single point of keeping in touch Greek and Czech public agencies for cooperation and interchanging experiences.

References

1. Samou, B.: ICT Facts and Figures, The Word in 2013. International Telecommunication Union (ITU) (2013). http://www.itu.int/en/ITU-D/Statistics/Documents/facts/ICTFacts Figures2013.pdf
2. Funk, J.: Key technological trajectories and the expansion of mobile internet applications. Info. **6**(3), 208–215 (2004)
3. Carter, L., Belanger, F.: The utilization of e-government services: citizen trust, innovation and acceptance factors. Inf. Syst. J. **15**(1), 5–25 (2005)
4. Kushchu, I., Kuscu, H.: From E-Government to M-Government: Facing the Inevitable. In: The proceedings of European Conference on E-Government (ECEG 2003), Trinity College, Dublin (2003). www.mgovlab.org
5. McMillan, S.: Legal and regulatory frameworks for mobile government. In: Proceedings of mLife 2010 Conferences. Brighton, UK (2010). http://www.egov.vic.gov.au/trends-and-issues/mobile-government/legal-and-regulatory-frameworks-for-mobile-government.html
6. Madden, G., Bohlin, E., Oniki, H., Tran, T.: Potential demand for m-Government services in Japan. Appl. Econ. Lett. **20**(8), 732–736 (2013)
7. Ntaliani, M., Costopoulou, C., Karetsos, S.: Mobile government: a challenge for agriculture. Gov. Inf. Q. **25**, 699–716 (2008)
8. ITU: M-government: Mobile Technologies for Responsive Governments and Connected Societies. ITU-OECD (2011). http://www.itu.int/pub/D-STR-GOV.M_GOV-2011
9. ITU: Mobile Cellular Subscriptions (2013). http://www.itu.int/en/ITU-D/Statistics/Pages/stat/default.aspx
10. ILO-International Labour Organization: Employers' Organisations Responding to the Impact of the Crisi. Working Paper No. 2, Bureau for Employers' Activities (2010)

11. Stamati, T., Karantjias, A., Markatos, D.: E-government service maturity and development. In: Survey of Citizens' Perceptions in the Adoption of National Government Portals. IGI Global Publications, USA (2011)

12. Doolittle, J., Moohan, A., Simpson, J., Soanes, I.: Building a mobile application development framework. Intel IT White Paper, Cloud Computing and Compute Continuum (2012). https://canada-it.intel.com/wp-content/uploads/2013/09/mobile-app-development-framework.pdf

13. ITU: Bhutan Project Report on Emerging Mobile Applications Opportunity (2012). http://www.itu.int/ITU-D/asp/CMS/Docs/Bhutan%20EV4.pdf

14. Roberts, K., McIntosh, G.: Use of mobile devices in extension and agricultural production – a case study. In: Proceedings of 16th Australian Agronomy Conference 2012, Armidale, NSW, Australia. http://www.regional.org.au/au/asa/2012/precision-agriculture/8224_robertsk.htm. Accessed 2012

15. Karetsos, S., Costopoulou, C., Sideridis, A.: The use of smartphones in agricultural m-Government. In: Agricultural Informatics 2013 International Conference, "The past, present and future of agricultural informatics". Hungary (2013)

The Strategy and the Progress Made on E-Government Services in the EU

L. Protopappas[(✉)] and Alexander B. Sideridis

Agricultural University of Athens, Iera Odos 75, 118 55 Athens, Greece
loucas.protopappas@gmail.com, as@aua.gr

Abstract. The need for the provision of a new generation of e-Government services able to meet the requirements of modern technological societies of the member states of the European Union (EU) was quite evident since the end of the previous century. To this end, the EU urge its members to actively participate on its 2020 strategic plan for the "provision of a new generation of e-Government services" [1]. The European Union's goal is to incentivise the participating states to further develop and evolve the current e-Government services in order to promote interoperability and better e-relations between states with the introduction of e-Signatures and e-Identification (STORK 2.0 project). Even though Europe is trying to achieve an ideal by implementing eGovernment 2.0, a dipole has formed in the sense that Europe is pushing for the 2020 goals on the one end, and on the other end the countries with a high percentage of public sector corruption are prioritising e-services centered mainly on tax collection, at the expense of other objectives. In this paper, an effort is attempted to make an up-to-date review of the criteria and benchmarks used in evaluating e-government services worldwide. Also, an assessment is contacted on how the member states of the EU conform to the EU's 2020 strategy.

Keywords: E-Government · e-services · e-Democracy · e-Government indicators · Public administration

1 Introduction

In modern societies, with complex day to day activities, in order to meet the rising citizens' needs, Information and Communication Technologies (ICT) have to play an even bigger part in the public sector's transformation. As evidenced by the recent changes, the technology readiness in e-gov services is a prerequisite not only for the constantly demanding citizen's needs, but also in the sustainability of a country [2].

Considering the latest e-government development indices and the latest reports from the European Commission and other organisations, it is abundantly clear that the member states of the EU are attempting to implement better and more reliable e-gov services for their citizens and businesses. Nonetheless, ambitious plans like the above are not easily implemented due to the economic crisis and end up significantly hampered, and also, because in many countries the public sector's corruption has changed their development plan and implementation schedule, resulting in priority e-services centered on tax collection services.

© Springer International Publishing Switzerland 2014
A.B. Sideridis et al. (Eds.): E-Democracy 2013, CCIS 441, pp. 192–201, 2014.
DOI: 10.1007/978-3-319-11710-2_18

The European Union is aiming to help and supervise EU member states' efforts in developing fully implemented e-gov services. It was on March 2010, when The European Commission (EC) launched its strategic program *"Europe 2020"*. This program aims to help the countries implement specific services, following a common developmental model [3].

Considering the last 10 years, while the number of twelve services provided to citizens and eight services provided to SME's has not changed, the EU strives, with its Europe 2020 strategy [4], to improve these services in order to achieve greater participation and a fairer e-Government policy. Although the public's and the SMEs' usage of the internet and interaction with e-Gov services has increased lately, the challenge remains to provide even better solutions and services.

To this end, the EC called the member states to participate on its "eGovernment Action Plan 2011−2015" [5]. This plan was included on the "Europe 2020" strategy and, in fact, was inspired by the Malmö Declaration of four political priorities, for the European Public Administration's 2011−2015 timeframe: *"to empower citizens and businesses, to reinforce mobility in the Single Market, to enable efficiency and effectiveness and to create the necessary key enablers and pre-conditions to make things happen"*.

2 Information Society: Overview of E-government Development in European Union

The last decade, E-government in Europe is characterized, in general, from inadequate ICT infrastructure, "cloudy" technological background and disappointing figures in Internet usage and e-services participation among the EU member states. Moreover, particular reflection was the digital divide and the digital inequality among northern and southern European countries. So, the European Commission should specify a clear strategy with the following goals: (i) to implement ICT technologies in order to provide safer and quicker internet access, (ii) to encourage citizens to use the internet and finally (iii) stimulate the role of EU in the global aspect of the Information Society.

2.1 The E-Europe 2002 Action Plan

The first well-structured program by the European Commission, with clear objectives, launched on March 2001. The e-Europe 2002 Action Plan belongs to a general pattern, following Lisbon's pursuance of transforming the European States in a powerful union of knowledge economies that could be competitive worldwide by the year 2010. This plan is aiming to increase Internet connectivity in Europe. This may had been the motivational kick off for a digital era, as lots of innovative challenges are emerging, such as intelligent transport systems, health services, electronic access to public services and the overall maturity of e-commerce [6, 7].

2.2   The e-Europe 2005 Action Plan

The e-Europe 2002 Action Plan was completed, having put the basis for the digitisation of society, achieving most of its main goals. The EC sustained momentum and proceeded to a second phase of its strategy towards an e-competitive Europe. By e-competitive Europe, the EC actually meant stimulated e-government services with applications and content providing better and cheaper services to citizens, SME'S and public authorities. As a consequence, emphasis should be given in the development of broadband infrastructures [8].

By 2005, the aim was to support new projects in e-government, e-health, e-inclusion, e-learning and e-trust/security. More specifically, the main proposed actions for the e-Europe 2005 action plan were: to implement interactive public services in order to reduce costs thought supply chain management including e-procurement, to create public Internet Access points that all citizens could have easy access to the Internet and to promote tourism and culture. The current action plan was trying to improve education and e-leaning with the provision of equipment and thus, most schools are now connected, and work is underway in order to provide convenient access to the Internet and to multimedia resources for schools, teachers and students [9].

2.3   The i2010 E-Government Action Plan

The 3rd in a series of programs, the i2010 Action Plan finds the situation of e-government in Europe slightly improved. The figures in 2009 were the following: Internet usage had reached nearly 49 % and EU members had implemented well- structured e-Government strategies and policies [10]. The most important thing was that in 2009, 29 countries overall presented E-Government strategies, in comparison with the year 2005 that there were only twelve. It is obvious that Action Plan programs have succeeded in the majority of their main objectives [11].

Consequently, with the i2010 Action Plan, the European Union is aiming to stimulate and update the efficiency of public administration services, keeping up with the daily needs of citizens and businesses. According to the EC plan, the five new objectives that were defined are: *(i) Inclusive eGovernment, (ii) Efficiency and Effectiveness of e-services, (iii) High Impact Services, (iv) Key Enablers and (v) e-Participation.* Thus, the EC was again directed in designing and implementing of cross-border services allowing citizens to establish across borders e-relations. Evidently, this necessitates e-IDentification (eID) for all citizens of the EU and improvement of the overall framework of e-government services throughout Europe [9, 29].

2.4   European eGovernment Action Plan 2011−2015

Action Plan 2011−2015, the last, and current, EC plan, is a part of Digital Agenda 2020. As it was emphasized above, it is urging for the provision of a new generation of eGovernment services. The ICTs should become an important enabler in the development of innovative ways to provide reliable e-services to citizens who are facing constrained public resources [12].

The 5th Ministerial eGovernment Conference (the 'Malmö Declaration') was a milestone in defining new critical priorities of this new action plan. The 'Malmö Declaration' recognised 4 challenges that the European Commission should overcome in order to establish a stable background and aspire for open, flexible and collaborative relations between European Governments and their citizens and businesses [13, 14].

With an informal deadline in 2015, all European Public Administrations should implement the following 4 policy priorities:

- *Citizens and businesses are empowered by eGovernment services designed around users' needs and developed in collaboration with third parties, as well as by increased access to public information, strengthened transparency and effective means for the involvement of stakeholders in the policy process,*
- *Mobility in the Single Market is reinforced by seamless eGovernment services for the setting up and running of a business and for studying, working, residing and retiring anywhere in the European Union,*
- *Efficiency and effectiveness is enabled by a constant effort to use eGovernment to reduce the administrative burden, improve organisational processes and promote a sustainable low-carbon economy,*
- *The implementation of the policy priorities is made possible by appropriate key enablers and legal and technical preconditions [15–17].*

2.5   Cross-Border Pilots

The EC's Action Plan, described above, is considered as a framework for the development of e-government services in both national and European level. Reliable cross-border services are now needed allowing increased citizens' mobility within the European states. By these new generation applications, personal documentation and data are following citizens throughout Europe. Obviously, this comes to reality by the development of an environment which promotes the interoperability of systems and key enablers such as eSignatures and eIdentification.

In order to bring public authorities, service providers and research centres, all over the EU, onboard, large scale pilot projects (LSPs) have been created and operate under the ICT Policy Support Programme in five prime sections: eID, eProcurement, eBusiness, eHealth and eJustice. Cross-border digital services in the aforementioned policy sections become feasible by a number of solutions or building blocks that the Seven LSPs are conveying [22].

Every block includes various components (common code), makes use of various standards and blueprints, and all have an identical attribute: they aim to be occupied as piece of online services which craft these online services 'cross-border enabled'. Also there are future challenges in order to entirely employ cross-border digital public services such as the LSPs expansion and to formulate the building blocks that could be applicable in other policy sections [18, 19].

The four LSPs that are running at this time are:

e-SENS (Electronic Simple European Networked Services) is aiming to facilitate the administrative procedures by enabling internet access and thus, to develop the European Digital Single Market and thought ICT technologies. This project involves 100 partners from 20 countries, including Greece, it started on April 1, 2013, and its duration is 36 months [20, 21].

e-CODEX (e-Justice Communication via Online Data Exchange) concentrates in the improvement of access in legal information (laws, procedures) across European borders. In a nutshell, the main objectives of the project are to contribute the implementation of the EU legal framework and modernise the judicial systems, so that the European Union Members can provide a safer environment for their citizens and their businesses. This project has started on December, 2010, it will be complete on February, 2015 and it involves 26 participants [23, 24].

EpSOS is a European project that is focusing in the area of e-Health. It is the first European e-health program which connects a large number and variety of countries in a practical cooperation. Also, epSOS is a project for the interoperability of eHealth services, funded by the European Union, and it aims to build and evaluate a service infrastructure that will allow cross-border interoperability of electronic health records in Europe, but not more than laws and existing national systems. As a consequence, the member states of the EU are trying to develop electronic health records for every citizen in order to improve the quality and efficiency of its healthcare system. This project is very important because, on the one side, it is trying to unify the health systems of all European countries, so that every citizen's medical data could be available in every country and on the other side to forward the use of electronic prescriptions ("ePrescription"). The project has started on July, 2010, it will run for 6 years and it involves 25 participants (22 EU member states and 3 non-EU member states) [25].

STORK 2.0 (Secure idenTity acrOss boRders linKed 2.0) is a 3-year project. It was which has been launched to promote the creation and development of an integrated and sustainable workplace for eID and e-Authentication in Europe, for both legal entities and individuals. STORK 2, a continuation of STORK 1, allows businesses and citizens, through a common architecture and standards, use their national electronic identities (eID), in order to obtain secure electronic access to public services across the EU.

The four main objectives of the STORK 2.0 are:

- Accelerating the development of electronic identification for eGovernment services, by coordinating the National Community initiatives in support of a federal structure for the management of electronic identification across Europe.
- Maximizing the uptake of scalable solutions across the EU, with a strong commitment to open standards and long-term viability, with a vision to evolve electronic identification in service (with the support of the participating European countries and industry).
- Facilitating convergence of private and public sector into a fully functional framework and infrastructure, using electronic identification (eID) for safe and consistent certification of legal and natural persons across the EU.

- Operation of four cross-sectoral pilot to test and demonstrate the capabilities and benefits of interoperable electronic identification (eID) environments factual circumstances.

STORK 2.0 is attempting to (i) enable the Digital Single Market focusing on legal entities & attributes which is important for boosting SMEs & private sector, (ii) Facilitates cross border eGovernment applications and (iii) Reduces administrative burdens for the companies & individuals wishing to provide services across borders. In this project, there are 58 partners from 26 participating countries [21, 26].

3 Evaluation of Implemented e-Government Services

In the last decade, the EC has been attempting to supervise the governments of the European Union members in order to implement a series of essential and simultaneously innovative e-services. The remarkable action plans that are designed by European Commission and implemented by the European governments are strictly related to the ICT technologies of each country. So, it is evident that the sophistication level of e-gov services is related to the technological framework of ICTs, a fact that the first action plan tried to address.

The lasting and honorable efforts of European governments in the development of eGovernment services, in the local and national level, yielded results but not as expected. On the one hand, the European Programs have really high demands and on the other hand, the economic crisis and the financial problems that hit many European countries, in the last 4 years, have slowed down the planning and the expenditure for the implementation of e-services. Surveys published by the EC and other authorized organizations provide reliable statistics and benchmarks. These surveys have shown that the existing e-government services fail to meet the citizens and businesses needs in a Government to Citizen (G2C) or Government to Business (G2B) mode. Proportionate failures are also recorded in a Government to Government (G2G) mode [27, 28].

3.1 The Current Situation

The EC released on May 28, 2013, a very important survey that was carried out by the Capgemini Group, which showed that citizens and businesses are recognizing the efforts for the full implementation of e-gov services, but there was still room for improvement. The survey looked into 19 public services and involved 28.000 European citizens. The key findings are very significant as (i) 46 % of respondents use online services but 28 % expressed reluctance to continue using them, (ii) Between 19 electronic services, the majority of European residents use tax collection services (73 %), 57 % claimed they use the service to change their address and 56 % is enrolling a studenst in higher education which is the third most widely used service, (iii) the less used e-gov e-services include: 'reporting a crime' (41 %), 'starting a new job' (41 %) and 'starting a procedure for disability allowance' (42 %) and finally (iv) 47 % of respondents claimed they got all they wanted from the public administration, 46 % of respondents partially fulfilled and 5 % encountered problems while interacting with the public administration services [30, 31].

Moreover, the present survey approaches the barriers that prevent the use of e-government and present the E-government satisfaction and the benefits of use of E-government services. In a nutshell, 21 % (mostly students) indicated incomplete information on the availability of relevant websites and e-services, 80 % of respondents (women and elderly) do not find interest in the use of electronic services, 11 % said their personal data are not protected and overall the satisfaction in eGovernment services decreased by 1,3 %, with the service of finding a job presenting a low score of satisfaction, reflecting the current economic conjuncture of corrupted countries. Finally most of the respondents claimed that even though a service provides simplicity, transparency and is time-saving, the quality of a service is less relevant to citizens (Fig. 1).

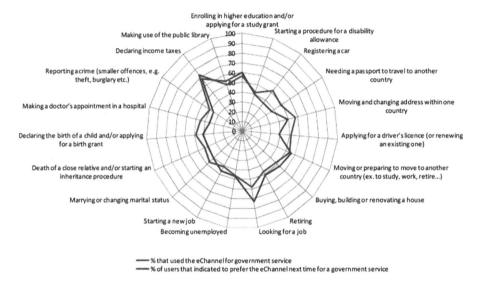

Fig. 1. Preference eChannel vs. traditional channels for 19 citizen services (EU-27 + , %). Source: Government Benchmark 2012 – INSIGHT report, Available at: https://ec.europa.eu/digital-genda/sites/digital-agenda/files/eGov%20Benchmark%202012%20insight%20report%20published%20version%200.1%20_0.pdf

3.1.1   The Use of the Internet in the EU27

The abstinence of citizens and businesses from e-gov services, as mentioned above, can be explained by many reasons. One of these is the inadequate ICT infrastructure and results in the limited use of the internet, and consequently, limited use of electronic services. Nowadays, according to European Commission, more than 60 % of individuals in the EU27 use the internet daily and more that 79 % of users have access to internet from their mobile phones. However, the three barriers that prevent citizens to become internet users are the lack of skills, the lack of internet access and the cost. The lack of skills and the cost are the major factors for many European countries, such as, Bulgaria, Greece, Hungary, Portugal and Slovenia (Fig. 2).

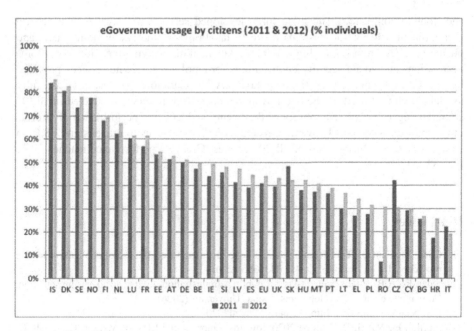

Fig. 2. EGovernment usage by citizens (2011 & 2012) (% individuals). Source: https://ec. europa.eu/digital-agenda/sites/digital-agenda/files/DAE%20SCOREBOARD%202013%20-% 203-INTERNET%20USE%20AND%20SKILLS.pdf

The last two years, the use of eGovernment services saw moderate growth, raising the percentage from 41 % to 44 %. 88.8 % of European countries improved their percentage in 2012 (23 of 27 European Countries). Some of them have recorded large increases in the use of E-government services, such as Romania (+24 p.p.), Croatia (+8 p.p.) and Greece (+7 p.p.). At this point, it is very important to look at the reasons why many citizens don't use the interactive e-government services. The survey showed that 10 % of respondents cite security issues, lack of skills (8 %), lack of supply (4 %), and quality of supply (2 %) [30, 31].

3.1.2 The Case of Greece

Greece demonstrates significant developmental effort in the implementation of eGovernment services, utilizing national and European resources, through the National Strategic Reference Frameworks programs. Also, it is actively participating in the implementation of cross-border services, contributing significantly to the technological maturity of these services.

Greece is trying to get back on track and achieve a growth trajectory, by (1) improving the sophistication level of 20 major e-gov services (twelve services for citizens and eight services for businesses) and (2) by implementing a series of pilot e-services in order to reduce bureaucracy, to fight unemployment and to stimulate factors in the local level, such as health, justice and education.

According to the Information Society [32], for the year 2013, only seven of the twenty services are handled entirely electronically, three of which relate to the citizens and, four to companies. The three fully developed services provided by the general secretariat of information systems relate to taxation (income tax by individuals and businesses, VAT refund), finding a job, the statement of changing the address, customs declarations and social security contributions for employees. Online services provided by the GSIS to businesses (income tax, VAT declarations to customs) are fully available online. Based on the latest available data, from research conducted in all EU countries regarding the availability of the twenty services, the performance of Greece, in comparison with the EU average, reached 65 % in services to citizens and 78 % in business services. In the total of all 20 services, Greece's performance reaches 70 % [31, 33, 34].

References

1. Chen, Y., Gant, J.: Transforming local e-government services: the use of application service providers. J. Gov. Inform. Q. **18**, 343–355 (2001)
2. Sideridis, A.B.: e-Government-Useful Public Administration. Invited speaker's presentation, Conference on ICT Developments, Ionian University (2006)
3. European Commission. http://ec.europa.eu/eu2020
4. Marlier, E., Natali, D.: Europe 2020: towards a more social EU? In: Marlier, E., Natali, D. (eds.) Work & Society. vol. 69(277), p. 2. Peter Lang Publishing Group (2010)
5. European Commission. http://ec.europa.eu/digital-agenda/en/european-egovernment-action-plan-2011-2015
6. EU Commission, eEurope – an Information Society for All. http://eur-lex.europa.eu
7. Council and the European Commission. http://eur-lex.europa.eu/LexUriServ/LexUriServ.do?uri=com:2000:0330:fin:en:pdf
8. European Commission. http://ec.europa.eu/information_society/activities/ict_psp
9. European Commission. http://ec.europa.eu/cip
10. Internet World Stats. http://www.internetworldstats.com
11. Council and the European Commission. http://eur-lex.europa.eu/lexuriserv/lexuriserv.do?uri=com:2005:0229:fin:en:pdf
12. European Commission, The European eGovernment Action Plan 2011–2015 Harnessing ICT to promote smart, sustainable & innovative Government (2010). http://eur-lex.europa.eu/LexUriServ/LexUriServ.do?uri=COM:2010:0743:FIN:FR:DOC
13. E-practice.eu. http://epractice.eu/en/events/292867
14. European Commission, The European eGovernment Action Plan 2011−2015 (2012). http://ec.europa.eu/digital-agenda/en/european-egovernment-action-plan-2011-2015
15. Ministerial Declaration on eGovernment (2009). http://ec.europa.eu/digital-agenda/sites/digital-agenda/files/ministerial-declaration-on-egovernment-malmo.pdf
16. Commission of the EU. http://ec.europa.eu/eu2020/index_en
17. European Commission, Benchmarking Digital Europe 2011−2015 a conceptual framework (2009). https://ec.europa.eu/digital-agenda/sites/digital-agenda/files/Benchmarking%20Digital%20Europe%202011-2015%20post%20Visby.doc
18. O'Dowd, L., Anderson, J., Wilson, T.M.: New Borders for a Changing Europe: Cross-Border Cooperation and Governance. Routledge, London (2005)
19. Gouscos, D., Kalikakis, M., Legal, M., Papadopoulou, S.: A general model of performance and quality for one-stop e-Government service offerings. J. Gov. Inform. Q. **24**, 860–885 (2007)

20. E-SENS. http://www.esens.eu/home
21. European Commission. http://ec.europa.eu/information_society/apps/projects
22. European Commission. http://ec.europa.eu/digital-agenda/en/ict-policy-support-programme
23. E-CODEX. http://www.e-codex.eu/home.html
24. European Commission. http://ec.europa.eu/justice/criminal/european-e-justice/e-codex
25. EpSOS. http://www.epsos.eu
26. STORK 2.0. https://www.eid-stork2.eu
27. Fang, Z.I.: Government in digital era. the internet and management. IJTM 10, 1–22 (2002)
28. Sideridis, A.B., Tsakalidis, A., Costopoulou, C., Pucihar, A., Zorkadis, V.: E-Government for small and medium sized enterprises (SMEs) in rural areas. J. IJED 1, 119–123 (2009)
29. Danish Technological Institute, i2010 eGovernment Action Plan Progress Study (2009). https://www.tno.nl/downloads/i2010_progress_study_final_report_november_2009.pdf
30. European Commission: Public Services Online (2013). http://ec.europa.eu/digital-agenda/sites/digital-agenda/files/eGov%20Benchmark%202012%20insight%20report%20published%20version%200.1%20_0.pdf
31. European commission, Digital Agenda Scoreboard 2013 (2013). http://ec.europa.eu/digital-agenda/en/digital-agenda-europe
32. Information Society. http://www.infosoc.gr/infosoc/en-uk
33. Papadomichelaki, X., Koutsouris, V., Konstantinidis, D., Mentzas, G.: An analytic hierarchy process for the evaluation of E-Government service quality. IJEGR 9, 19–44 (2013)
34. European Commission. http://ec.europa.eu/information_society/newsroom/cf/dae/document.cfm?doc_id=2231

PERIKLIS - Electronic Democracy in the 21st Century

Emmanuel Sardis[1(✉)], Panagiotis Kokkinos[2], and Magdalini Kardara[1]

[1] Institute of Communications and Computer Systems/ICCS,
National Technical University of Athens/NTUA, Athens, Greece
{sardism,mania}@mail.ntua.gr
[2] Computer Technology Institute and Press "Diophantus", Patra, Greece
kokkinop@ceid.upatras.gr

Abstract. PERIKLIS platform encourages citizen participation and supports sophistication of electronic government services by leveraging the capabilities of location based services, social networks and web 2.0 technologies. In this paper a structured analysis is adopted for identifying the advantages, from the digital transformation of the government transactions and the electoral processes, exploring the notion of society members and the benefits for better life conditions through electronic transactions in a Municipality. Adopting a computing approach for e-government and voting methodologies with an easy setup and completion by its members is investigated, reviewing the availability of services through mobile and web based systems, coupled with geo location services. Furthermore, PERIKLIS proposes a high level e-governance and e-voting solution for a municipality while investigating issues that require further research for exploitation and interoperability with more than one Municipalities.

Keywords: E-government · E-democracy · SOA platform · Web services · Social networks · Voting system

1 Introduction

New trend technologies and their capabilities can assist e-government applications by enhancing user experience and thus encouraging the participation of citizens. In this paper, we present PERIKLIS, a platform that enhances interaction between citizens and between citizens and public services, through the use of mobile and social network technologies.

E-democracy builds online public space in the heart of real democracy and community [1, 2]. Our aim is to harness the power of online internet based tools for supporting the participation of city residents in public life activities, strengthen communities, and build democracy relationships. The integration of ICTs methodologies and tools into governance transactions contributes to informed populations, which are a basis for effective participatory governance. Mobile technologies have reached almost more than 90 % of population usage in many cases, increasing the related platforms and applications for e-government services for cities residents and visitors. Despite the relative infancy of technology especially in developing countries, anecdotal evidence

© Springer International Publishing Switzerland 2014
A.B. Sideridis et al. (Eds.): E-Democracy 2013, CCIS 441, pp. 202–212, 2014.
DOI: 10.1007/978-3-319-11710-2_19

suggests that access to government information has a beneficial economic impact [3]. Some developing countries are already engaged in transformation of the governance process through increased citizen participation and are attempting to create an open, transparent environment through convergence of information and services [4].

The e-government sector is beginning to encapsulate new trends and technologies like cloud computing, green e-government, mobile services, whole-of-government approaches that attract the citizen participation and especially the young people residents in cities. Various published studies [5] have ranked the following countries as leaders in e-government during 2011 and 2012: Australia; Canada; Denmark; Finland; France; Japan; Republic of Korea; Netherlands; Norway; UK and Northern Ireland; USA; Singapore; Spain; Sweden; Taiwan.

PERIKLIS platform attempts to create an open, transparent environment for municipalities through convergence of information and services. Reaching these ideas and transforming them into an electronic tool faces a lot of problems. A number of important issues already exist, as Big Data is changing the face of customer analytics, giving organizations new insight into customers' wants and preferences. A similar phenomenon is going on nowadays in the realm of politics and e-government [6, 7]. Many world cases like the 2012 U.S. national elections for the Democratic National Committee leveraged Big Data analytics to better understand and predict voter behavior and alliances [9, 10]. PERIKLIS platform's modules harness the power of social networks, couple them with services for e-government and voting. Also, PERIKLIS platform covers many of the Municipality needs utilizing big data manipulation techniques, statistical analysis and geo-location services. The aim of PERIKLIS platform is to present to the authorities a framework that will help them to develop thinking and planning about the approach that best fits their particular environment and purpose for e-services integration into their municipality.

2 E-Democracy

Information and communication technologies (ICT) present benefits and challenges to democratic development, since they can be used in a crosscutting manner, strengthening initiatives in governance, political parties, election processes, citizen participation, and gender programs.

Democrats and institutions in emerging democracies can be empowered to use ICTs as a tool to enhance the information sharing, efficiency and transparency which are crucial to build and sustain democracy.

Providing access to all city citizens, old people with no internet access but with a mobile phone on their hands, to young people that participate in city areas like schools where only them could investigate and report possible problems, giving voting capabilities between unknown people, residents of a huge area, etc. particularly those in less developed socioeconomic areas in developing and developed nations, presents a related developmental challenge. Many cities around Europe have started promoting and enhancing strategies for using the Internet, and related technologies, but are not withstanding the technological divide which is critical in beginning to narrow the gap and enhancing participation by those currently disconnected either due to economic reasons, or due to no knowledge to participate in these platforms. In particular, the critical factors that hinder access to Internet and related technologies for the populations are:

- level of technology and infrastructure,
- cost of equipment,
- cultural, linguistic or other social barriers, and/or
- low political will to address these issues.

Also there are thousands of very important organizations, and millions of people, who do not necessarily face these problems and conditions and who reside in emerging democracies. In many countries these are civil servants, members of government organizations and staff, civil-society organization staff and members, teachers and students, employees in all spheres of the private sector, political party members, and more. These people are leaving in disconnected communities from government transactions, but work or are involved with organizations that could and should have to be connected and plugged into social events and transactions.

In most cases the above organizations are disconnected due to not recognizing the importance of getting connected and communicating or sharing information with other residents. The economic resources make them to remain disconnected, or they do not have the related technical and managerial expertise to adequately plan for and procure the needed equipment, systems and services in order to be connected. These are cases and areas where we believe PERIKLIS platform can be very useful and supportive.

As a democracy practitioner [12], PERIKLIS platform provides useful support to enhance democratic development in a society, making its members active, through Internet and related technologies, which will not increase the cost for the end users. The only requirement is a mobile phone from them. Integrating PERIKLIS within society sectors and making practical end users applications provides an add-on for democracy activities into e-activities. In doing so, we inevitably bridge people within these societies from one side of the divide to the other.

PERIKLIS services apply both an in-depth knowledge of the democratic workings of its partners (an involved Municipality) gained over time, the research aspects (Universities involvement) and the technical and project management expertise (involved IT Companies) needed to work with information technology (IT) vendors. In addition, PERIKLIS [12] success is linked to that of the corresponding project and the partners, with the ultimate goal being the development of sustainable systems that will support the community, the Municipality without using expert staff, or costly equipment but instead working with open source tools and cheap IT equipment that will support the democratic processes of the Municipality [13].

3   E-Democracy, E-Voting and E-Participation Status

Organizations like Facebook, internet blogs, the wikis, and a host of other technology based tools are transforming the ways that citizens interact with others and with government. Indeed, technology is transforming our democracy. Sites like the e-democracy.org are creating online communities for presenting and discussing issues about city life problems in UK [23], Zealand, and the U.S. [14].

Software platforms like the "athenabridge" are manipulating online discussions of specific statements/hypotheses, plus related voting tools for quick identify the areas of consensus [15]. European projects [17, 18] for e-government and e-participation models [19] implemented in an electronic format have already been online.

Organizations like the gov2u [20, 22] have a list of related projects executed under the umbrella of e-government and e-participation of EU citizens in related countries. PERIKLIS has evaluated their contributions and is focusing to develop an online platform for the 'Maroussi' municipality as a starting point aiming to grow in more municipalities in future. The aim of e-democracy tools [26] is to provide in more people choices about how they can participate and make them feel that their opinion input makes a real difference in their society, eventually resulting in more trust. Starting from a municipality level this will grow in a government based tools and levels. Social and economic variations between citizens in terms of gender, age, resources and income, geographic location, education, etc. are expected to influence their level of trust in ICTs, a research that PERIKLIS already evaluates and measures in its developed modules covering this aspect for successful project deployment in the municipality area The basic aim is to provide the necessary e-tools for helping the local authorities to communicate with citizens.

In Greece e-government programs like 'Cl@rity' portal [26–28, 31, 32] are examples of ICT involvement in e-democracy activities between municipalities. PERIKLIS provides a more simplified method for attracting residents in a easy for them way through social networks and mobile easy access in e-activities. In the following sections we present the main architecture and components characteristics of PERIKLIS platform.

4 PERIKLIS Platform Characteristics

The objective of PERIKLIS platform is to provide an interaction between citizens and public bodies that leverages the popularity of social networks as well as the capabilities of modern smart phones that will trigger related web services of an internet based web platform which in the other end will support the Municipality e-government transactions and in parallel will inform online the end users with direct analytical and evaluated democracy results. Users are able to login using their existing social network accounts via their smart phones or tablet devices the platform and perform a variety of actions such as gather the opinion of fellow citizens on a specific matter, report a problem, raise awareness or recruit users to their causes. The functionality of the platform is enhanced by a number of data analytics and location based services that bring added value to the platform.

The basic architecture of the platform PERIKLIS is presented in Fig. 1. In the design of PERIKLIS we have followed the principles of Service Oriented Architecture. SOA is an architectural paradigm based on reforming application functions and pieces of information into a "service" that can be accessed through a common interface regardless of the location of the function or of the piece of data. As a result, applications using this paradigm are more adaptable to changes and its components are reusable.

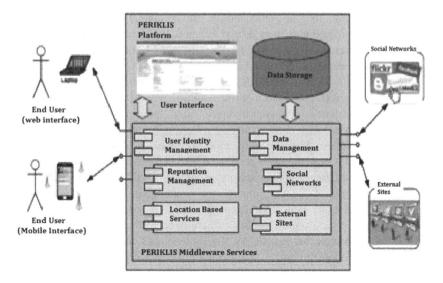

Fig. 1. PERIKLIS basic architecture.

Following the SOA paradigm, PERIKLIS has been designed as a set of loosely coupled services. We have two types of services: the PERIKLIS core services and the PERIKLIS added value services. The main functionality of the platform is implemented by the PERIKLIS Core Services. These services implement functions such as the creation and management of actions and participation information as well as storage and can operate as a standalone entity (i.e. without the added value services described below). Their functionality is exposed through a SOAP API [16].

In addition to the core services, four added value services have been developed in the context of PERIKLIS. The objective of these components is to enhance the functionality of the platform by providing specialized analysis on top of the user generated data (e.g. data analytics, location based analysis), in order to bring some added value to the end users. As explained in previous paragraphs, the platform is highly adaptable and can easily accommodate new services so that it can be used for a variety of e-government applications providing interoperability services and interconnecting more than one Municipality online like a puzzle.

5   PERIKLIS Core Benefits

PERIKLIS provides the following benefits through its platform services and tools [21].

5.1   Democratic Governance

PERIKLIS governance work is emphasizing the political dimension of democratic governance, within four main practice areas:

- constitutional reform,
- society participation
- legislative development,
- local/municipality government, and
- public integrity.

PERIKLIS provides a tracking mechanism for geo-location based notifications and matters that should be noticed and resolved. This technological characteristic can assist municipality related services that are based on geo-location attributes and enhancing the related organizations in it to plan and develop services that will support these reported problems and case studies from residents and city visitors.

5.2 Sustainability

Common practices of e-government ICT systems provide related value to end users, which comes through sharing knowledge and experience among democratic leaders, or documenting and sharing democracy building experience. Technology programming typically involves building systems (websites, databases, communication networks, etc.) and thus requires organizational changes within our partner institutions in order to maintain these systems. These changes drive planning, assessment, implementation and program evaluation.

Sustainability means that development of the Internet or other IT system must happen in parallel with a process of building capacity within the partner organization to support and maintain the system [24]. The partner must form the necessary relationships within its country to meet its ongoing needs for equipment, support and services. This approach needs higher initial investment, and possibly requires a longer-term engagement with the partner organization, as it aligns its staffing and budgeting to meet the long-term commitment of supporting the systems.

In PERIKLIS the Municipality services can be interconnected through the PERIKLIS platform and get online notifications directly for issues that relate to their daily operations. In this way, Municipality services efficiency is increased, bringing value to its municipality citizens, and supporting democratic development.

5.3 Elections and Voting

One of the most interesting PERIKLIS feature relates to elections and voting system, where PERIKLIS users can use smart phones for municipality election observation [28]. Combining a web based environment through a smart phone and locating the position of the user, the PERIKLIS reporting system provides a rigorous observation methodology, where the municipality administrators can enhance the integrity of elections, by alerting authorities to problems early enough to allow remedies. The speed of web based reporting with a usage of social networks combination allows the Municipality partners to publicize an assessment of the quality of polling and tabulation, exposing problematic elections and increasing public confidence in credible elections.

5.4 Municipality Residents Participation

People involvement in their neighborhoods problems is a potent force for dealing with local problems and a huge benefit for democracy. Through research, coordinated planning, and actions, they can accomplish what individuals working alone cannot. This is a nice idea but cannot be completed due to current city conditions. People have no time to do that. Many reasons and fast track life conditions isolate them from this societal involvement.

PERIKLIS platform enables partners and civil groups to be involved. There is no need for extra effort and coordination activities from their side, everything is covered automatically through this platform and its functionalities. Coordinate training activities, organize focus groups, distributing materials and information for events and problems in the city, but also generating statistical reports that evaluate human transactions is key value for a Municipality that gets automatically feedback from its residents. The available platform technological support in developing civil society can also include assistance with online discussion groups to help sustain networks of activists, and developing secure intranets that incorporate collaboration tools, so member groups can work together in confidence on policy or planning documents.

5.5 Social Media and Mobile Phones

People will only choose and transact with government services that digitally supported. Technology solutions that have been integrated in PERIKLIS platform like social media and mobile platforms [6, 11] integration for direct information transfer in the core platform provide enhanced tools, for information visualization for the end users and citizens participation in democratic governance processes.

5.6 Cooperation Improvement

PERIKLIS will support improved digital capabilities across municipality departments in order to resolve the reported and published problems from citizens. Municipality departments could better cooperate by exchanging direct and online data for geolocation support and reaction [25]. Municipality PERIKLIS digital services will:

- increase support to municipality departments and corresponding services, like roads recovering and service.
- Help departments to improve their digital capability,
- develop extensive support for team leaders and service managers,
- develop digital awareness training for civil servants.

All municipality departments involved in digital services should ensure that they have appropriate in-house digital capability, including the management of their portfolio of digital services. This capability will vary in size and skills depending on the balance of information and services the department is responsible for. For example voting services could be served by only one person that upload a vote case and the same person collects and evaluates the results, but in case of a road reported problem a dedicated service team (with more than five persons and related materials, dedicated tools, etc.) will be needed. It will typically include a balanced government team design to support the reported issues from the residents.

5.7 Better Life Conditions

Residents will be able to make their city work better. Giving them some responsibility for looking after their part of town is a way of effectively addressing local preferences and priorities. Understandably, boosting citizen participation improves live ability [30]. The city is a source of potential conflict, between residents and government, between different residents groups, but resident's participation in civic affairs can reduce all of these sources of conflict. In particular it can prevent the problems occurred and associated with changes in growth and renewal.

5.8 Strong Democracy

When residents get together, they generate a number of remarkable side effects. One of these is strengthened democracy. Democracy means that the people decide. Political scientists describe our system of voting every few years, but otherwise leaving everything up to government as weak democracy. In weak democracy, citizens have no role, no real part in decision-making between elections.

EU many countries are supporting especially during the last decade the stronger democracy in corporations, institutions and governments. In many cities, this has resulted in the formal recognition of neighborhood groups as a link between people and municipal government, and a venue for citizen participation in decision-making between elections [8].

Providing an automated mechanism, through PERIKLIS platform that brings thousands of different resident's ideas and thoughts for their city problems, in a very friendly way with no extra costs, as social networks do, and advertising to the municipality their thoughts, problems and solutions, is a strong democracy achievement.

6 PERIKLIS Platform

PERIKLIS provides all the above characteristics through a web based environment that works in all platforms that are using Internet. Some related screenshots from its environment are provided in the Figs. 2–3.

The programming of PERIKLIS has used open source tools for development and deployment. Cloud storage facilities and web services SOA interconnections with external services. It is based on a flexible SOA Architecture allowing for the addition of any number of added value services. The system is working as a pilot in municipality of 'Maroussi' in Athens city and already has been interconnected with municipality services for resolving the posted problems from residents [12].

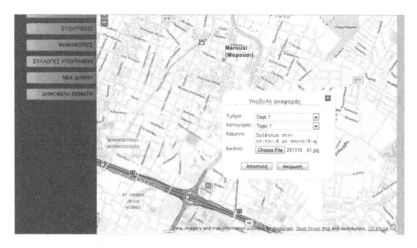

Fig. 2. PERIKLIS web interface

Fig. 3. Mobile interface

7 Conclusions

Technologies abound that could be harnessed to cheaply bring governance services nearer to citizens so that self-serving government activities may be transformed to e-governance service platform. This manuscript presented a framework for harnessing the potential of current developments in mobile and web technologies to provide e-governance services to help residents in a Municipality to participate in governance and democratic activities. The residents by accessing and contributing to their neighborhood problems and supporting the local government services and teams to respond on them, using user friendly web tools from their mobile phones are increasing the democracy rules in their society, providing better city conditions for them. Also through this paper the authors are triggering points that could present research topics, which can be used to adapt e-governance for societal transformations.

The use of emerging technologies like mobile applications and web 2.0 computing, has enhanced the interactions between online services and governance services. Providing web tools to these organizations that improve the management of their teams operations, and triggering the reengineering of government systems, their planning and policy making processes have many benefits for the residents. Also, the capability to monitor the implemented policies and recording either the physical or the social changes in the community of a municipality, makes PERIKLIS platform an important tool for every Municipality. PERIKLIS improves the quality of life of citizens and transparently activates and enhances their e-democracy activities. Through this tool every local community can promote aspirational openness, neighborliness, inclusion and integration for all kinds of people and neighborhoods. In parallel provides challenges for building new bridges, increase civic trust and embrace public life.

Acknowledgments. This research has been co-financed by the European Union (European Social Fund – ESF) and Greek national funds through the Operational Program "Competitiveness and Entrepreneurship and Regions in Transition" of the National Strategic Reference Framework (NSRF) – National Action: "COOPERATION 2009 - Partnerships of Production and Research Institutions in Focused Research and Technology Sectors". PERIKLIS program code [09SYN-72-948].

References

1. E-Democracy.org. http://www.slideshare.net/netclift/inclusive-social-media-webinar-slides
2. http://www.infohelp.co.nz/politics.html
3. Brewer, E., Demmer, M., Du, B., Ho, M., Kam, M., Nedevschi, S., Pal, J., Patra, R., Surana, S.: The case for technology in developing regions. Comput. Publ. **38**(6), 25–38 (2005)
4. Okoronkwo, M.C., Monica, N.A.: Providing e-governance services to technologically challenged grassroots environments. Int. J. Soft Comput. Eng. (IJSCE) **3**(1), 107–111 (2013). ISSN: 2231-2307
5. http://www.budde.com.au/Research/Digital-Economy-E-Government-Transforming-Services.html
6. Garcia, A.C.B., Vivacqua, A.S., Tavares, T.C.: Designing mobile interaction to elicit alternative solutions for participatory decision-making. In: 14th International Conference Computer Supported Cooperative Work in Design (CSCWD), pp. 461–466 (2010)

7. http://www.ecommercetimes.com/story/Turning-Politics-Into-Political-Science-With-Big-Data-79232.html#sthash.VcY8PtRA.dpuf
8. http://www.rialtas.net/blog/#sthash.vyv93FOc.dpuf
9. Wigand, R.T., Agarwal, N., Osesina, O.I., Hering, W., Korsgaard, M.A., Picot, A., Drescher, M.: Social network indices as performance predictors in a virtual organization. In: Fourth International Conference on Computational Aspects of Social Networks (CASoN), pp. 144–149 (2012)
10. http://www.futuregov.asia/
11. http://gov20.govfresh.com/election-2012-social-media-big-data/
12. http://Periklis.eu
13. Lazovic, V., Durickovic, T.: Democracy in the electronic government era — challenges and opportunities for development in Montenegro. In: 2011 Proceedings of the 34th International Convention, MIPRO, pp. 1365–1369 (2011)
14. http://pages.e-democracy.org/Neighbors_forums
15. http://athenabridge.wordpress.com/
16. Orellana, F., Niinimaki, M.: Distributed computing with RESTful Web services. In: 2012 Seventh International Conference on P2P, Parallel, Grid, Cloud and Internet Computing (3PGCIC), pp. 103–110 (2012). doi:10.1109/3PGCIC.2012.30
17. http://www.isi.fraunhofer.de/isi-de/t/projekte/bb-stoa-e-democracy.php
18. http://www.isi.fraunhofer.de/isi-de/t/projekte/rl-huwy.php
19. Päivärinta, T., Sæbø, Ø.: Models of e-democracy. Commun. Assoc. Inf. Syst. **17**, 818–840 (2006)
20. http://www.gov2u.org
21. Anderson, S., Felici, M.: How democratic will e-democracy be? In: 29th Annual International Computer Software and Applications Conference, 2005. COMPSAC 2005, vol. 1. IEEE (2005). doi:10.1109/COMPSAC.2005.85
22. http://www.gov2u.org/index.php/research-centre/projects
23. http://www.e-democracy.gov.uk/
24. https://www.ndi.org/democracy-and-technology
25. Guo, Y.: Analysis on how to enhance e-democracy through e-government. In: 2011 International Conference on Management and Service Science (MASS), pp. 1–4 (2011). doi:10.1109/ICMSS.2011.5999004
26. http://www.itas.kit.edu/english/projects_henn10_e-d.php
27. http://eparticipation.eu/2012/12/clrity-program-every-government-decision-on-the-internet/
28. Katakis, I., Tsapatsoulis, N., Triga, V., Tziouvas, C., Mendez, F.: Clustering online poll data: towards a voting assistance system. In: 2012 Seventh International Workshop on Semantic and Social Media Adaptation and Personalization (SMAP), pp. 54–59 (2012). doi:10.1109/SMAP.2012.19
29. http://www.diavgeia.gov.gr (Clarity Portal)
30. Web 2.0 to Government 2.0 in Ireland. http://www.rialtas.net/blog/
31. http://www.OpenGov.gr (Open Government Programme)
32. http://eparticipation.eu/2012/12/network-of-ict-collaboration-of-municipalities-of-south-western-greece/

Zeus: Bringing Internet Voting to Greece

Panos Louridas[1]([⊠]), Georgios Tsoukalas[1], Kostas Papadimitriou[1],
and Panayiotis Tsanakas[2]

[1] Greek Research and Technology Network, Mesogeion 56,
115 27 Athens, Greece
{louridas, gtsouk, kpap}@grnet.gr
[2] Department of Electrical and Computer Engineering,
National Technical University of Athens, Polytechnioupolis,
157 73 Athens, Greece
panag@cs.ntua.gr

Abstract. Zeus is an internet voting platform, in which all the steps of the voting process can be verified using well-established mathematical tools. It has been developed with the goal that the voters can be confident that their votes are counted correctly and their anonymity is guaranteed, without needing to trust the operators of Zeus that they do not behave improperly: the assurances provided by Zeus are at least as strong as those in traditional elections. Zeus has been used in more than 120 elections, involving more than 22000 voters, and is continuously in use. It has shown that it can be used when traditional elections cannot take place, due to hostile conditions, and is actively being developed and evolved.

Keywords: Electronic voting · Cryptography · Elections

1 Quis Custodiet Ipsos Custodes?

Or, who guards the guardians? The Roman satirical poet Juvenal (his Latin name was Decimus Iunius Iuvenalis) asked that question in his poem Satire VI (lines 346–348), and refers to the guardians or wives. Romans may have had watchmen watching over their wives' behavior; but who watched the watchmen?

It seems that the problem predates Juvenal and had been posed by Plato some five centuries earlier. In Plato's Republic, an ideal society is imagined. The society is protected by specially appointed guardians. The guardians must behave properly, and in particular, drunkenness and sloth is unbefitting to them (Republic, Book 3, 398e). Moreover, Glaucon, who is in dialogue with Socrates, argues that it is absurd that the guardians should need to be guarded (Republic, Book 3, 403e).

In elections, we place our trust in the hands of the people counting the votes; usually the election committee. We normally take it for granted that they will behave honestly, they will follow due process, and the elections will be fair. The point has not been lost to those whose purpose is the opposite. Boris Bazhanov, in The Memoirs of Stalin's Former Secretary (Saint Petersburg, 1992) quotes Staling in 1923 "I consider it completely unimportant who in the party will vote, or how; but what is extraordinarily important is this – who will count the votes, and how". Otherwise put: the people who cast the votes decide nothing. The people who count the votes decide everything.

© Springer International Publishing Switzerland 2014
A.B. Sideridis et al. (Eds.): E-Democracy 2013, CCIS 441, pp. 213–223, 2014.
DOI: 10.1007/978-3-319-11710-2_20

We describe here the history and development of Zeus, a system for voting via the internet. Our aim in Zeus was to make a system realizing Glaucon's point. Zeus is a system that intends to implement internet voting in a way that it is absurd to argue that the people running Zeus are not to be trusted. This is not because these people are not trustworthy (we hope we are), but because were we not trustworthy we would be caught with certainty. It would therefore be foolish to try and rig an election. Interestingly, Glaucon's word for "absurd" in The Republic is γελοῖον, which in modern Greek means exactly that – foolish.

2   The Problem

Electronic elections have been the subject of much negative publicity, especially as a result of botched implementations, bugs, opaque implementations, and lack of transparency in the selection of the digital voting systems [4].

Traditional paper-based ballots, have a good track record. Advantages of such ballots include:

- Low barriers for voter participation. Essentially, no familiarity with technology is assumed. Even literacy is optional, since it is possible to vote with picture-based ballots.
- Low barrier for ballot counting. As long as counting is carried out by a trusted entity, the only requirement is the secure transmission of the results to a central electoral authority, when the election involves multiple electoral districts.
- Even the secure transmission of results mentioned above is not essential, since at any doubt ballots can be recounted.
- Recounts are possible and based on the physical properties of the ballot: as long as the ballots counted are the ballots submitted, the result can always be verified.
- Elections take place at specific premises where coercion is not possible and the voter's actions may not be monitored.

The disadvantages of paper-based ballots follow from the physicality of the voting medium:

- Counting is tedious and can be slow and costly. If counting equipment is used, then this can be complicated and expensive, and subject to arguments against electronic voting.
- Counting can be disrupted and the whole elections procedure invalidated by taking hold of the actual ballots.
- Large scale fraud is possible by exchanging whole ballot sets with fake ones, in places with extreme political corruption.

Internet voting tries to address the shortcomings of traditional elections by leveraging developments in cryptography and information technology. In internet voting the whole voting process takes place electronically, via the internet; there is no physical voting booth, or any non-digital medium that is used throughout the election process. In this way, internet voting is distinct from other forms of electronic voting, such as voting via dedicated voting machines and booths. In internet voting all interactions happen through a typical browser. This includes both voters' actions, and the actions performed by the election committee.

In electronic voting in general, votes are no more than patterns of digits stored in computers and transported through computer networks. Patterns of digits are infinitely malleable, and it is therefore always possible to alter the contents of a vote. Moreover, internet technology was not designed with security and privacy in mind, so it is relatively easy to find the person behind an internet transaction (a voter in our case). This breaks anonymity.

In order to make internet voting work, therefore, one must ensure that:

1. Any attempt at altering a vote can be detected.
2. It is impossible to trace the person behind a particular vote.

These two requirements do not guarantee that elections are fair: it is still possible not to count some votes at all. Therefore an additional requirement for internet voting is that:

3. It is possible to verify that a vote has been counted correctly in the results.

These three requirements rule out most naïve voting implementations. For example, a voting platform in which voters are given some confidential credentials through which they can access the system, vote, and check that the vote has been counted, does not pass muster since the system administrator knows what each voter has done and how they have voted.

In traditional elections, the only requirement for them being fair is that election committee members are honest. Similarly, in internet voting, the only requirement should be that the committee members are honest; there should be no requirement that the system programmers and administrators are honest. In short: in internet voting you should not need to trust the system.

That brings us to the problem we tried to address with Zeus: build a production-quality electronic voting platform, for which voters would not need to trust us. They would only need to trust the appointed election officials, as in traditional elections.

There exist proprietary solutions that purport to do exactly that. They fail, however, at one crucial aspect: they require voters to trust the people that have created the system. Proprietary electronic voting platforms do not reveal their exact workings to the public; at best, they provide access to selected experts, who can verify that the voting system performs faithfully as intended.

Such guarantees were not sufficient for us. Simply put, we ourselves would not agree to vote in an electronic voting system that we do not know exactly how it works. This means that we would never agree to vote in an electronic voting system that is not completely open source, allowing everybody to check its internals. This brings us to the fourth requirement for Zeus:

4. An electronic voting system should be completely open source, and all its code, documentation, and development should be readily available to everyone.

In what follows we present how we went to solve the problem composed of those four requirements, which led to the creation of the Zeus voting system, and our experience with it. First, we provide some background on the events surrounding the birth of Zeus.

3   The Genesis of Zeus

In 2011 law 4009 (partially amended by law 4076 in 2012) came into force in Greece. The law brought fundamental changes to the structure, governance, and working of Greek higher education (which is exclusively provided by the state). It met considerable resistance from some political parties, students, and unions of academics.

Among the provisions of the law was the institution of new Governing Councils responsible for the management of the universities (as distinct from academic affairs, which remained under the remit of University Senates). A widespread means of protest was then to disrupt the election of those Governing Councils. Disruption took the form of sit-ins, obstructing access to the ballot box, or taking hold of ballot boxes. The situation remained at stalemate for several months, which would endanger university funding (installment of Governing Councils was a prerequisite for receiving funding from the state).

At this juncture, in September 2012 a decree was passed that allowed the elections for the Governing Councils to take place electronically; we were also assigned the responsibility of implementing a system for the electronic vote. The system was to become Zeus, and the overall charged political atmosphere meant that Zeus was brought into the controversy surrounding the new university law. In particular, it meant that some political parties were against the use of Zeus, or any form of electronic voting.

We were pressed for time, as the system had to be operational in a couple of months time. We therefore turned our attention to existing available work, and came across Helios [1], a respected system for electronic voting with a good publishing record over the years, during which no serious weaknesses had been detected. Helios was, and is, open source, and it meets all four of our essential requirements. The current version of Helios (version 3) allows internet elections from end-to-end: from the moment the voter casts an encrypted ballot through a web browser to the publication of election results. It does that by never actually decrypting the ballots but performing a series of calculations on the encrypted ballots (the mechanism was different in earlier versions of Helios, such as the one in the original publication). At the end, the results of the calculations are decrypted and published. The calculations are called homomorphic and have the mathematical property that when decrypted they will be equal to equivalent calculations on the decrypted ballots, had they been decrypted previously. The homomorphic property is what allows Helios to dispense with decrypting the actual ballots altogether, an appealing solution.

Unfortunately, Helios could not be used as such, for several subtle reasons.

In the Governing Council elections, the voters are the faculty of the institution. The elections use the Single Transferable Vote (STV) system, in which the voters do not simply indicate the candidates of their preference, but also rank them. These ranks are then taken into account during the production of the election results. The idea behind STV is that votes are not "lost". The election of candidates proceeds in rounds. The first preferences in each ballot are counted. Then, if a candidate is elected because their vote count exceeds a defined formula, their surplus ballots (i.e., those ballots beyond the required quota) are used in the next round to elect the second candidate, based on the second preferences in these ballots, and so on, until all seats are filled. There are some complications when no candidate receives enough votes to pass the quota; for our purposes what is important is that it is not just the individual choices on each ballot that matter, but the whole ballot as an entity. That is in contrast to other voting systems, like approval voting, where individual choices on a ballot are just summed up. Whereas homomorphic calculations, like the ones used by Helios, can be readily used for approval voting, significant modifications are required for non-approval voting schemes. Although some published work on that front does exist [3], it is not implemented in Helios, we were not aware of it at the time, and it does not address other details of the Governing Council elections. First, there could be a set limit of candidates elected from one school in a university, which complicated considerably the standard STV algorithm. Secondly, during the STV algorithm it is possible to arrive at ties, which are resolved in random. The use of computer-generated random numbers was not deemed acceptable by the authorities, so in case of ties the system would have to stop, ask the electoral committee to pick between the tied candidates in some approved analog random way, input the result to the system, and let the system continue.

At that point we realized that it is not necessary to use Helios's homomorphic tallying capabilities. We decided to use Helios for counting the ballots, not for producing the election results. Once we do have a verifiable ballots count, this can be fed to an STV calculator, or indeed to a calculator of any voting system. Since the ballots are published, and the algorithm is also published, a third party can always verify that the results are correct. In other words, if we have a voting platform that only tallies ballots verifiably, and a clear, published algorithm that takes the tallied ballots and produces the election results according to the selected voting system, the process is verifiable from end to end.

Zeus was developed in autumn 2012. It was open sourced from the start, and all development was carried out in a publicly accessible GitHub repository. We welcomed constructive criticism or the exposure of unknown vulnerabilities, but we did not receive any. We did receive letters and comments, or some open letters circulating over the web, but they referred either to vulnerabilities in older versions of Helios, or objected to electronic voting in general. The atmosphere was at times vitriolic, as when a mainstream political party called the people behind Zeus "techno-fascists", thus introducing a new term in the Greek lexicon and bemusing the people involved in the whole effort.

The first real elections with Zeus took place successfully on October 19, 2012 at the Harokopio University of Athens. It has been in continuous use ever since. Due to the need to move away from homomorphic tallying and other requirements and refinements that we implemented, the Zeus software only retained 50 % of the original Helios source code, and the ratio is declining as we continue to evolve the system.

4   The Zeus Election Process for the Voter

The election process for a voter starts with the receipt of an e-mail containing a link to the election page. That link is personal, and serves as means of authentication. It must be kept private, since anybody with possession of it will be able to vote for that voter – although the voter will know about it.

By clicking on the link, the voter's browser goes to the voting booth. The voting booth displays the election questions and possible choices. Zeus is also capable of using "write-in" ballots, although we have not implemented the functionality yet. The voter specifies the ballot contents using a mouse, or, if using a phone or a tablet, finger gestures. The ballot is cast when the voter proceeds to submit the vote to Zeus. At that point, the ballot is encrypted with the election key and sent in encrypted form to Zeus. The ballot cannot be decrypted since Zeus does not have the decryption keys. Only the election committee can decrypt the ballots, at the appropriate time.

In contrast to traditional voting, and in accordance with best practices in electronic voting, a voter can vote repeatedly. This is to thwart coercion. In a traditional voting booth, it is assumed that the voter is alone, and nobody can check what the actual vote is. There is no way to offer such guarantees with internet voting. If the voter is not careful, an onlooker may get a glimpse of the ballot contents. Worse, a coercer may force the voter to vote then and there what they want. If this occurs, the voter can go back and vote again.

Each time the voter casts a vote they receive an e-mail with a digital proof of their vote. This proof can be used to verify that the vote has been counted correctly, when the results are published. If somebody has stolen the voter's link, the voter will receive a proof for a ballot they have not cast, so they will know that something is amiss.

5   The Zeus Election Process for the Election Committee

The election committee is responsible for the overall election process. The process starts with the election operator – usually a technically savvy member of the election committee. The election operator enters into the system the specifics of the election – starting time, ending time, the contact details of the committee members themselves, and the election questions. The system then sends an e-mail to each member of the election committee. The e-mail contains a personal and private link. By clicking on the link, the browser takes the member of the election committee to a web page in which they generate their part of the election key. The key for each committee member is composed of two parts: the private key, which is used for decryption, and the public key, which is used for encryption. The election key, in turn, comprises all the keys of the election committee, plus one key generated by Zeus itself; hence, even if the election committee colludes, they cannot decrypt the votes unless they have internal access to the Zeus system.

The generation of the election keys happens entirely on the browsers; the private keys are never sent to Zeus, so Zeus itself and its administrators are not able to decrypt the votes. The members of the election committee are responsible to store their private keys securely. Once this happens, Zeus can send the voters the invitation links in order to take part in the election.

During the election itself the election committee is responsible for any problems that may arise with the voters. Voters may have deleted their invitation links by mistake, in which case the election committee may send a new e-mail. It may transpire that a voter's e-mail is no longer functional, so that the election committee will change the voter's details and send a new invitation link (invalidating the old one). It may also happen that a voter should not be allowed to vote at all, and that the election committee must remove the voter from the electoral register, including any votes cast by that particular voter.

When the election ends the election committee members are responsible for decrypting the vote, but only after the votes have been anonymised.

6 Anonymisation of Votes

Although the votes arrive at Zeus encrypted, they are linked to the voter that submitted them. To ensure voter anonymity it is necessary to sever that link prior to decryption. This is achieved by mixing the votes, without decrypting them. The output of the mixing process is again a set of encrypted votes; in fact these votes are encryptions of the already encrypted votes, so that by looking at them it is not possible to identify which re-encrypted output corresponds to which encrypted input. The only way to derive this information, is by tracing the operation of the mixing server itself. But if we then add another mixing server that takes as input the output of the first one, then the only way one can link the output of the second mixing server with the original encrypted votes is by having traces of the operation of both mixing servers – that is, either cracking into both of them, or corrupting their operators. We may proceed in this manner, adding mixing servers run by independent entities, for as long as we do not have enough confidence in the operators of the existing mixing servers.

Since the output of each mixing server is an encrypted set of votes, each mixing (also called shuffling) must be done in a way that makes it possible to verify that each input vote is present in the mixed output. It turns out that there are cryptographic protocols with these properties [2], which we used in Zeus.

7 Decryption and Election Results

The cryptographic protocols used in Zeus are such that at the end of the mixing process, when we have a set of re-encrypted votes that we cannot link to the original votes cast by the voters, we can still decrypt the re-encrypted votes with the original election key. At the end of the mixing process a notification is sent to each member of the election committee. The notification contains a link; by clicking the link, the votes are downloaded to the committee member's browser and decrypted there with their private key. The result is sent back to Zeus. The votes become readable, i.e., completely decrypted, when they have been decrypted by every member of the election committee, and also by the Zeus server itself, each using their own private key.

The final of decrypted votes can then be published and used to produce the actual election results, according to the voting system in effect.

8 Quis Custodiet Ipsos Custodes, Redux

We stated at the outset that our goal was to make foolish any attempt to compromise elections with Zeus. It would be foolish, because it would be detected, in one of the following ways.

The voter challenges that their vote has been counted in the results
Each time the voter submits a vote, they are sent an e-mail containing a proof of the submission of their vote. That proof does not reveal the contents of the vote. It can be input to a special program that will show, based on the mathematical properties of the cryptographic protocols used by Zeus, that the vote has indeed been counted.

The voter argues that a retracted vote has been counted in the results
Since a voter can vote repeatedly, they may worry that some other vote, apart from their final one, has been counted in the results. They may check, as previously, that the final vote has been counted correctly, while all their previous votes have not.

Voters do not trust the election committee
As Zeus itself has a part of the election key, elections cannot be compromised by the election committee alone. They can only be compromised by the whole election committee and the Zeus operators being in cahoots with them. This is a stronger assurance than traditional elections, where the election committee can breach voter anonymity or fake results.

Voters worry that Zeus does not work as described
As Zeus is completely open source software, anybody can check that the code implements the correct cryptographic protocols.

Voters worry that the whole process is a charade
Although we have published information on the workings of Zeus, and we have made the Zeus code available on the web, voters may question that the computer they interact with runs the published code; it could be a clever trick, behaving as Zeus, but doing something else entirely behind the scenes.

If voters express such worries before hand, they can always appoint somebody else to run Zeus for them – since the software is open source, it is possible to download it and run it in whichever environment, and by any particular operator is deemed trustworthy.

If the voters express such worries after the elections, they can always download the Zeus code, get the encrypted votes, and run the mixing and decryption process again; the results should be identical to the original ones.

9 Cryptographic Machinery

Votes are encrypted on the voter's browser with the election public encryption key. Zeus uses the ElGamal encryption scheme. We give a brief description of the mechanism here, as it can be found in any standard cryptography textbook. We select a large prime, p, so that $q = (p - 1)/2$ is also prime and two random numbers g and x such that $g < p$, $x < p$, $g^q \equiv 1 \bmod p$ and $x^q \equiv 1 \bmod p$. The public key of the ElGamal scheme is the number $y = g^x \bmod p$ along with g and p. The private key then is x.

To encrypt a message M we choose a random k, such that k is relatively prime to $p - 1$. Then we compute $a = g^k \bmod p$ and $b = y^k M \bmod p$. The ciphertext is the tuple (a, b). To decrypt the ciphertext we calculate $M = b/a^x \bmod p$.

A key characteristic of ElGamal is that it allows us to re-encrypt the ciphertext and yet be able to decrypt to the initial ciphertext. Suppose we have a ciphertext $c = (a, b)$. If we choose a random r such that $r < p$ and calculate $c' = (g^r a, y^r b)$, then c' decrypts to the same plaintext M.

The ElGamal re-encryption underlies the anonymisation process. Having an initial set of encrypted votes, they are re-encrypted so that we arrive at a set of newly encrypted votes, which we shuffle, so that cannot be linked to the original encrypted ones. We then decrypt those votes and perform the ballot tally.

Of course, if somebody traces the operation of the mixing server, they will be able to maintain the correspondence between the original encrypted votes and the re-encrypted ones by tracking the shuffle; for this reason, and in order not to trust the operators of the mixing server, it is necessary to have at least an additional, independent, mixing server. This would require both mixing servers to be compromised in order to break anonymity. Since it is possible to add any number of mixing servers, we can further reduce the probability of compromise.

A final piece of the machinery is the guarantee that, when the ballots were mixed, no ballots were substituted. That is, to guarantee that the set of re-encrypted ballots do indeed decrypt to the initial set of plaintext ballots. This is achieved by a zero knowledge proof, in which we can show that the shuffle is correct (no substitutions were made), while revealing nothing about how the shuffle was performed (which would make the shuffle pointless), except that it was done correctly. In the Sako and Kilian protocol that we follow [5], we perform a large number of shadow shuffles. We cannot reveal the original shuffle, but for each shadow shuffle we may reveal either how the ballots were re-shuffled, or how we get from the shadow shuffle to the original, real shuffle. The probability that we could cheat is $1/2^n$, where n is the number of shadow shuffles; so for a large number of shuffles (currently 128) it is extremely unlikely.

10   Experience

Zeus was initially intended to be used for the elections for the appointment of Governing Councils in universities in Greece. There were 23 such elections, mired in controversy for political reasons. In this charged climate, Zeus was successfully in all 23 of them. Despite the controversy, the average turnout in these elections was 80.76 %, widely judged as very high. This was not lost on the Zeus development team, since we therefore had an indication that we did not do something against the will of the people. During these elections we noticed several attacks on Zeus, of varying sophistication, all of which were thwarted. The interested reader can read Sect. 6.1 of Tsoukalas et al., 2013, for more details.

To this day, electronic elections are usually promoted for economical and practical reasons. The use of Zeus showed that electronic voting is a viable solution when traditional elections cannot take place because of hostile conditions. As long as the computing and communications infrastructure is intact, elections can proceed as normal; in fact, even if computing and communications are under attack, elections can still take place by transporting computing resources (an easy task given the facilities offered by cloud computing), or using alternative communication channels (such as substituting SMS messages for e-mails).

Following this initial set of elections, we started receiving requests to use the system for other kinds of elections in the universities (e.g., deans, chancellors, department presidents, etc.), from a political party (to use in their party congress), even from the private sector (the Hellenic Chamber of Hotels). As a result, to this date we have run more than 120 elections, involving more than 22000 voters.

Even though we designed Zeus so that voters and election committees would not need to trust us, it turned out that they did trust us, to an unexpected degree. In particular, voter anonymity even in the presence of corrupt Zeus operators can be maintained by having a series of vote mixing servers. It turned out that in no elections to this date has a separate mixing server been set up by the election committee. On the one hand we are happy that people trust us; on the other hand, we want to make sure that distributed mixing does take place. We have been working on making its use as easy and as unobtrusive as possible, although we do not have a strong indication that technical difficulties prohibited its use (it has been a matter of command line tool installation and execution).

Electronic voting does not relegate humans to an auxiliary role. The election committee is the entity really pulling the strings in each election, responsible for election setup, settlement of any disputes, election close, and publication of final results. Also, as with any information technology, Zeus must cater for its users, so its operation is accompanied by a helpdesk that guides the election committee through the election steps, compiles manuals, and responds to questions that arise during elections.

11 Conclusions

Zeus has been a success, despite having been introduced in a very adversarial setting. We have been improving Zeus throughout this time, based on the feedback we have received from voters and election committees. To the best of our knowledge, it is the only system that has been used to substitute for traditional elections when these could not take place due to unfavourable conditions on the ground. The requests that we receive to use Zeus indicate that voters and election committees involved seem to have caught on the convenience offered by electronic voting. We hope that its use will spread even more, as it could be a vital tool in expanding direct democracy, and fostering consultation processes, while keeping costs down and logistical requirements low.

More details on Zeus can be found in [6]. The full source code of Zeus can be found at https://github.com/grnet/zeus.

References

1. Adida, B.: Helios: web-based open-audit voting. In: Proceedings of the 17th Conference on Security Symposium (SS'08), pp. 335–348. USENIX Association, Berkeley, CA (2008)
2. Benaloh, J.: Simple verifiable elections. In: Proceedings of the USENIX/Accurate Electronic Voting Technology Workshop on Electronic Voting Technology Workshop (EVT'06). USENIX Association, Berkeley, CA (2006)
3. Benaloh, J., Moran, T., Naish, L., Ramchen, K., Teague, V.: Shuffle-sum: coercion-resistant verifiable tallying for STV voting. IEEE Trans. Inf. Forensics Secur. **4**(4), 685–698 (2009)
4. Jones, D.W., Simons, B.: Broken Ballots: Will Your Vote Count?. CSLI Publications, Stanford (2012)
5. Sako, K., Kilian, J.: Receipt-free mix-type voting scheme. In: Guillou, L.C., Quisquater, J.-J. (eds.) EUROCRYPT 1995. LNCS, vol. 921, pp. 393–403. Springer, Heidelberg (1995)
6. Tsoukalas, G., Papadimitriou, K., Louridas, P., Tsanakas, P.: From Helios to Zeus. USENIX J. Election Technol. Syst. **1**(1) (2013)

Author Index